Technobabble

John A. Barry

The MIT Press
Cambridge, Massachusetts
London, England

First MIT Press paperback edition, 1993

©1991 John A. Barry

All rights reserved. No part of this book may be reproduced in any form by any electronic or mechanical means (including photocopying, recording, or information storage and retrieval) without permission in writing from the publisher.

This book was set in Sabon and printed and bound in the United States of America.

Library of Congress Cataloging-in-Publication Data

Barry, John A.
    Technobabble / John A. Barry
        p.   cm.
    Includes bibliographical references and index.
    ISBN 0-262-02333-4 (HB), 0-262-52182-2 (PB)
    1. Computers and civilization.   2. Technology—Philosophy.
    I. Title.
    QA76.9.C66B375   1991   77078
    004' .014—dc20   91–12488
                                                                                 CIP

This book is dedicated to Eva, without whose assistance I would never have made my deadline, and to Sean, for sacrificing some of his time so that I could make time to write.

AUGUSTANA UNIVERSITY COLLEGE
LIBRARY

AUGUSTANA UNIVERSITY COLLEGE
LIBRARY

Contents

Foreword

The United States was once a nation of farmers, but by the turn of the century most of us had moved away from the land. Today we city dwellers have lost contact with the down-to-earth figures of speech so deeply planted in the humus of our language. But a little digging uncovers the rich, earthy metaphors from which grow so much of our speech and writing.

• The lines in a worried forehead resemble the grooves in the earth made by a plow. We describe such a forehead as furrowed.

• Like well-farmed land, the fertile mind of an intellectual man or woman is carefully tended and yields a bountiful harvest. We say that such people are cultivated.

• Among farm equipment is a cultivating implement set with spikes and spring teeth that pulverizes the earth by violently tearing and flipping over the topsoil. That's why we identify an emotionally lacerating experience as harrowing.

Through history, emerging technologies have yielded new terms and catchphrases that have become embedded in our language—"suits to a T" and "dead as a doornail" from carpentry, "free-lance" and "last-ditch effort" from military conflict, and "touch and go" and "scuttlebutt" from sailing, to name a few.

The most far-reaching, dramatic, and accessible technology of our age is the computer, in which many of us find our hopes and our fears, our realities and our dreams. Any activity that exerts such an enormous influence on our lives is bound to affect our vocabulary.

This process has needed a chronicler, and John Barry has brought his broad talents to the task. Because of John's deep coverage, his authoritative research, and his rich and colorful descriptions, I'm confident that

Technobabble will appeal to experienced hackers, computer neophytes, and word lovers alike. John's compendium is at once a dictionary, a reference resource, and a collection of lively anecdotes, all of which chronicle what is sure to be the lasting impact of a major technology on our language and culture. Best of all, because John writes so comfortably and colorfully, this user-friendly book is a delight to read.

Richard Lederer
Concord, New Hampshire

Acknowledgments

In addition to the people listed in the book and endnotes, I would like to thank the following for their contributions: Michelle Arden, Allan Ball, Lorrie Duval, Tom Fussy, Jennifer Gill, Martin Hall, Roger Knights, Eva Langfeldt, Lisa Levine, Erica Liederman, Dave Needle, Anne Pettigrew, Jackie Rae, Dave Raether, Carol Ranalli, Ron Richardson, Chip Salzenberg, Laura Singer, Dina Toothman, Peter van der Linden, and Rich Wyckoff. For moral and technical support, I want to thank Midori Chan, Martin Hall, Bill Kennedy, Carla Marymee, and Roger Strukhoff. Finally, I especially want to thank those who reviewed and critiqued manuscripts: Mark Hall, Eva Langfeldt, Richard Lederer, Laura Singer, Mike Swaine. Special thanks to Bill Gladstone of Waterside Productions for finding a publisher.

Introduction

This paper-based, productized bookware module is designed to support the robust implementation of a friendly, context-driven interface between the developer and the end-user. Did you understand this sentence? If so, you are fluent in technobabble.

Technobabble. The word connotes meaningless chatter about technology. And often that is just what technobabble is. But it is also a form of communication among people in the rapidly advancing computer and other high-technology industries. By implication, the term *technobabble* could refer to the gamut of languages that describe the areas subsumed under the rubric of high technology: computers, biotechnology, aerospace, robotics, and the like. For the purposes of this book, technobabble refers almost strictly to the language of the computer industry.

This industry is advancing so rapidly that the language describing it is as volatile as the industry itself. Any attempt to maintain an up-to-date compendium of computer technology in book—rather than electronic, online—form is next to impossible, because things change faster than books can be reprinted. Still, an examination of the phenomenon of technobabble is overdue, because of the lasting effects of computer technology on society and on language.

My guiding premise is that what used to be called "computerese" has transcended its fundamental purpose: to describe and explain computing. Although it still fulfills its original function, it frequently steps outside these bounds to describe the human condition. Conversely, in the computer industry, the human condition is frequently explained in terms of technological metaphors.

About the Book and the Author

The computer industry is a network of interrelated disciplines. Its two most general areas are hardware and software, although these two often overlap. Just a few of the scores of aspects of hardware, for example, are mainframe computers, minicomputers, personal computers (PCs), and workstations. The last two categories are increasingly overlapping, to the point where it has become difficult to determine what is a PC and what is a workstation. Another component of the hardware category is peripherals, which includes printers, plotters, disk drives, and tape drives. The point of the preceding technotaxonomy is to illustrate the size and scope of the computer industry. A book that adequately covered its entire lexicon would be larger than the fattest computer dictionary now in existence. And many computer dictionaries are currently available.

The goal of *Technobabble* is to pinpoint and examine the roots of computerese and to discuss its influence on our society and our language. My overall approach is inductive, although I do define many specific terms in my quest for a broad understanding of the phenomenon.

My interest in technobabble began in the late 1970s, before the term was even coined. I was abruptly exposed to it as managing editor of a computer "hobbyist" magazine called *Kilobaud*. Even though this was around the same time that computers, and by extension their lexicon, were becoming available to the masses, *Kilobaud*'s content was opaque to readers who were not "techies." With no previous exposure to computers, I quickly realized that, to paraphrase Gatsby, "The very technical do not talk like you and me."

After three years of absorbing this new language, I moved in the summer of 1980 to the Silicon Valley area to work for the newly formed *InfoWorld* magazine. A couple of years later, with the encouragement of the editor, I started to write a column called "Computer Illiteracy," a take-off on the then-popular term "computer literacy." The column, which explored technobabble trends and terminology, ran for nearly two years. Shortly after its demise, I left *InfoWorld* for five years of firsthand experience within the industry—at the marketing level—at the phenomenally successful Sun Microsystems. During my tenure at Sun, I cofounded an internal magazine, *SunTech Journal* (now called *SunWorld*), for which I still work, although under the aegis of an independent publisher, and for which I write a technobabble-examination column called "/lex."

Research

Whenever possible, I have identified sources of information I used in writing *Technobabble*. In some instances, however, full identification was not possible. Some of the materials in my files (of the paper variety) were completely or partially unidentified photocopies handed or mailed to me by various people. I have so noted these references in the book's endnotes. Research materials cover the period from the mid-1940s to the time when the book went into production in early 1991.

As a follow-up to this book, I am compiling a list of computer-industry words and terms. If you have run across any

- neologisms
- anthropomorphic computerese
- people described in terms of computer technology
- nouns as verbs
- verbs as nouns
- acronyms as parts of speech
- entertaining gaffes, including, but not limited to
  —misspellings
  —misplaced modifiers
  —solecisms
  —malapropisms
  —factual information

or anything else of note, such as recursive acronyms, eponyms, and onomatopoetic words, please send them to me c/o The MIT Press. Please cite source and include a photocopy or tear sheet if possible. All entries used in future publications will be acknowledged, unless anonymity is requested.

Technobabble

1

What Is Technobabble?

Technobabble—to use the appropriate bit of computerese—is becoming "fully integrated" into American conversation.
—Lead sentence of magazine article[1]

Technobabble, like any argot or specialty language, reflects that which it chronicles and describes. It is a relatively new phenomenon, born after World War II with the advent of digital computers. As such, it might be thought of as a baby boomer[2]—one that today is perhaps settling into mature middle age?

Hardly. Because it advances so rapidly, computer technology never has time, like wine, to mature. No sooner does a computer company announce its latest "hot box" than some competitor surpasses the accomplishment—in both performance and price. An ever-changing array of concepts, technologies, and products requires an expanding vocabulary to keep pace, even if much of the technology is transient and most of its attendant language ephemeral. The vocabulary of every technology has to evolve to keep up with the latest developments, but no technology, it seems, changes as fast as computer technology or is as pervasive in everyday life—in part because nearly every process that was once entirely mechanical is now, at least in part, controlled by computers.

Vocabulary as Reflection of Technology

Every technology, no matter how much it changes over the years, retains vestigial terms that bear no tangible relation to the current "state of the art." Take the printing industry. Until the middle of this century, typesetting involved casting forms for pages of a publication with melted lead, one line at a time. (This "line of type" approach gave us the Linotype machine—the Linotype company is still in business, but today it produces computerized, digital typesetting systems.) If typesetters—the people doing the typesetting—needed to add space between lines of type, they would add thin strips of lead. The term *leading* came into being to describe the process of adding space to texts. Typesetting technology is now computerized. Hot metal type is a thing of the past, but the word *leading* lives on, still indicating the amount of space between lines. *Kerning*—the addition or subtraction of space between individual letters—was performed mechanically from the seventeenth century, when the term was coined. Today, kerning occurs digitally. The graphic-arts industry has also provided its share of terms based on physical processes that now can be replicated on a computer screen: *cutting, pasting, copying, drawing,* and *painting.*

The lexicon of computing also retains carryover terms that arose in the early, mechanical days of computing. One example is *batch processing,* a term that refers to a type of data processing in which jobs are grouped and performed during a single run of the computer. This approach to computer processing is mainly restricted to mainframe computers, although the term is sometimes employed generally to differentiate older styles of computing from newer ones. Although *The Random House Dictionary of the English Language,* 2d ed., unabridged, indicates that the term *batch processing* dates from the period 1970–75, its origin can possibly be traced to the 1950s, when stacks, or *batches,* of punched cards served as input for early mainframe computers.

Another example of antiquated terminology surviving in contemporary computerese is the term *core dump.* Early computers used ferromagnetic cores for memory and program storage; copying the contents of one of these devices to a printer or disk was called a core dump. Core memories are a thing of the past, but the term persists, having shifted contexts to become mainly an anthropomorphic expression meaning to get something off your chest, to express everything you know or feel about a given subject.

The term *machine* persists to this day as a synonym for *computer,* even though, as MIT computer scientist Joseph Weizenbaum has noted, "The machines that populate our world are no longer exclusively, or even mainly, clanking monsters, the noisy motion of whose parts defines them as machines. The arrival of all sorts of electronic machines, especially of the electronic computer, has changed our image of the machine from that of a transducer and transmitter of power to that of a transformer of information."[3]

From the Back Room to the Living Room

Technobabble is so pervasive and significant today because computers have become so accessible. In computing's early days, only select, highly trained individuals could put their hands on computers—behemoths that cost millions of (1950s) dollars. Today, anyone can wander into a corner computer store and, for less than $3,000, pick up and carry away a machine that packs more power than a multimillion-dollar room-sized device offered less than thirty years ago.

In the half century since the development of the first electronic digital computers, technobabble has transcended its origins. Whereas it initially served a specific purpose—to enable a small, select group of people to communicate with each other—it is now on the tips of the tongues of millions, from knowledgeable "techies" to flacks, who often seem to gauge the success of their press releases by the amount of gratuitous jargon they can include, to people discussing aspects of their personal lives.

Technobabble is an offshoot of *computerese,* a word coined as early as 1955, according to the second edition of the Random House unabridged dictionary. (It also goes by other names, as noted in the glossary under *technobabble.*) About a decade after the beginnings of electronic computing, a mildly derogatory term for its lexicon was already in use.[4] Computerese is still around, and its lexicon is increasing year by year: Witness the number and size of general and "niche" computer dictionaries in print.[5] Two main characteristics differentiate technobabble from computerese: the heavy influence of marketing and public relations (PR) and the extracomputer contexts in which it is used.

Technobabble's Origins

The word *technobabble* first cropped up in the early 1980s, derived from or inspired by *psychobabble,* the title of a 1977 book by Richard Rosen and an entry, credited to Rosen, in the Random House unabridged dictionary. This dictionary defines *psychobabble* as "writing or talk using jargon from psychiatry or psychotherapy without particular accuracy or relevance." The definition of technobabble is similar, but a key difference between psychobabble and technobabble is that the former borrows clinical terms from psychotherapy and glibly applies them to everyday life. Technobabble takes terms from the computer industry and puts them into extracomputer—often anthropomorphic—contexts. In technobabble, technical and colloquial terms from computing are applied to human thoughts, processes, and interactions—and vice versa. When people break into the conversation of others or are interrupted by someone, they are said to be in "interrupt mode," whereas two computers interchanging data are "talking to" each other. Psychobabble is mostly self-indulgent palaver; technobabble personifies technologies and objects and objectifies people. At their worst, they both serve as "noise," signifying little or nothing, or as an obfuscatory mechanism.

The Random House unabridged dictionary defines *babble* as "inarticulate or imperfect speech; foolish, meaningless, or incoherent speech; prattle; a murmuring sound or confusion of sounds." The telecommunications community has its particular definition of the word: "a confused mixture of extraneous sounds in a circuit, resulting from cross talk [interference heard on a telephone or radio because of unintentional coupling to another communication channel] from other channels." The *Oxford English Dictionary*, which gives 1668 as the first recorded use of the noun *babble*, indicates that it most likely derives from the repetition of "ba, ba," "one of the first articulate sounds made by infants." Most Indo-European languages have a near equivalent in sound and meaning: *babiller* (French), *babbeln* (German), *babollare* (Italian). Although they seem to be related, *babble* and *Babel* are merely homophones; the "Babel" in Tower of Babel is a Hebrew word based on Assyrian roots.

What puts the babble into technobabble is less its incomprehensibility to those outside its purview than the ways in which it has come to be employed. Computer jargon devolves into babble under the following—among other, secondary—circumstances.

When it is used as filler or decoration. An example is the pandemic appearance of the word *support* in writing and speech about computers. So pervasive and nebulous is this word that it frequently serves as little more than an interlocution or punctuation mark in written and verbal communication.

When it is employed intentionally for obfuscatory purposes. Technobabble is frequently obfuscatory. The main culprits in intentional confusion-by-technobabble are people in the industry who have a vested interest in hiding bugs, delayed delivery dates, and the like.

When it is employed gratuitously. Use of any jargon can become habitual or unthinking. Some people become so accustomed to technobabble that its use becomes second nature.

When it is used obsessively. Technozealots and technophiles are most likely to fall victim to this affliction, in large part as a reflection of their obsession with computer technology.[6]

When it is used by those unfamiliar with its meanings in an attempt to sound as if they know what they are talking about. Rather than admit semantic defeat or try to find alternatives to jargon, many not-too-technical residents in technical environments opt for the parrot approach: simply repeat words heard from others.

Today, technobabble fulfills two fundamental purposes: (1) to describe computer technology and related phenomena among like-minded people in a profession, and (2) to serve as a lingua franca for describing everything from human interaction to the state of the world. The second of these two purposes is the major focus of this book. Technobabble has in many ways transcended the first purpose, although that original objective is still important and necessary. Anthropologists, linguists, and historians of the future will study surviving texts to determine how we lived. Presumably, they will note the influx of technobabble into our language in the second half of the twentieth century and use technobabble as evidence to construct theories about the critical role of computer technology in our society.

Technobabble is not the first specialty language that has infiltrated the mainstream lexicon. When the U.S. space program heated up in the early 1960s, terms such as *A-OK* and *blast-off* became popular. The late 1970s was the high point of psychobabble, as captured by Rosen and novelist Cyra McFadden in *Serial,* her account of Marin County, California, mores. Phraseology such as "I can relate to that" and terms such as "wellness" are still part of the American lexicon. The 1980s witnessed an infusion of businessbabble into the language: *bottom line, greenmail, leveraged.* If these three patterns are representative of the extent of adoption of argot outside its original bounds, there is a direct relation between the degree of adoption and the degree of exposure to the phenomenon the argot represents. Computer use and "computer literacy" are increasing daily, and so is the use of technobabble. The public's interest in computer technology shows no signs of waning.

As the epigraph at the beginning of this chapter notes, technobabble is becoming an increasingly noticeable part of the American English landscape. And as Appendix A shows, American English is not the only language experiencing computer-related changes. Computers are everywhere, and although the world's languages have borrowed heavily from American technobabble, speakers of many other languages have also crafted their own terms to describe computer phenomena.

Whatever the language, technobabble is not only the argot of people in the computer industry; it is also a general method of communication that exhibits these primary characteristics:

• It applies an essentially mechanistic lexicon to human thought processes, interactions, and endeavors.

• Conversely, it describes computer processes in human terms.

• It exhibits an identifiable style and structure.

• It has connotations outside the realm of computing, in addition to the anthropomorphic ones already mentioned.

• It exhibits noticeable influences from marketing and PR.

Technobabble is both the jargon, argot, slang of the computer industry as used within that industry and, more significantly, that special language freed of its industry confines and applied in new and different contexts. Computerese has been around almost since the appearance of computers in the 1940s, but technobabble took almost three decades to come into full flower.

2

Genesis and Evolution

But it is the jargon phrases of Silicon Valley, reapplied to noncomputing circumstances to make a kind of high-tech slang, that may eventually prove as influential on the language in the long run.
—*The Story of English*[1]

In part because of the military origin of computer development, technobabble was initially a kind of secret language developed by a special technological priesthood. But the cabalistic nature of technobabble was not strictly a result of the military foundations of computing. Early computers were as difficult to operate and as unreliable in service as early cars and aircraft. The unreliability of these early machines required a leap of faith to undertake their use. They demanded patience and expertise not available to anyone outside a small, discrete group. The very first computers and those that were developed in the early years of the computer industry were accessible only to a select few whose power and prestige derived from keeping their minions in thrall.

One of the first functional computers, ENIAC (Electronic Numerical Integrator And Calculator), and one of the first computer-industry acronyms were developed at the University of Pennsylvania in 1946. Even at that early date, one of the hallmarks of technobabble, non-standardization, was in evidence. The February 18, 1946, issue of *Newsweek* referred to this new device as "Electronic Numerical Integrator and Computor." Not only were people unsure whether to call this electromechanical marvel a "calculator" or a "computer," but the now-standard spelling, "c-o-m-p-u-t-e-r," was not even fixed.[2]

As with most computer technology, ENIAC's development owed much to the military—in this case, the U.S. Army's Ordnance Department, which needed new ballistics tables for calculating the trajectories of various shells. ENIAC never got a chance to fulfill its original mission, however, because it was commandeered to work on calculations for nuclear-bomb theories at Los Alamos, New Mexico.[3] But it could not be moved to Los Alamos. It weighed thirty tons, stood two stories high, covered 15,000 square feet (it had what today would be called a "large footprint"), and was filled with thousands of vacuum tubes. Although subsequent computers became more compact—covering hundreds rather than thousands of square feet—they were literally and figuratively locked away from the majority of their users. System administrators kept them operational, and programmers processed the jobs submitted by worshiping supplicants.

This environment, shrouded as it was in secrecy, and dedicated to complex and arcane technology, was the breeding ground of a new lexicon to help make sense of it all. How computers actually worked was a secret known only to a select group of initiates, but that some of the devices' functions bore striking resemblances to human characteristics was recognized even by common mortals. Computers could, for example, "remember" things once data had been put into their "stored memory," a concept developed by computer pioneer John Von Neumann. Not only could they remember but they could also "think."

Nonetheless, in spite of their capacity to perform seemingly cerebral functions, early computers were not much more than a notch above steam engines in mechanical sophistication. They were machines: very big, very heavy, and made mostly of metal. These devices were hybrid entities. Mechanically and aesthetically, they were products of the industrial revolution. Conceptually and functionally, they seemed to signal the dawn of a new age.

Because the public knew little or nothing about these miraculous devices, the job of educating the masses fell to such interpreters of culture as magazine writers and editors. As the creators and users of computers set about inventing a technical vocabulary—replete with arcane acronyms but also employing anthropomorphic metaphors—the interpreters needed terms for their audiences.

An examination of *The Reader's Guide to Periodical Literature*, starting in mid-1945, throws light onto the origins of technobabble. The May 1945–April 1947 edition contains twenty-eight article references to computers, although not under that rubric. The heading "Computing Machines" refers readers to "Calculating Machines"; the word *computer* does not even appear in the index. Of those twenty-eight entries, appearing in magazines ranging from *Life* to *Aviation,* five have the word *computer* in the title (example: "Desk Electric Computer Aids Chemical Research" [*Science,* June 29, 1946]). Only three titles focus on the machine aspect. Five of the articles refer to the devices as *robots,* a word coined by Czech playwright Karel Capek in his 1920 dystopian drama *R.U.R.* Other terms for nascent computers are "electronic tubes," "differential analyzer," and "fortune teller."

Anthropomorphism was already in evidence, as the following sample demonstrates:

Electrical Memory (*Newsweek*)

It Thinks with Electrons (*Popular Science*)

MIT's 100-Ton Mechanical Brain Is Now Ready to Tackle Problems of Peace (*Popular Science*)

100-Ton Brain at MIT (*Scholastic*)

Great Electro-mechanical Brain (*Life*)

As the years pass, the number of references to "calculating machines" increases—along with titles containing such words as *brain*—but it is not until the March 1965–February 1966 edition that the discrete index entry *computer* appears. In retrospect, calling these first machines "calculators" is ironic, given that modern calculators are often smaller than a deck of cards and pack more power than ENIAC did in 1946. The definition of *computer* was still "one [i.e., a person, not a machine] who computes."[4]

While the noncomputing public (almost everyone in the 1940s and 1950s) read about computers in articles whose writers relied heavily on science-fiction vocabulary ("electronic brain" and "robot"), the small but growing number of people who depended indirectly on the machines began, usually out of professional necessity, to incorporate into their vocabularies some of the professional jargon that was developing in the labs and back rooms where the machines resided. These people had jobs to be *processed,* the jobs consisting of punched cards that the machines could *read.* Anthropomorphic terms such as the latter suggested that a computer could "read" a card with patterns of holes punched into it.

Punched cards and paper tape were an early form of *input*; *output* was the result of processing the cards and produced more cards or tape to be read and deciphered, which in turn produced more input.

The appearance of minicomputers eventually gave people who depended on computers access—albeit limited—to the computers through terminals (initially just keyboards and then keyboards with video displays). Still, these users were limited as to when they could *log on* (a term derived from sailing) to the system and how much time they could have once logged on. Advances in computing technology brought new, more-egalitarian-sounding terms into play—*timesharing,* for example. Computer users were now sharing the power of the machines rather than merely being subjected to it.

What freed access to computers for large numbers of people were "microcomputers," later called "personal computers." True, you had to be a hacker to operate the first "micros," also called hobby computers, which appeared in small numbers in 1974–75. By the late 1970s, computers from Apple, Radio Shack, Commodore, and other, now extinct companies, were easier to use than the hobby computers, but they too were limited in computing power. One of the reasons these little systems were not truly easy for tyros was the appalling manuals that accompanied them. Written in computerese by hackers for hackers, they were all but opaque to the non–"computer literate." Still, they opened the floodgates—to a profusion of computers, and a spill of technobabble.

To help explain the development of technobabble, an overview of the technological evolution it mirrors is worthwhile.

The Phases of Computer Technology

When Bernie Lacroute was the executive vice president and general manager of Sun Microsystems, a workstation manufacturer based in Mountain View, California, he presented a historical model of computing. Lacroute wrote, "Digital computing is less than half a century old, yet it has gone through four distinct phases of evolution. Each generation was spurred by the emergence of new hardware technology and software advances, resulting in new applications and an increasing number of users. Concurrently, the level of user sophistication necessary to master the new systems decreased substantially."[5] What Lacroute did not mention in his essay—but what his model also illustrates—is the evolution of technobabble. Each phase of Lacroute's technological evolution is mirrored by a phase in technobabble's own evolution. Lacroute broke the "less than half a century" history of computing from the late 1940s to the late 1980s down into four phases, or generations:

- Back-room, or one-on-one, computing
- Shared interactive computing
- Isolated one-on-one computing
- Networked, or distributed, computing

First Generation: Back-Room Computing

In Lacroute's model, back-room computing is the first generation of computing, which "stems from the invention of the transistor and the later introduction of batch operating systems in the 1960s." He notes that IBM was built on "this mainframe/batch concept." The concept is "batch" because "the entire computer is devoted to the processing of a single task." For this reason, the user is "positioned one-on-one with the machine."[6] This is not to say that such users are actually operating the machine themselves. A specialist runs their jobs for them; but the specialist can run only one job at a time—thus the one-on-one concept. As Lacroute points out, "Back-room computing isolates the user from the machine, locating the computer in a specially built room."[7]

Second Generation: Shared Interactive Computing

The shared interactive approach was brought on in the 1970s with the creation of the minicomputer by Digital Equipment Corporation (DEC), according to Lacroute. He notes that the minicomputer industry coincided with the invention of the integrated circuit (IC) and timesharing operating systems. Minicomputers and timesharing brought users into more-direct contact with computers: Instead of having to carry cards and lists to programmers, who would then run their jobs for them, users could interact with the machine themselves by using a keyboard and a primitive alphanumeric display.

Interaction was actually less direct than it was in back-room computing, however. What made it seem direct was manipulation of data by means of a keyboard, rather than through an intermediary person, and the considerably shorter response time. Timesharing measured response time in minutes or seconds rather than in hours and was less expensive. It is the province of "departmental organizations" (thus the term *departmental computing*), in which groups of users have common missions. Timesharing also introduced "networking," by which the members of a group could communicate electronically with each other.

Third Generation: Isolated One-on-One Computing

The late 1960s saw the invention of the microprocessor and the liberating force of the microcomputer.[8] Although the first microcomputers (later called "personal computers," or PCs) were primitive and ungainly, they did, as Lacroute put it, free users "from the burden of sharing the system or suffering the headaches of a centralized system-administration bureaucracy." Users were still "one on one," but interaction was, well, up close and personal.

Fourth Generation: Networked Computing

This type of computing, according to Lacroute, is also one-on-one, but it is "distributed," meaning that computing resources can be routed around the network to wherever they are needed. Lacroute notes five technology advances that were responsible for the advent of networked computing:

- High-performance 32-bit microprocessors
- High-speed networking
- High-resolution bit-mapped graphics displays and mice
- Windowing software
- Networkwide, multitasking, virtual-memory operating systems such as UNIX[9]

Lacroute wrote of the fourth generation that "The interaction between the computer and the user takes places graphically as well as alphanumerically via keyboard, mouse, windows, and icons. Information exchange among users occurs on a direct, one-on-one basis, and shared resources, called servers, are available networkwide to all users. Because the operating system was designed up front to handle networking, distributed computing permits the use of 'diskless nodes.' Diskless nodes reduce the cost of computing and facilitate the management of tasks such as archiving data and backing up databases."[10]

Distributed computing is "heterogeneous," meaning that through the use of certain communication protocols users of, for example, Apollo workstations can gain access to files on a DEC minicomputer and manipulate them as if they were running on the Apollo machines.

In Lacroute's generational model, computing has gone from being a cloistered, priestly environment to a populist phenomenon, a sort of "computing socialism": from each [computing resource] according to its [his] [cap]ability, to each according to its [his] need. Terms such as "collective computing" and an organization named SPEC (Systems Performance and Evaluation Cooperative) have helped foster this idea of "computer socialism."

Waves and Nodes

Lacroute is not the only industry insider or observer to draw this evolutionary conclusion. Take a look at part of the introductory note S. Henry Sacks wrote to readers of *SunExpert* magazine when he assumed the role of publisher:

I've been in publishing since 1957. During that some thirty-odd years, I've watched computing change beyond recognition. And, guess what? There's a pattern to the way this industry changes.

When I founded *Computer Design* in 1962, the word "computer" meant "mainframe." When I began *Modern Data* in 1967, minicomputer was a contradiction in terms. . . . But it wasn't long before you could see the handwriting in very large letters on a lot of walls. The minis were coming, and they would shake computing to its core. It wasn't long before *Modern Data* was re-titled *Mini-Micro Systems*.[11]

But note the word *micro*. Suddenly, microcomputers—in the form of [personal computers] in the business environment, and workstations in the scientific environment—made it possible to take computing out of the glasshouse and drop it on the desktop.

But, all of that's history. What's the next wave? Networked computing. This wave is embodied in general by the workstation.[12]

This notion of four phases of computer evolution, like a myth or an archetype, crops up in various guises throughout the industry. In July 1990, for example, Wavefront Technologies, a Santa Barbara, California, producer of "visualization" software, announced some new products at a press conference at the Mark Hopkins hotel in San Francisco. Bud Enright, the company's president, alluded to four "classes of computer users," which Enright said exemplified the evolution of visualization technology:

• Lab curiosity. The technology's practitioners were initially a small, select group of highly trained specialists.

• Dedicated groups. Next, the technology was in the hands of a larger but still specialized group of professionals.

• Commonplace. The technology became much more widespread and now was employed by a larger, more general, less expert group of people.

• Pervasive. Now in widespread use, the technology is the province of people who are merely interested in its application and perhaps know little about its inner workings—nor do they particularly care.

The technically minded Lacroute writes about generations of computing; the Toffleresque Sacks terms the phases waves. Enright's classes are roughly equivalent to the concepts of generation and waves, and their invocation in an evolutionary context ties in with a presentation that occurred a couple of months earlier in San Jose, California.

Concerning the evolutionary trends in computing, Ira Goldstein, president of the Open Software Foundation (OSF), waxed metaphorical. Goldstein was one of the keynote speakers at Xhibition 1990, Xhibition being the small but growing trade show devoted to developments in the X Window System developed at MIT. The focus of the keynote speeches was "computing in the 1990s." "The transition in computing is similar to what went on in biological evolution," Goldstein proclaimed. Early computing, he suggested, consisted of individual, or specialized nodes, which he equated with single-celled organisms from which more-complex creatures evolved. In the "fine-grained [computer] architecture" of the 1990s, specialized nodes interoperate with other nodes to give us what Goldstein referred to as "collective computing," to differentiate it slightly from what others are calling "networked, distributed, or client/server computing." Briefly, Goldstein saw the 1990s as "collective entities consisting of specialized nodes." Another term for this structure is "workgroup computing," the evolutionary result of Lacroute's "departmental computing."

The Phases of Technobabble

With the exception of some terms that were carried over from earlier technologies, technobabble, like computing, was born in the 1940s. Its purpose was to give computer professionals—and everyone who talked about computers in the early days was a professional—a common language with which to communicate about their work. It still serves that purpose, but it has also transcended it. We can apply Enright's—or indeed Lacroute's or Sacks's or Goldstein's—model of computing's evolution to the evolution of technobabble.

First Generation: Lab Curiosity (Back-Room)

A few years elapsed before ENIAC's immediate successors made it out of defense-research laboratories and into the world. When they did, though, they were cloistered in Enright's "labs," Lacroute's "special rooms," Sacks's "glasshouses." So, mainly, was the argot that sprang up for talking about computers. Outside the labs, the language that was used to describe the machines was either passive and aloof or anthropomorphic. Passive language resulted from the uninitiated's total lack of contact with the machines. Active language was reserved for the closeted wizards who ran the machines ("Joe just ran my job for me."). Anthropomorphic language seemed the only appropriate way to describe these new machines that seemed to replicate human thought processes. Terms such as "human brain" and "electronic brain" began to sprout up in popular culture.

As with the first generation of computer technology, the first generation of technobabble was the longest, lasting approximately a chronological generation, from around 1946 to about 1970.[13] During this period, the building-block terms of technobabble arose: *memory, program(mer), computerese, input/output, hardware, software,* and others. When the industry decided that programmers would "write" programs that would make the machines work, they needed "languages" in which to write the programs.

The invention in 1957 of the integrated circuit (IC), which eliminated vacuum tubes and prompted miniaturization, propelled the growth of the industry and of technobabble. The 1960s was a fertile period for the creation of technobabble—particularly for the transmogrification of nouns into verbs. About a decade after the IC's invention came the microprocessor (1968), which put the entire central processing unit (CPU) of a computer—once a large, ungainly hardware device—onto a chip of silicon. This development ushered in an age of smaller, more powerful computers, and an expanded lexicon.

Second Generation: Dedicated Groups (Shared Interactive)
The next phase was minicomputers and timesharing. Computers were interactive in that groups of users could "timeshare" them. These groups' members could also more easily share among themselves the vocabulary required to describe the tools with which they worked. Whereas vocabulary and technology had evolved relatively slowly over the first generation, the second generation reflected the rapidity with which computer technology could now advance—thanks mainly to the microprocessor itself. Technology may have produced miniaturization in computer size, but this process stimulated the growth of computer-related vocabulary. This second generation also produced an offshoot of networking called electronic mail (e-mail), a primary vehicle for the instantaneous dissemination of technobabble.[14]

This second generation ended with the availability of personal computers. But in that short time, the number of people using and communicating about computers jumped astronomically—especially in the marketing and public-relations sectors. As the 1980s approached, another generation was on the horizon.

Third Generation: Commonplace (One-on-One, or Personal)
Microcomputers did not instantaneously make computers commonplace. The first units were primitive and sold in kits that only proficient hardware hackers could assemble. By 1977, though, anyone could plunk down a few thousand dollars at one of the increasing number of computer stores, take home a machine such as a TRS-80 Model 1, an Apple II, or an Exidy Sorcerer, and try to figure out how to use it by struggling through the documentation. In part because of the ready availability of these little machines, the word *microcomputer* increasingly gave way to the more congenial-sounding term *personal computer.*

Diverse groups of people also started to get personal with industry jargon, which was appearing in more and more places: new magazines, such as *Byte, Kilobaud,* and *Personal Computing,* that had been started to serve the users of personal computers; advertising; press releases; and, most significantly, everyday conversations. The majority of the population was not talking about "interfacing" and getting "on line," but increasing numbers of people were.

Fourth Generation: Pervasive (Networked, or Interpersonal)

Today, in the fourth generation, which started in the early 1980s, computers are pervasive and their use is second nature to many people. Even if we aren't obsessive hackers, nearly all of us encounter computers in some form in daily life. We also encounter and employ technobabble. Some commonplace terms in the mainstream lexicon—*networking, connectivity, workgroup, user friendly, database, interface*, and many others—originated in the computer industry, and most have taken on connotations outside their original denotations.

What started out as a "pure," dispassionate, scientific, and academic lexicon has evolved into a popular phenomenon in the process, migrating from the lab to the glib lips of a large, though disparate, community. Computer technology will soon be omnipresent. Its advances will include sophisticated speech recognition and prosthetic medicine. Technobabble will perhaps never become as widespread as the technology that spawns it. The question is, Will it come to dominate general communication?

3
Proliferation

Spreading the Words: How Computer Terminology Wends Its Way from "Computerese" to Webster
—Headline for airline-magazine article[1]

In the 1950s, the pioneering days of computing, before the thaw of the Cold War, the message of many science-fiction (SF) films was ominously apparent. Movies such as *The H-Man, The Incredible Shrinking Man, Invasion of the Body Snatchers, Them,* and *The Thing* offered none-too-subtle warnings to watch out for "them." In the downbeat ending of *Body Snatchers*, for example, lead actor Kevin McCarthy vainly warned an oblivious populace, "They're coming!" In the 1990s, with the fall of the Iron Curtain, computer companies are eyeing markets in countries that represented the dreaded "them" thirty and forty years earlier. The inhabitants of those countries will soon have to cry: "They [the promulgators of technobabble] are coming!" In the United States, they have been coming in phases since about the dawn of the Cold War. Even today, to listen to them communicate, you may sometimes think they are aliens, communicating, as they do, in acronyms and obscure terms such as "register" and "integer unit." Lest this book start off by conveying the idea that "they" constitutes a homogeneous community, an overview of the denizens of the fragmented computer community is in order.

Who's Who

If the computer community includes everyone who, even tangentially, uses, works with, produces, promotes, or analyzes computers, the resulting group is huge and diverse. Even if the tangential users—those who have bought a "home computer" and only "boot" it up once or twice a month—are discounted, it is still a large group, which can be broken down into the following categories.

Workers

Workers differ from "users" in that they may have no interest in the machines once they have logged off and gone home for the day. Although they may in fact be quite knowledgeable about computers because of their constant exposure to them, these people view them only in the context of their work. Word processors and airline reservations clerks, for example, can be thought of as constituents of the class of disinterested workers.

Users

For the most part, users are enthusiasts. These are people who have actively sought ownership and/or use of machine(s). Casual users are a little more active than the tangential users noted above. Moderate users purchase machines to accomplish personal tasks, to help run small businesses, or to run educational software for their children. Serious users tend to have one or more machines at home, as well as attendant gadgets such as laser printers, fax machines, and portable telephones. They buy a lot of software—unlike moderate users, who tend to copy it—and they devour computer magazines. Users in this category are often employed in or on the periphery of the computer industry, so a lot of overlap occurs between this group and the industry groups, especially "Producers," that follow.

Producers

Broadly speaking, producers are the hardware and software engineers who design the chips, boards, and boxes; write the code that runs on them; and write the documentation that accompanies them—as well as the managers of these people. This category does not include the actual production personnel: the blue-collar workers on the assembly lines and in the "clean rooms," many of whom could as easily be working in sweatshops of another variety. Assemblers and others are more likely to fit into the "Workers" category.

Promoters

These are the people who market the products. The more technically oriented of this group, the product marketers, are likely to have been apprentice producers before they got into marketing. The less technical ones are in PR, marketing communications, and the like. This latter segment is the most prone to liberally slinging the jargon of the industry without a clear or complete understanding of what it means. This group tends to typify the adage that a little knowledge can be dangerous.

Sellers

Salespeople either work for manufacturers and sell directly to business customers, or they work in computer stores and sell the products of several makers to consumers. Resellers buy manufacturers' products, augment them with specific added value, or "value added" as the phrase is inverted in the industry, and sell them to a particular market. Walk into a computer store and talk to a salesperson, and you will be inundated with technobabble—even though the salesperson may be using it to wow you into buying.[2] In his 1983 book *Computer Wimp,* John Bear warns about encountering technobabble as soon as you walk into a computer store.[3]

Analyzers

This group includes reporters, magazine writers, consultants, and market researchers. Many of these people write for or otherwise contribute to widely circulated vehicles for the dissemination of technobabble. Until ten or fifteen years ago, these vehicles were limited to trade and specialty magazines. Today, every major newspaper and many smaller ones have computing sections. Airline magazines regularly carry articles about computers,[4] as do other mainstream publications.

The "Technical" Versus the "Marketing" Mind

Although all the categories discussed here do not fit neatly into a technical or a marketing niche, the distinction is valid. As the authors of *Silicon Valley Fever* put it, "There is a natural tension between technical people and the marketing department in every high-technology company."[5]

Initially, computers and computer jargon were almost solely the province of "technical" minds. These people were professionals whose work was mostly incomprehensible to anyone outside their specialty, but their foreign-sounding lingo served a professional purpose: to further the new phenomenon of computing. Increasingly, people of a "marketing" mind have largely usurped the technical professionals and put technobabble into the public domain.

The technical types wrote and spoke strictly for each other. They assumed that anyone who was hearing or reading their words knew exactly what they were discussing. Those listening or reading did, and the words stayed within a closely knit community. Like the technology, the words were not "real," according to the editor of *MacUser* magazine. "Words are a way to tell when a technology is becoming real," wrote Jon Zilber in his November 1990 editorial, "with real companies developing real products for real customers at realistic prices that don't leave them reeling." What Zilber was *really* writing about was the widespread availability of inexpensive, relatively reliable computer products for the masses. In the process, however, he touched on the two minds: "When the language used to discuss it changes from the jargon of engineers (numbers and esoteric details) to the parlance of marketeers (buzzwords and meaningless neologisms), it's time to take a technology seriously."[6] *MacUser* is a "consumer" computer magazine, so Zilber was perhaps being only partially facetious. He could have easily, and perhaps more accurately, substituted "technobabble" for "a technology" in his last sentence.

The spelling out of acronyms is an area that illustrates the sometimes oppositional nature of the two mentalities. Debate rages intermittently in the industry as to whether the meanings of acronyms and abbreviations, especially commonly understood ones, should be spelled out following the first use of the acronym, as in this example from a letter to *InfoWorld* submitted by a reader:

A 62K (Kilo or 1024) RAM (random-access read/write memory), 2K ROM (read-only memory) computer with IEEE-488 (a standard for device interconnection proposed by the Institute for Electrical and Electronic Engineers) and serial I/O (Input/Output), ASCII (American Standard Code for Information Interchange) terminal, and an 8-bit [the reader neglected to identify bit as a combination of binary and digit] D/A (Digital to Analog) converter.

As the reader noted, without all the identifying "noise" this phrase could be rendered simply as "A 62K RAM, 2K ROM computer with IEEE-488 and serial I/O, ASCII terminal and 8-bit D/A."

This reader was taking issue with another one, who had written in the magazine that acronyms should be identified because "regardless of the level of the readership, it helps to make the articles clearer." Possible solutions to this dilemma are to define as necessary for the perceived audience or to append a glossary, including acronyms, to articles, books, etc. The latter approach makes it easy for technonovices to locate the meanings of unfamiliar terms and equally easy for sophisticates to skip them altogether. Overall, the industry tends to assume that everyone is on intimate terms with its terms, which is increasingly the case.

Computer technology is everywhere, and so, it seems, is the lingo. "It seems like everybody these days is talking about 'networking,' 'accessing databases,' and 'interfacing.' These words may have begun with the clip-on-ID-badge set in Silicon Valley, but they have spread to Main Street, USA, in what seems like only nanoseconds. Call it high-tech talk, Silicon Valley-ese, or technobabble, chances are that some computer buzzwords already are creeping into your vocabulary," wrote a *San Francisco Examiner* writer in late 1984.[7] While technical professionals still inter-communicate with this lingua franca, many more people outside the technical fraternity can understand them—many more than in 1984—or at least have a familiarity with the terms they hear, owing largely to the efforts of people in marketing. Both the technical and marketing types speak the language, and both also have a variety of vehicles for disseminating technobabble by means of the written word.

Documentation

"Users, reviewers, and computer professionals regularly lament the poor quality of software documentation. Increasing numbers of people new to personal computing are forced to learn from confusing, disorganized, and unforgiving manuals." So started an article submitted to *InfoWorld* magazine in the mid-1980s. *PC* magazine put it more forcefully in a headline: "Why Computer Manuals Drive Everyone Stark Raving Mad!"

As anyone who has tried to assemble or learn to use a fairly complex product knows, the instructions that accompany products can be maddening. Convoluted or inaccurate descriptions of assembly processes, inaccurate parts lists, indecipherable illustrations—all these elements and more make much product documentation difficult to use. Frequently the problem can be traced to the foreign manufacture of the product and the translation of the instructions by a foreigner whose fluency in English leaves much to be desired. But sometimes even instruction manuals produced in the United States for English-speakers appear to have been written on another planet.

Computer documentation, among the first vehicles that materialized for technobabble's spread, has long had a well-deserved reputation for being abysmal. Two main factors account for this poor quality. First, the development cycle of a computer product makes accurate documentation of the product nearly impossible. The exigencies of the highly competitive computer market demand that a finished manual be ready when the product is ready to go out the door. Against this backdrop, the term "accurate computer manual" is often an oxymoron. Second, the lamentable state of computer manuals can often be traced to their creators, hackers who write for other hackers rather than for users of the product. "The average computer manual is supposed to be read by a human being," said Carnegie-Mellon University English professor David Laufer optimistically, "but most of them are just indiscriminate 'memory dumps' of some computer systems engineer who just pours out what he knows."[8] Although many technical writers are not hackers, these people too have soaked up the jargon of the industry and needlessly confuse documentation readers by subjecting them to a foreign vocabulary. A second characteristic of bad documentation is logorrhea. Many technical writers are unable or unwilling to state things concisely. The result is meandering prose and paper waste.

Admittedly, these scenarios have changed a lot of late. Until average people started buying and using computers, documentation was essentially an afterthought. So were production values. Manuals often consisted of nothing more than the free associations of some engineer, which were then cranked out on a dot-matrix printer with a faded ribbon, photocopied, punched, and stuck into a binder. Not that it made all that much difference: Early users of computers were as sophisticated as, or even more knowledgeable than, the people building the machines and writing the code. All they needed to see were schematics and specification (spec) sheets. To explain to them in simple linear detail how to use computers might have been perceived as an insult.

The scenario has changed, because the profile of computer buyers has changed. Apple Computer was the first company to make a commercially available, easy-to-use computer ("for the rest of us," as the ad slogan went). Not surprisingly, Apple was also one of the first companies to produce comprehensible documentation. Computer companies that pitch their products to a more technical audience continue to believe that documentation is nothing more than a high-level reference source.[9] But most companies are beginning to aim at more general markets and are attempting to make their manuals and other support materials accessible to less technical users—with varying degrees of success. The companies that have the toughest time are the ones that make and sell very complex computers. In spite of "user-friendly" interfaces and other such decorations, these machines are still difficult to operate and therefore difficult to explain.

Highly technical documentation is not the only culprit. In the early 1980s, the toy company Coleco tried to get into the computer business with a machine called the Adam. In late 1983, hundreds of the machines were returned because customers said they were defective. Coleco, however, claimed that the problems stemmed "from poorly written manuals for the Adam, and not from defects in the machine."[10]

The Laws of Technical Communications[11]

In technical writing, there is always an easier way, always a clearer way, always a more accurate way to say something. Unfortunately they are not the same way.

Once you get it grammatical you'll find its [sic] technically inaccurate. And vice versa.

If you don't understand something, use longer words. Share the ignorance with your readers.

Normal sequence of product design:

1. Management announces the product.
2. Technical writing publishes the manual.
3. Engineering begins designing [the product].

No engineer or programmer ever finished his design before seeing the typeset, printed, perfect-bound manual.

Write a manual that an idiot can understand, and only an idiot will. The author.

The more things a publication tries to explain, the fewer things it does explain.

If you can't convince, then confuse. If you can't bedazzle, then baffle.

The quality of the text varies inversely with the opulence of the cover.

The less time it takes the engineer or programmer to make a change, the more time it takes the writer to describe it.

Exercise abstinence from proclivity toward grandiloquent sesquipedalian verbalizations.

The passive voice should not be used.

DO NOT OVERCAPITALIZE.

One remaining bastion of awful documentation is the variety that comes "on line." This is information you can call up on a screen to help you get through a problem. It is not all bad, and much of it is based on the principle of "hypertext," which enables you to do substantial cross-referencing by clicking on icons and dialog boxes on your screen. But if the prose you obtain is as murky as an algae-choked swamp, all the cross-referencing in the world will be of little value.

Regardless of the quality of computer documentation, it is a major vehicle for the dissemination of technobabble. A lot of people are buying computers, some for the first time. Although they probably have already been exposed to some forms of technobabble, documentation may be their first in-depth exposure to relentless use of it. Inevitably, they will incorporate some of what they encounter into their own vocabularies and, in turn, disseminate it to others. Many will be so put off by the documentation, however, that they will turn to one or more of the three main alternatives to documentation: magazines, books, and oral tradition.

Magazines and Newspapers

Almost from the inception of the computer industry, it had its own magazines. The first publications were industry trade journals such as *Datamation* and *Electronic Engineering Times* that circulated strictly among computer professionals; nobody else would have been able to comprehend them. It was not until the mid-1970s—with the arrival of personal computers—that magazines intended for a more general audience began to appear. These publications were not necessarily any less opaque than their predecessors; since the first microcomputers were things only a hacker could love—and use—anyway, the publications devoted to them were laden with obscure industry argot.

The first microcomputer, the Altair, appeared in early 1975,[12] and the January 1975 issue of *Popular Electronics* magazine had a photo of the machine on the cover.[13] *Popular Electronics* may have dabbled in stories about computers, but it was not until the middle of the year that the first publication resembling a mass-circulation computer magazine debuted.[14] As its title, *Byte,* suggests, its content was technical, and its audience, at least initially, was limited. Less than a decade after *Byte*'s debut, more than 200 computer magazines were available on newsstands. A shakeout was inevitable—it came in the mid-1980s—and today the number is probably less than 100.

Today, magazines that spread technobabble can be divided into two categories: general interest and special interest. Examples of the former are airline and business publications. The latter group ranges from in-house PR disguised as magazines to computer- or area-specific magazines, such as *PC* and *Publish*, to technical trade journals. General-interest titles and the less technical of the computer magazines serve as one of the most significant vehicles for the propagation of technobabble. The audience for technical and trade journals is still essentially limited to professionals, whereas general-circulation computer magazines such as *Macworld* reach hundreds of thousands of readers, from beginners to experts. As more people are introduced to computers, they tend to use these publications as references.

A variant of computer magazines is newsletters with specialized computer-related content. Sometimes it seems that everyone in the computer industry is producing a newsletter. Newsletters are a gold mine of technobabble—and subscribing to one may require a gold mine. Most of these publications are expensive ($500 and more for twelve issues a year is not uncommon). Liberal and gratuitous use of technobabble occurs in slick in-house magazines that promote the companies' products.

Newspapers are oriented toward general audiences. Most major ones, and even many small ones, carry computer stories in their business or technology sections. The major metropolitan papers located in high-technology areas—the *San Jose Mercury News*, for example—have special sections devoted to computer products and developments. Although the computing section of the *Mercury News* is geared primarily to people in the industry, it also includes articles aimed at novices. An August 5, 1990, article that informed beginners about how to select a machine for purchase included a sidebar full of terms, such as *bit*, *display modem*, and *wait state*. "Computers have their own jargon that can be confusing and intimidating to novices," the sidebar started. "But understanding just a few basic computer terms can go a long way toward helping you get the right computer for your needs."[15] Within the industry, understanding a few terms, or at least having passing familiarity with them, can go a long way toward using them with abandon.

Computer Books

The primary purpose of early books about computers was either to translate the documentation into something more comprehensible or to fill huge information gaps in the manuals. A lot of these books were not much more coherent than the documentation they supplemented, but they did provide missing information. In any case, they helped spread technobabble to those who purchased them in hopes of learning more about computers. As computer use grew, the number of companies that published computer books proliferated—to a point at which the market became glutted with titles. A few publishers went out of business, others dropped the computer-book line from their lists. Successful publishers that remained in the business reduced the number and improved the quality of the titles they published.

Different computer-book editors take different approaches to their wares. Some attempt to beat technobabble-laced manuscripts into clear prose, and others just let the authors have their head. Since most people who write technical computer books are techies first and writers second, heavy editing is frequently indicated but not always provided.

A more important factor than cursory editing is the author-as-publisher syndrome. A few years ago, publishers discovered that they could save time and money on production if they required authors to submit camera-ready pages. The publisher would pay an author a per-page production fee that was generally well under what the publisher would pay customary suppliers of production services. Publishers not only saved money, but, ideally, they also got titles to market sooner, since authors had a special incentive to speed production of their own books.

The authors formatted pages themselves, employing page-layout software, or contracted the work out—generally to friends or associates. The periodic problem with the approach was that some publishers were seduced into thinking that because it was "state of the art," employing as it did desktop-publishing tools, it was good. That seduction sometimes bred laziness. Some publishers conveniently forgot that they still had to participate in the process—namely by editing. In leaving the editing to authors, they overlooked a cardinal fact: Authors are rarely editors. Predictably, the publishers who left editorial decisions solely to the authors often ended up with inferior products. The good editors, in all areas of computer publishing, help keep technobabble at bay and technical writing reasonably coherent.

Dictionaries

The 1969 edition of the *American Heritage Dictionary of the English Language* lists the primary definition of computer as "a person who computes." Yet the copyright page mentions that the book was "computer-composed by Infonics, Inc., in Maynard, Massachusetts." It seems astonishing that well into the age of computers, a dictionary would still consider as the primary meaning of this word a person performing calculations. By 1969 there was no doubt in most people's mind about what a computer was.

The article "Spreading the Words" deals briefly with the selection process used by the editors of the Merriam-Webster dictionaries for admitting definitions of computerese.[16] After noting that, starting in 1983, the *Ninth New Collegiate Dictionary* was the first of the publisher's dictionaries to list the date of coinage or first appearance of words, the author wrote about Merriam-Webster's authority for dates and definitions, a "vast citation file: bank upon bank of long, narrow drawers resembling the card file of a gargantuan library." A single word may have several citations. But "making it into the file is no guarantee that a word will make it into the dictionary," the article notes, giving *hacker* as an example. In 1983, Merriam-Webster had not admitted it, even though the file held about half a dozen citations, the earliest being from a 1972

Rolling Stone article by Stewart Brand. (Brand called hacker "a term of derision and also the ultimate compliment.")

Whether a word finally gains admittance to the dictionary's pages or languishes in the citation file depends largely on "spread," citations from different sources over an extended period. "A word can be rejected despite a thick wad of citations if all instances of its use are clumped together in a period of a few months, indicating a faddish usage rather than an enduring addition to the language."[17]

Editors at Merriam-Webster comb industry journals for technobabble, but they also look closely at "nontechnical sources as evidence that a word has gained some degree of general use." In 1983, Merriam-Webster had only three citations for the now pandemic *gigabyte,* and two of the three had come from *Datamation,* an industry trade magazine.

Merriam-Webster is cautious in its approach to admitting technobabble. The publisher tends to steer away from regional proper nouns (in 1983 it considered *Silicon Valley* a regional term) and trademarks. At the time "Spreading the Words" was written, Merriam-Webster was "still waiting to hear from IBM about the etymology of 'Winchester hard disk.'"[18] Some people, however, do not believe that Merriam-Webster is cautious enough. Several readers of *InfoWorld* (one of the Merriam-Webster editors' sources listed in the article) wrote around the time of the publication of "Spreading the Words" that the *Ninth New Collegiate Dictionary* was too liberal in its admission of technobabble. One reader, who worked for a Silicon Valley PR firm, bemoaned the *Ninth*'s descriptive versus prescriptive approach to etymology. "Access as a verb! The dictionary probably also includes the definition 'to impact: to greatly affect.' Just because we hear those around us use nouns as verbs doesn't mean the usage is correct."

Advertising

According to a computer-industry adage, serious computer enthusiasts are more interested in looking at the ads in computer magazines than in reading the articles. The articles, this line of thinking goes, are not necessarily objective, because some magazines are a little too cozy with advertisers. Ads, of course, are full of hype and outlandish claims, but at least they let readers know what products exist and sometimes how much they cost. A given issue of a magazine can cover only so many products, but a weighty issue packed full of ad pages is almost like a directory of products and services. Many of the ads are laced with technobabble. Their readership is generally steeped in or at least familiar with the language of the industry. You would not expect to see this kind of advertising in mainstream media. Or would you?

TV Ads

Although the practice is not yet widespread, ads featuring technobabble have appeared on network television. The campaign that kicked off the practice on a national scale was initiated by the Lowell, Massachusetts–based computer company Wang in 1988. In this series of ads, computer-industry male Yuppies discussed their technotravails in language heavily laced with corporate technojive. In one ad, a man explains "how Wang's integrated image system would handle an [insurance claim]":

Adjuster comes out, takes a picture of the fender. Signs off on an adjustment. Handwritten document. Photograph—an image. All go back to home office via electronic mail. Touch a button and you got a data window, text window, image window right in front of you . . . That's integrated imaging, and Wang has it. Another example: customer service—guy calls EBC. [fade out]

In another ad, a troubleshooter talks to his supervisor:

I was hired midway into the revolution. The independent forces, you know, PC users, had begun to form guerilla groups hooked together like tinker toys. Stubbornly independent, but cut off from the main source of power. No electronic mail from one outpost to the other. No shared resources. Chaos was the price they were paying for freedom. So we put up Wang's PC LAN. It networks PCs, yes, but it also networks the networks. [fade out][19]

What was the rationale behind such a campaign? The ad was seen by millions of people, but how many of them were likely to have understood what they were hearing, much less be in a position of responsibility for the purchase of lots of expensive computer equipment? Similarly, how many television viewers who saw Sun Microsystem's April 14, 1991, saturation ad were likely to understand the tag line that served as the ad's finale: "Sun Microsystems. The purest form of client/server computing"?

Another company that has used TV advertising is Apple Computer. Apple took off like a rocket in the late 1970s with its Apple II personal computer. Yet by the early 1980s, the company had already stumbled when its Apple III turned out to be bug-ridden. Almost concurrently, the

Lisa was a disaster. The Macintosh revived Apple's fortunes for several years. Then, it seemed, Apple forgot its roots: inexpensive computers "for the rest of us," as an Apple ad slogan once put it. Shortly after the Macintosh's introduction in 1984, Apple cofounder Steve Jobs was ousted by the man he had brought in to boost sales, chairman John Sculley, formerly of Pepsico. (Sculley's early success at increasing sales seemed to indicate that selling computers was like selling any other commodity.)

Reportedly, one of Sculley's reasons for axing Jobs was that the latter personified the brash old Apple that in 1981 had run a full-page ad in the *Wall Street Journal*, proclaiming,

Welcome, IBM. Seriously.

Welcome to the most exciting and important marketplace since the computer revolution began 35 years ago. And congratulations on your first computer. Putting real computer power in the hands of the individual is already improving the way people work, think, communicate, and spend their leisure hours. Computer literacy is fast becoming as fundamental a skill as reading or writing. When we invented the first personal computer system. . . .[20]

Whereas Jobs was brilliant but volatile—Apple's Dionysian side—Sculley was ascetic and buttoned down—the Appleonian side. Advertising was one of the areas in which the two men reportedly disagreed. Two Jobs-inspired TV ads allegedly helped hasten his ouster. Both took heavy swipes at IBM. In the infamous "lemmings" commercial, blindfolded men in blue-gray suits marched in lockstep over a cliff.

Apple's subsequent campaign featured a string of staid commercials with the self-actualizationish tag line "The power to be your best." In one of these ads, which started running in late 1989–early 1990, a forty-something executive peers out of a glass-walled office at well-scrubbed and -coiffed younger colleagues going busily about their computer tasks among their cubicles . . . worker bees scurrying in a hive is the impression conveyed. A contemporary of the contemplative executive inquires, "What are you looking at?" He replies that he is trying to determine which computer among the variety of brands out on the floor is getting the most use. (Hint: Everyone is crowded around a Macintosh, while all the other brands are not even turned on.) "That's easy," reasons his colleague alliteratively. "The one with the most MIPS, megaflops, memory." "I don't think so," counters the observant executive, who informs his technobabbling colleague, "I think it's the one people use the most."

MIPS? Megaflops? On prime-time network TV? The difference between Wang's and Apple's approaches to technobabble for the masses is that Wang made vocabulary the central focus of its ad. Apple inserted technical language only briefly, giving it a mildly pejorative slant in the process. Sun used technobabble as a grabber at the conclusion of an ad that had already tossed off jargon in a voiceover.

The appearance of technobabble in advertising that is reaching a wide audience, most of whose members don't have a clue about what it means, is likely to increase. In early 1990, New England Telephone (NET) ran an ad that featured a balding, well-dressed Yuppie conversing with a smartly attired female colleague on a business flight. They discuss the respective merits of their telephone companies, when the conversation turns to ISDN. The woman informs her bemused traveling companion that this entity is within NET's repertoire of services. "NET handles ISDN?" he inquires in acronymic amazement. So what is ISDN?[21] inquire Joe and Jane Average Television Viewer. It stands for Integrated Services Digital Network—an increasingly important technology as more and more digital information is sent across antiquated analog phone lines. An ISDN digitally encodes voice, data, fax, and other forms of communication for transmission over fiber-optic as opposed to multistrand copper-wire lines.

As these and other technologies become more pervasive, the terminology that describes them is going to be on the lips of more and more people, in part because advertising is going to start using such terminology more and more, increasing the general public's awareness and use of it in the process. In this post-McLuhan era, we are all aware of the significant influence of TV on everything from fashion to language. Although you are likely to hear increasing amounts of technobabble in TV advertising, do not expect it to dominate the copy the way it did in the Wang ads. It will probably occur as an intriguing allusion rather than as a theme.[22]

Classified Ads

Classified advertising by high-tech companies accounts for a wealth of technobabble. The want-ads sections of Sunday newspapers in urban areas with a high concentration of computer and software companies are loaded with solicitations for hardware engineers, programmers, and others who maintain the infrastructure of technology companies.

One such area is the Virginia suburbs of Washington, D.C. What used to be a lethargic rural area is now an ocean of concrete and gridlock. In 1983 *Washington Post* columnist Phillip Godwin wrote about the difficulty of deciphering job postings in classified ads. Godwin was responding to the benighted pronouncement by then-president Reagan that the unemployed merely had to open their papers to the classifieds to find work. Godwin noted that Reagan's critics had claimed that most jobs listed required advanced training that the unemployed tended to lack. Godwin decided to find out who was right by checking out the Sunday paper. He discovered an entirely different problem: "How do you know if you qualify for a job when the title reads like a foreign language?" Predictably, perhaps, most of the obtuse titles he listed were for computer-industry jobs. "What," wondered Godwin, "does a Configuration Management Specialist do? Or a Verification-Validation Software Analyst?" Some of the titles had accompanying descriptions, Godwin acknowledged, "but the descriptions are just as puzzling as the titles, as in the following: 'Are you looking for a technical challenge in the area of DARPA and DOD technologies, implementing Data Base Management Systems and developing micro, mini, and host applications for worldwide DODIIS?'"

"What normal American isn't?" Godwin asked rhetorically. "Reagan should hire a translator to clarify for the public what these jobs are. People may realize that they are qualified for these jobs once they understand what they involve."[23]

High-tech classifieds are laden with jargon as well as the usual euphemistic personnel babble, but anyone who is qualified to apply for these kinds of jobs should have no trouble deciphering them. To get an idea of what Godwin was complaining about, though, take a look at the following excerpts, selected randomly from the September 9 and October 7, 1990, Sunday editions of the *San Jose Mercury News:*

CIM Professionals

Kernel Development Manager

Distributed Environment Manager: Supervise a team of Software Engineers in the development of distributed environments (NFS and RFS) for an SVR4-based operating system for large systems

Port and enhance UNIX device drivers as well as optimize device support for our System/370 XA platform

Leverage your training expertise to help our customers understand and learn to implement complex internetworking systems
Senior Bring-up Engineer
Strong experience with INGRES RDBMS, specifically ABF, is essential
Engineering: ASIC (MCU/MPU) . . . design svcs. to gate array/standard cell customers

Only a techie could love or understand these descriptions. One San Francisco–area company tried an altogether different approach, one that eschewed professional technobabble for the much more colloquial and direct variety—and threw in a little sex for good measure. "TECHNO-WEENY" was the ad's all-caps lead. "Are you the Bay Area's greatest computer nerd? We need you. Must have carnal knowledge of computers, memory boards, hard drives, upgrades, modems, cables, terminals, etc." Demonstrating that it was looking for fast-track nerds, the ad listed only a fax number, to which it directed those interested to send their résumés.

PR and Marketing

Among the most prolific purveyors of technobabble are the people who work in PR and marketing departments. Their dissemination of the industry's argot is natural, because their objective is to carry their companies' messages to the world. Many computer companies have in-house groups performing the requisite tasks, other companies use outside agencies, and some combine in-house and contract approaches. Whether the function is provided in or out of house, the primary duty of these practitioners is to present companies and their products in the best light. Doing so involves carrying a lot of messages to a variety of audiences.

Public-relations and marketing people are schooled in communication, but they do not necessarily know much about technology. Their introduction to a company and its wares may come in large part from the oral tradition (see below). Since their main function is to dispense "messages," they constitute a primary conduit for industry jargon.

Some PR/marketing types believe in the value of clear, concise communication; others are more interested in boosting the buzzword quotient. One PR firm that is aware of the technobabble-glut problem, at least on the PR end, is McGrath/Power West Public Relations. In 1988 this Santa Clara, California, company presented its "Wordy Awards" to "the most overused words in high-technology press releases." According to the firm, the awards were based on a survey of high-technology and business journalists. (The comments following some of the words in this list are mine.) Awarded top honors were *easy to use, first, functionality, high performance, implement, integration, interface, synergy, unique,* and *user friendly.*

A partial listing of "other nominees" includes *architect* (the awards-givers do not indicate whether this is the noun or verb form of the word), *alliance, allows, configure, enhanced, high-tech, industry-leading, information management, innovation, leading-edge, low end/high end* (meaning the bottom and the top of a product line), *monolithic, open, platform, powerful, power user, price point* (take off the word *point,* and you have the meaning), *productivity, provides, solutions, sophisticated, super computer* (more often this term is closed up: *supercomputer*), *transparent interface, user, utilization,* and *vaporware.*

Missing from these lists are such obvious candidates as *support, array, suite, develop, offer, leverage, impact* (as a verb), *benchmark,* and *deliver.*

According to an informal survey conducted by *Wall Street Journal* reporter Michael Miller in 1989, the 11 most overused words in "high-tech hype" are *leading* (appeared in 88 of 201 press releases Miller collected over a one-month period; the number of occurrences of the words appears in parentheses in the rest of this list), *enhanced* (47), *unique* (35), *significant* (30), *solution* (23), *integrated* (23), *powerful* (20), *innovative* (18), *advanced* (17), *high-performance* (17), and *sophisticated* (17). "Writing press releases for high-tech products is a feverish game without rules," Miller concluded. "The world's electronic industries bring out hundreds of new products daily, each attended by professional hyperbolists."[24]

In a market characterized by technological Darwinism, getting products out fast is crucial. Miller identified four characteristics of high-tech hype that reinforce this urgency:

• "Forced firsts." Miller noted that "there is no verbal hoop through which [high-tech publicists] won't jump to make the claim" of being the first.
• "Mystery market research." Numerous market-research firms sometimes produce dubious and inflated data, and one firm will often make calculations that diverge widely from those of another firm in the same product category. Nevertheless, Miller noted, computer companies have

been shown to take the most speculative market-research projections and then inflate them.

• "Measurement mania." When PR people are stumped, Miller says, "It's never hard for companies to find a number to brag about."

• "Gobbledygook." "Again and again," Miller stressed, his sample showed a "curious reluctance" of companies to "come right out and say what it is they are announcing. The gobbledygook quotient was high even in releases written by outside [PR] firms, whose fortunes often depend on how many newspapers decided to run stories about the companies they represent."

One account manager from a PR firm said she had tried to persuade her client to "drop the techno-babble [*sic*] and instead emphasize the long-term economic impact of the product." The company would have none of it. "They're all engineers," she said. "They say, 'This is a neat whizzy thing and engineers love it.' Talking about things like productivity, it's like 'Don't bother me with those details.' "[25] Another firm tried to explain such terms as *dual-channel, SCSI,* and *Multibus,* but the client insisted that the explanations be cut. "These companies are very snobby," said one of the firm's publicists. "They just figure, how could you not know that dual channel means you can hook up two peripherals on one board and free up a slot?"[26] Inherent in technobabble is the assumption that everyone else knows what the users of the technobabble are talking about.

Some marketing people argue that their releases are aimed at technical publications and have to be written accordingly. NCR's director of public relations, Gary Stechmesser, explained, "There is a fear that editors who receive [a less technical release] would believe they are being talked down to."[27] This explanation, however, does not jibe with the expressed desires of editors of technical magazines editors (noted below). Jargon-laden releases may have the desired effect because of the very problems Miller identified. "If we aroused your curiosity to the point where you were interested in talking to us, then we succeeded in the primary goal of getting some press attention," said Caine O'Brien, a marketing manager at a company called MicroCASE.[28]

Miller made his observations about technobabble in 1989. The examples he cites—this one, for example: "a joint development effort between Cadre Technologies and MicroCASE that tightly links structured analysis and design CASE tools to software development and test tools in support of real-time embedded system design"—are not nearly as opaque

as those dredged up by another newspaper writer about six years earlier—
one reason being that the overall quality of press releases has marginally
improved over the years. In 1983, *San Jose Mercury News* columnist Steve
Lopez took industry press releases to task by conducting the "Valspeak
[Silicon Valley Speak] Contest." "The challenge," as Lopez put it, was "to
create a press release of 25 to 100 words, with the most technical
buzzwords and the most confusing purpose." Lopez offered some examples from press releases that had prompted him to create the contest:

The 4019NYS and 4019NYO Single Monitor Units upgrade a Western Electric
551A Channel Service Unit to provide a self contained, in line, signal monitor,
loopback and performance diagnostic system.

The DM5213 is specified at 350 ns read access times and 10 ms byte write over
the full military operating range of −55 degrees C to +125 degrees C. The military
temperature range DM5213 is available for prototyping, and a DM5213/B
screened to military standard 833, level B, is available for production. Both are
organized 2K by eight bits in the JEDEC (Joint Electronic Device Engineering
Council)-approved, metal-oxide semiconductor (MOS) byte-wide memory configuration. They are available initially in a 24-pin dual-in-line package (DIP) and
will be available in a 32-pin chip carrier.[29]

At the time, I was working at *InfoWorld* magazine, and some colleagues
and I decided to enter the contest with this "press release":

For Immediate Release

XERCOM today announces a state-of-the-art CMOS-based EPROM module
conforming to all MIL-SPEC parameters and interfacing to ROMable/RAMable
ASCII/ANSI devices.

The ABC-PDQ 381 EPROM environments into hex and alphageomosaic applications virtualized to PIA DIP switch functionality at 1200_{10} baud. A download-
ing EBCDIC-oriented uploader enhances the enhancements of the enhanced
IDRIS protocols that talk to the PABX store-and-forward interface bread-
boarded into the unit.

Available in 16, 32, and 48-bit configurations, the 381 utilizes user-keyboardable
softkeys and display functionalities maxing out at 265 colors on an RGB CRT
configured for modemized operation that concatenates with a 4MHz, 12 VAC,
155 cps, VAX-alike, DEC-emulating, annualized, prioritized, PROMized, and
user-friendlyized operation for easy understanding and utilization in an
environmentalized environment.

For knowledge workers everywhere.

To our dismay, we placed only third in the contest.

Similar to this and other contest entries was a piece of corporate
folklore circulating at the time. It was a template for producing computer-
industry press releases:

NEWS RELEASE

FOR RELEASE AFTER *date*

FOR MORE INFORMATION CONTACT *Flack A* OR *Flack B*

Company name OR *Geek name*

SUPPORTS OR RELEASES OR PROMOTED TO

INTEGRATED *what* SYSTEM

OR VICE-PRESIDENT, CORPORATENESS

FOR HIGH-END END-USER

MARKET DEVELOPMENT TECHNOLOGY

SUNNYVALE, CA—*Company's* marketing technology group has signed an exclusive contract with *some other company's* technology marketing group to cross-license the subcontracting of all third-party agreements to market third-generation technologies or to technologize third-generation markets, announced *Geek name*, newly promoted Vice-President, Corporateness for High-end End-user Market Development Technology.

"We consider *company name's* commitment to third-generation market technologization to be a milestone in the history of the newly formed Division of Corporateness for High-end End-user Market Development Technology," said *Geek name*. "We are proud to be a part of *other company's* strategically aggressive move to incorporate innovative integrated desktop thinking into its technology marketing endeavors."

Company name is a publicly held corporation traded OTC under the name *company acronym*. *Company name* is headquartered in *company California address*, with manufacturing facilities in Bangladesh.

CP/M is a registered trademark of Digital Research.
i is a registered trademark of Intel.
Arabic numerals are a registered trademark of *company name*.
Editors, please note: Company name must be spelled with Greek es and with odd-numbered letters capitalized. To spell it otherwise is to invite lawsuit and loss of advertising revenue.

Around this time, *InfoWorld* reporter Scott Mace attended a meeting of a Silicon Valley advertising association. Also present were representatives from the *San Jose Mercury News, BusinessWeek,* and *Electronic Design*. These press people were there to tell advertisers and PR people what they did and did not want to see in press releases. They wanted to receive releases that were short and succinct and read like news stories rather than ad copy; they did not want to receive badly written, jargon-laden, hyperbolic releases. Yet the trade and business press often does nothing more than reproduce the releases that cross editors' desks, with much of the technobabble intact. Here is a short piece that appeared in the business section of the *Peninsula Times Tribune,* a daily newspaper serving communities between San Francisco and Silicon Valley:

ParcPlace Systems of Mountain View announced the availability of its Object-works for the Smalltalk-80 object-oriented programming system for Microsoft Windows 3.0.

This new product, named Objectworks for Smalltalk-80/Windows 3.0, brings workstation performance to the PC and allows programmers to port graphical-user-interface (GUI) programs across PCs and workstations.

Under Windows 3.0, Objectworks for Smalltalk-80 allows programmers to create sophisticated and graphical applications that run identically on all major platforms.[30]

Although this particular newspaper does cover the northern reaches of Silicon Valley, many of its readers are likely to be nearly as baffled by this story as most of the nation was by the dialogue in the Wang ads mentioned earlier in this chapter.

Product "Rollouts" and Trade Shows

Major product introductions, to large groups of people, are often forums for the rollout of "technoneologisms" or the perpetuation of existing ones. When Apple, for example, introduced the Macintosh in early 1984, Apple executives Steve Jobs and John Sculley tossed off such terms as "radical ease of use," "power curve," and "knowledge worker."[31] *Knowledge worker* is a term that started gaining popularity in the early 1980s. By the end of the decade, these workers were clustered in *workgroups*, to which Sun Microsystems' vice president of engineering paid homage at the July 1990 introduction of Sun's SPARCstation IPC. Eric Schmidt said that Sun's vision was to "empower the workgroup." He also referred to "diskful Sun desktops." In attempting to explain what *IPC* stood for, Schmidt rattled off a litany of possibilities: Integrated Power Computer, Integrated Personal Computer, Instead of a Personal Computer. He did not mention what the abbreviation was commonly understood to denote: Interpersonal Computer, after the psychobabble-tinged term coined earlier by Steve Jobs.

If you stroll the endless corridors of major computer trade shows, such as Comdex, Uniforum, and Interop, technobabble assaults you from the mouths of live actors, people in videos, banners, and neon signs. Often the babble is thematic; a networking show will be laced with *connectivity, interoperability,* and, of course, *networking.* Also sure to be out in force will be the usual lexical suspects: *powerful, sophisticated, advanced, solutions,* and superlatives galore.

The largest computer show in the world is Comdex, held each year in Las Vegas. The 1990 edition saw nearly 150,000 people exploring hundreds of thousands of square feet of exhibits that numbered in the hundreds. One of the exhibitors was Pick Systems, named after its founder, Dick Pick, which makes an operating system tailored for large business applications. At the Pick booth, a rap group belted out tunes under the slogan "Pick's Got the Power." The lyrics evoked a phrase from an early 1980s song, "Psychobabble," by the Alan Parsons Group: "It's all psychobabble rap to me." In this case, it was all technobabble rap:

I bought applications to run the firm.
Shellin' out money at every turn.
Sticker shock brought me to my knees.
Time to buy ten more PCs. . . .
LAN cards, PCs, cable it by hand,
It's still every user on their data island. . . .
And just when I thought I knew true pain,
Along comes this box from Hell they call a "Main-Frame!". . .
All I'm ascertaining is complaining
Of downtime backups, bugs, and crashes.
Even when it's up, it runs like molasses! . . .
The dictionary tells you how the data is viewed.
You can have your data any way ya like it, dude!
Conversions, correlative, ASCII crude. . . .
It's "virtual memory," the hot, hot ticket;
If it's in RAM, use it; if it's not, pick it
Off the disk in a hurry and store it in RAM. . . .
Flush it back out to disk, and now your data is saved.
When you need it again, you get it, "Demand Paged."[32]

Oral Tradition

In light of the technological meshes that surround the world, it is tempting to lapse into a McLuhanesque assessment of technobabble. Wide-area networking has all but realized McLuhan's vision of the "global village." Communications today are much more rapid and widespread than anything McLuhan knew and wrote about in the 1960s and 1970s. Ironically, perhaps, despite all this technology, oral tradition remains significant, particularly when it comes to the propagation of technobabble. In preliterate societies, the oral tradition was the method by which a people communicated and perpetuated their culture and myths. With the advent of papyrus, paper, printing, and other technologies, oral tradition diminished in importance, although even in today's global village, isolated preliterate societies continue to exist.

With its magnetic and optical storage media, video, voicemail, speech generation and recognition, data communication, and all the other technological triumphs of the "information age," the computer industry is a kind of postliterate society—so-called computer literacy and product literature notwithstanding. But as in a preliterate group, oral dissemination of culture is crucial to this postliterate society. A predominant characteristic of the computer industry's culture is volatility—in relation to both technology and people. Technological innovations and developments occur at an ever-accelerating pace. Workers, particularly "knowledge workers," are expected to do more and do it faster. The accelerated pace leads to an inevitable proliferation of information: trade journals, documentation, competitive reports, newspapers, white papers. The laughable utopian notion that computers would lead to the "paperless office" has been entirely discredited as people drown in a sea of documents (Xerox even bills itself as "The Document Company").

A human aspect of this volatility is mobility. Workers in the computer industry tend not to stay put. Better opportunities always seem to beckon over the horizon. People go from startup to startup in hopes of getting lots of cheap stock options and cashing in big when the company goes public. Employment in the computer industry is much like working in professional sports: Long-term loyalty to a company (or team) is overshadowed by short-term monetary considerations.

New arrivals at computer companies soon discover that each one has its unique "corporate culture." Although a pink shirt and a flashy yellow tie may be suitable for an Apple salesperson, for example, such attire would provoke horror and derision at IBM. Given the mobility of the industry's work force, its members have to learn such distinctions each time they switch companies.

Although computer firms conduct new-employee-orientation sessions that tout the company line and purport to give basic training, these pat presentations ignore many of the real-world situations new workers are likely to encounter. Traditionally, DP (data-processing) managers have been responsible for technical training, but either they are too busy or they offer rarified, abstract assistance that, again, does not account for situations workers actually encounter.[33] Highly paid workers in these "high tech sweatshops" are expected to dive in and produce immediately, without much practical training. They often have to turn to knowledgeable colleagues to learn the ropes.

Against this backdrop of technological and human volatility, the oral tradition helps people keep up. In addition to transmitting and perpetuating technical and corporate conventions, the high-tech oral tradition is a fecund method of spawning and spreading technobabble. Success in the computer industry depends almost as much on sounding knowledgeable as on being knowledgeable, so the people who are most susceptible to the effects of oral tradition are the nontechnical types—especially those in marketing and PR.

Consider the marketing novices who enter an intensely technical milieu. Around them swirl perverse polysyllables, arcane acronyms, fractured syntax. The documentation, data sheets, and other materials are also replete with these elements. The concepts behind the terms and the technology represented by them are obscure, incredibly complex—fathomable only by the keenest of technical minds. Rather than sound ignorant in front of more-seasoned colleagues, many overwhelmed tyros opt for parroting jargon and buzzwords, sometimes with an inchoate idea or no idea at all of what the terms mean.[34] In the case of PR people, the rule of thumb often seems to involve the "TQ" (technobabble quotient): The more technobabble they can cram into a press release, the better. "Merely picking up the jargon will not substitute for some real knowledge or experience," however, warned the author of an article about job prospects in the computer industry. "Knowledge of the buzzwords and terminology may be necessary on the résumé or in an interview, but on the job it can lead to trouble, if the person really doesn't understand what he/she is talking about."[35] On the other hand, the larger the corporation and the more entrenched the bureaucracy, the more the knowledge of technobabble may lead the person to a promotion.

Technobabble creeps into casual conversation as well, which becomes filled with "interfacing," "interrupt modes," "disconnects," "offline discussions," "brain dumps," "environments," "implementations," and the like. The oral tradition in computing educates new employees about their companies, but it can also adversely affect concise, and often even coherent, conversation.

The functioning of the oral tradition was nicely illustrated in a 1985 installment of the comic strip "On the Fastrack" by Bill Holbrook. In the strip, two men are chatting at an office-automation show:

Bob: Well, Bud, have you seen any new equipment at this office-automation convention?

Bud: No, Bob, but I've picked up a new buzzword. It's "entry-freem." I found it in the brochure, and I have no idea what it means! But I didn't want to sound ignorant, so I've been saying it to everyone I've met!

Bob: Uh, Bud. That's just a typo in your copy. It's supposed to say "entrance fee."

Bud: Oh, no! You mean I've been making a fool of myself?

In the final panel, Bob says, "Not entirely," as he glances over his shoulder at a group of people, who are saying,

"It achieves high-density entry-freem."
"This product entries freemicly with multi-use functions."
"And it incorporates entry peripherals with modular freeming."
"This generation freems into your entry-environment."
"It's freemic-literate."

This strip offers a slightly exaggerated picture of how technobabble is perpetuated in the computer industry. But it is not just the nontechnical types who are subject to the effects of the oral tradition. All UNIX techies, for example, know—many down to the minutest level—what the *grep* command does. They use it and employ it in speech and writing with impunity. But do they know what its letters stand for? According to the glossary accompanying an article in the November 1990 issue of the *SunTech Journal,* the UNIX acronym *grep* stands for "Get Regular Expression and Print."[36] Unfortunately, the quest for standards in the industry has not necessarily filtered down to its terminology, according to what meets the eye. According to a column in the December 1985 issue of *UNIX World, grep* stands for "Globally search for a Regular Expression and Print."[37] A tech writer at Hewlett-Packard once proclaimed that it denoted "Generalized Regular Expression Parser" (two variations on this theme are that the *g* stands for General or Generic). The authors of *UNIX for People* claim that it means "Global Regular Expression or Pattern."[38] Not so, say Don Libes and Sandy Ressler in *Life with UNIX,* which lists *grep* as standing for "Global Regular Expression Print."[39] How about "Generalized Regular Expression [Pattern]"? That's the pronouncement of *An Introduction to Berkeley UNIX*.[40] That's eight prospects for the meaning of *grep;* recombining the words yields even more possibilities. The primary point here is not to single out semantic ambiguities but rather to reinforce the notion that technobabble often spreads without a clear or universal understanding of just what is spreading. As with other oral traditions, that of the computer industry is much like a line of people telling a story. The person at the head of the line whispers something into the ear of the adjoining person. That person in turn tells the story to the next but in the process adds, drops, or otherwise changes a few details, and so on down the line. By the time the final person recounts the story aloud, it bears only a slight resemblance to the original.

Once a technobabble term catches on and spreads, it will most likely crop up just about everywhere: in documentation, press releases, in brochures. Many of these terms will be like rock groups: They will experience brief popularity and then vanish. Others—*interface* as a verb, for example—will become widespread and even make it into dictionaries and popular media such as TV and film.

In 1978, Philip Kaufman directed a remake of *Invasion of the Body Snatchers;* Kevin McCarthy, the lead in the original film, even put in a cameo appearance. Although the basic plot of the new version was the same as that of the original, its emphasis and nuances were different. Because of such technological progress as the ubiquity of VCRs, the remake reached a wider audience than did the 1956 original. So it is with technobabble several decades after its inception.

4

High-Tech Tower of Babel

Dismantling the Computer Industry's Tower of Babel
—Newspaper headline[1]

As it deals with innumerable and diverse computer systems, programming languages, byte orders, and other such phenomena, the computer industry needs standards—not of behavior but of operation. A technology standard is an entity, such as a protocol, to which everyone in the industry—at least in a particular country—can conform to accomplish tasks. The 256-alphanumeric-character ASCII (American Standard Code for Information Interchange) character set is an example of a standard by which computers and their users can exchange information. The System Network Architecture (SNA) is a networking protocol, developed by IBM (International Business Machines), that has also become a standard.

Although some standards in the computer industry had been in place for years, the 1980s witnessed "standards wars." In the early days of computing, when IBM and DEC (Digital Equipment Corporation) and their ilk effectively dictated standards, competitors just fell into line. By the late 1980s, "open systems," personal computing, laissez-faire attitudes—all these things and more made standardization an elusive and sometimes fractious process. Companies and consortia attempted to "outstandardize" each other, each claiming to be the true bearer of a given standard. Ironically, these battles served mainly to further fragment some segments of the industry, thereby complicating the standards problem.

Mirroring this technological free-for-all was the language of the industry. Almost as quickly as some upstart company would develop a new technology or come up with a new variation on an existing one, someone would come up with yet another term or a variation on an existing one. The main difference between technology and vocabulary was that there were few standards unifying the industry's lexicon.

Standards arrive in the computer industry by two different routes. They can be mandated by a committee such as ANSI (American National Standards Institute) or its German counterpart, DIN (Deutsche Industrie Normen). Such standards are considered "de jure." The other method by which standards can arise is "de facto." In the early, autocratic days of computing, most standards were de jure, although an IBM specification could become a standard because, as the saying went, "IBM is not the competition, it's the environment"—meaning that IBM exerted such technohegemony that everyone else almost had to follow suit to survive. This is not to say, though, that IBM was an absolute dictator.

The accepted business practice in the computer industry—in both hardware and software—was to develop "proprietary" systems. Digital Equipment Corporation, for example, spent millions of dollars to create its exclusive VMS operating system. Once a customer bought DEC minicomputers, that customer was "locked in" to DEC. The equipment was so expensive that the customer had no choice but to continue to buy DEC's machines, to run DEC's operating system, and to upgrade when DEC decided to release a new version of VMS. Scrapping the DEC equipment for that of another vendor would have been prohibitively expensive. That philosophy prevailed into the early 1980s, when the advent of so-called open systems began to change things. Ironically, one of the catalysts for open systems was IBM. The IBM Personal Computer, introduced in 1981, was "clonable," which meant that smaller companies could legally produce "compatibles" at half the cost of what IBM was charging.[2] Another major catalyst was the UNIX operating system (OS), which could be licensed cheaply from AT&T. Companies that did not want or could not afford to create an OS from scratch worked hard to establish UNIX as the de rigueur operating system of the late 1980s and on into the 1990s. Why spend millions of dollars developing your own OS, the reasoning went, when you can take something that already exists and concentrate on developing your own enhancements to it? Besides, computer users were tired of the restrictions imposed by closed systems.

Populist postulations were heard: "Committees don't mandate standards; the market does." If enough people and companies wanted and used a product or specification, that should be enough to make it a standard. The new industry attitude had a free-market ring that echoed the laissez-faire attitudes of the decade.[3] Sure enough, certain computer phenomena did attain standards status simply because of widespread adoption—in some cases because they filled a void and were immediately needed, warts and all. A problem with de facto standards, however, is that because they generally arise quickly to fill a need, they often are hastily or imperfectly crafted—and eventually challenged. It also turns out that some standards are more equal than others.

UNIX has become a standard, yes, but which UNIX? Sun has a version, Hewlett-Packard/Apollo has a version, DEC has a version, Microsoft has a version, Apple has a version, IBM has a version, Unisys has a version. And, of course, AT&T, whose researchers created the operating system in the first place, has a version—as do several other companies. They all share the same foundation, but each has its particular strengths and weaknesses, its idiosyncracies, and its own "syntax" and "semantics." Each version even offers different ways to produce the same results (it is possible, for example, to create a registered-trademark symbol in a single version with a four-character command string or with one of twenty-plus characters). To prevent anarchy, the standard needs to be standardized, and open [systems] warfare has broken out over which version of UNIX will be ascendant.

Speaking in Technotongues

Because of their fervor, the standards battles in the computer industry have often been referred to as "religious wars." The discord they have wrought, coupled with the obscurity of much technobabble, has led some industry critics to equate the computer industry with the biblical Tower of Babel. In the Bible story, God becomes incensed at the hubris of a group of zealots who attempt to build a tower tall enough to reach up to the heavens. To thwart their success, He makes them unable to understand one another. This confusion, according to the Bible, is the basis for the world's many different languages.

The Giver of Data[4] may have had a similar intent in mind when he or she input the concept of "languages" into computing. Like technobabble itself, computer languages have evolved through four phases, or generations. The first generation was "machine language," the conceptual 1s and 0s that flow through a computer's circuits and gates and make the machine operate. Next came assembly language, a machine-oriented programming language, which was geared more toward understanding by humans than machine language was. Assembly language was followed by programming languages,[5] such as BASIC, COBOL, FORTRAN, Pascal, and Ada. These languages enable their users to interpret machine language and vice versa; programmers can "write" in these languages to make computers perform tasks. Programming languages consist of various categories: graphics languages (such as PHIGS), page-description languages (PostScript being the most common), and increasingly complex language "suites" (C, C+, C++). Sometimes operating systems are referred to as languages.

Fourth-generation languages (known as "4GLs" or "FGLs"), which have been around since the early 1980s, are more "English-like,"[6] in industry parlance, than were the three preceding generations. Database, artificial-intelligence, and other pattern-recognition software have "grammars," "parsers," and "syntax"—all bolstering the idea that advanced computer languages resemble human ones. Any computer language that enables a person to command the operations of a computer by using a human language is known as a "natural-language interface." To distinguish the Babel of computer languages from the Babel of human ones, the industry has appropriated the term *natural language* for those spoken by people.[7] This term, which originated in the field of anthropology, dates from about 1880. Its original meaning was "a language used as a native tongue by a group of speakers."

Received Standard Technobabble?

Some critics of the computer industry's lack of standards see a relationship between chaos in the industry and chaos in its lexicon. As an *InfoWorld* reader put it, "I believe that the primary purpose of the techno-babble generated by the micro industry is to cover up 'techno-bungle.' The American micro industry is a topsy-turvy basket case with little predictability or standardization. . . . Isn't it time we settled on something?"[8] The volatile computer industry might forever be in search of standards. When it was an oligarchy, standards tended to be mandated. Since it became democratic in the late 1970s, standards definition has become more egalitarian, perhaps, but it has also become more chaotic.

If standards are hard to come by in the computer industry, they are outright elusive in some quarters of technobabble. To paraphrase the one-time slogan of the *Realist* magazine, the meaning of words in the computer industry can be like Silly Putty: Denotations are so nebulous that certain words can mean almost anything. Different companies, even different divisions within the same company, have different names for the same thing. Marketing designates a term one way, PR another way, engineering yet another way. Unlike the efforts to standardize technology, imperfect as they may be, no comparable effort exists for technobabble.

Noise

Noise, which comes from the Latin *nausea,* took on its technology-oriented meaning, "an electrical disturbance in a communications system that interferes with or prevents reception of a signal or of information," during World War II. This new twist to the word, which entered the language in the late twelfth century, is attributed to MIT's Norbert Wiener, who also developed the theory of cybernetics, while working on radar technology. Wiener was a contemporary of Claude Shannon, a Bell Telephone Laboratories scientist who developed *information theory* and coined that term to describe his development in 1948.[9]

The Random House unabridged dictionary defines information theory as "the mathematical theory concerned with the content, storage, transmission, and retrieval of information, usually in the form of messages or data, and especially by means of computers." This dictionary defines *noise* as above and also points out its informal meaning: "extraneous, irrelevant, or meaningless facts, information, statistics, etc."

Today, the computer industry is awash in information—and in noise, which is often represented in technobabble. Noise does not have to be meaningless facts; it can also comprise words and terms made meaningless by their nonspecificity and their random concatenation. The computer industry's vocabulary has become so "noisy" in so many quarters that it is often a swamp of imprecision and vagueness. This chapter deals with several terms that effectively have no meaning because of their indiscriminate use. Other such terms abound. What, for example, is a "customer-support environment"? Or a "pen-input platform"? Public-relations firm Hodskins, Simone, and Searls provides the following examples of industry noise: "backwardly architected hyper-intelligent analysis inference leader," "digitally-driven compatibility-based internal availability phase-logic breakthrough-capable technology market," "upwardly seamless multi-object network compatible strategy solution," and "incrementally intelligent workgroup process topology vendor."

If you work in the industry, you may be able to figure out what the above strings of words mean; it you do not, best of luck. The reasons for noise in the industry are myriad, and many are examined throughout this book. The prevalence of technobabble noise is ironic—given the precise nature of computer calculations and technologies. If the industry communicated with anything like the precision of its machines' operations, the noise level would greatly diminish.

Definitions du Jour

What is an *application?* In the computer industry, this word most often means "product" or "package," not "a use to which something is put." Real-life examples of applications are word processing, computer-aided design, and illustration. A word-processing program is an application program, but in technobabble, the program becomes an "application"— as in, "That application [meaning "application program"] runs faster on the new systems." Employing *application* for *program* in this case is an example of the prevalent practice of synecdoche, the use of a part for the whole. Occasionally *application* is employed in an adjectival sense—as in the acronym ABI (application-binary interface). The word, however, has become such a lexical dumping ground that without a great deal of accompanying context, it can mean just about anything its user wants it to. Even with context, you sometimes cannot be absolutely sure what someone who employs this term is talking about.

At a computer-trade-show demonstration, the demonstrator puts his product through its paces. You can use it, he explains, to "build applications." But he does not mean application programs. In this instance, he is calling the dialog box he is constructing on the screen an application. Some people, however, would call the box he was building part of the graphical user interface (GUI, pronounced "gooey") through which users would gain access to or manipulate the application [program].

As a noun used in its true sense, *application* suggests a use of something, so references to "construction" or "building" of applications seem out of place, at least on a physical level, unless you are talking about building up layers of a substance (e.g., applications of paint). Although *application* has several meanings throughout the computer industry, its most common connotation is abstract: "application software" or "application program." But it can also apply to physical devices, as in this 1983 press release from Plessy: "[The FIFOs] are also well suited to such applications as computer-to-printer buffers, or type-ahead keyboard buffers."[10] Buffers are hardware circuits—sometimes; they can also be data-storage areas. *Electronic News* is a computer trade magazine for which devices are "applications," as this sentence indicates: "The LR33000 is designed for applications including laser printers, X Window terminals, disk controllers, protocol converters, and military/avionics products."[11]

Try as one may to pin down a standard definition for *application* in the computer industry, that goal remains elusive. One of the editors at a Macintosh magazine has claimed that in the Macintosh cosmos, an application program is called an "application," whereas those in the PC world refer to such a piece of software as a "program." This arbitrary approach may serve the editorial style of computer magazines, but it only further obscures words' meanings.

The word *application* appears in terms that form acronyms:

• An ASIC is an application-specific integrated circuit, an integrated circuit that is devoted to a specific task—image processing, for example. Here *application* clearly refers to a use rather than to a program.

• An API is an application-programmer, or programming, interface. In this case, the word modifies *programmer*. APIs are methods of interaction with computers for programmers who are writing applications—that is, programs.

Less nebulous than *application* but equally polysemous is the word *platform*. What exactly is a platform? In the computer business, it's not exactly anything. Rather, it has become a catchall term, standing for everything from a philosophy of computing to a chip architecture to a single product. It generally stands for "product line" or type of computer system, as in this turgid phrase from an April 1990 Spectragraphics press release: "The first company providing computer graphics technology solutions across the full range of computing platforms, from personal computers and technical workstations to mainframes." The Random House unabridged dictionary lists several definitions of the word that stem from professions: the building trades, the military, geology. Computing is not among the professions listed as having a specific definition of platform. Etymologically, *platform* means "flat form" and thus suggests a computer board or card.

Platform implies significant philosophical underpinnings and a belief system. That may seem a grandiose notion for the computer industry, whose goal is to sell computers and make money. Back when a few big companies dictated the rules, brand loyalty was a driving factor in purchase decisions. IBM, as the most obvious example, sold computers and service and did both well. It did not pontificate about philosophies of computing. As the industry opened up and the big established names were increasingly challenged, the challengers stressed approaches, beliefs, and philosophical stances as often as they emphasized products. For Apple, it was "evangelism," icons, and the "Macintosh Way." Hewlett-Packard employees lived in "The HP Way." Sun proselytized about UNIX and open systems with religious fervor. Companies no longer sold computer systems, they graced users with *platforms*.

You might think of a platform as providing support. *Support* is a term that crops up so frequently in computer-industry literature that to remove every instance of it might well chop page counts and save acres of forest in the process. *Support* means everything from, rarely, "supports" to "works with," "uses," "is compatible with," and "functions as as adjunct to." But *support*'s supporters are not content to employ this catchall verb for one of the above meanings. They throw it into a loquacious noun phrase: "Product X provides support for product Y." It is not uncommon to run across archipelagoes of *support*, in both verb and noun forms; in a piece of technical writing, ten or more occurrences per page are not uncommon. This glut of *support* is symptomatic of the tendency among many computer users to eschew the simple and concrete for the Byzantine and convoluted.[12] One of *support*'s meanings is "prop up." In light of some of the ill-conceived products the industry has produced over the years, it is perhaps not surprising that the word has gained such prominence.

In the early days of computing, when it was controlled by the likes of IBM, users were in the thrall of a few big manufacturers. These overlords may have enslaved their subjects technologically, but at least the relationship between lord and vassal did not end at the sale. If your IBM mainframe went down, an IBM support team was soon on the scene to repair it. Of course, you had automatically purchased a service contract along with the machine; you had no choice. What were you going to do? Fix it yourself? The same arrangement applied to DEC minicomputers and to the mainframe and minicomputer clone-makers, who had to emulate their masters.

Once PCs, portable computers, workstations, and the like blew the industry open, users were often left to fend for themselves. Support from the manufacturers was no longer a given—particularly in the case of overseas makers of cheap PC clones. Service contracts were optional and sometimes bought nothing more than an empty promise. "Customer support" was often a misnomer. Realizing that support was a problem, companies began to compensate by touting support. The word began to suffuse other areas of the industry until it took on its omnipresent and nebulous state.

To compensate for their deficiencies in this area, the companies, especially their marketing arms, boasted about how great their support was. Soon everybody was in on the act, and *support* assumed the prominent position it occupies today, taking on a nearly limitless number of connotations and denotations in the process.

The most nebulous word in the computer lexicon, however, has to be *interface,* which came into the language as a noun in the early 1880s and now serves with equal, or perhaps greater, frequency as a verb. Never mind that the word has taken on extratechnical connotations of human interaction ("Marketing will have to interface with Engineering on this project."), as a noun it doesn't even have a clear-cut or consistent definition, whereas it once did: "a surface lying between two portions of matter or space, and forming their common boundary."[13] Relative to computing, the word has come to have abstract or conceptual connotations, as have words such as *link, desktop*, and *frame.*

In computing, the word *interface* is frequently a part of the compound *user interface,* a phrase of dubious meaning. To convey a more specific denotation, the term should be something like "user/computer interface,"[14] since the interface is the surface—physical or conceptual—where the two entities meet. The most common connotation of the noun *interface* is the visual representation on the computer's screen of the operating system and application programs. It is by way of the interface that users interact with the computer.

But *interface* implies much more than human/computer interaction. In its most general sense, it connotes a connection, a relationship of some sort, between or among diverse elements. In this general sense, the author of an article entitled "Measuring Graphics Performance" refers to what are ordinarily thought of as "graphics standards" as "interfaces."[15] As the article portrays PHIGS (pronounced "figs") and GKS, two of the graphical entities with which the article deals, they may well function as interfaces between developers and the graphical applications they craft. To refer to them as interfaces, though, may confuse those who are not familiar with the world of computer graphics. With PHIGS, such ambiguity further clouds an already murky situation: The computer-graphics community has not yet been able to agree on a definition of this acronym. Depending on whom you interface with and what articles and papers you read, PHIGS stands for Programmer's [or Programmers' or Programmers] Hierarchical Interactive Graphics [or Graphical] Standard [or System]. But everyone seems to agree that GKS stands for Graphical Kernel System.

Interfaces can be of the software variety (e.g., PHIGS, GKS), of the conceptual variety (e.g., something you see on a screen), or of the physical variety (e.g., a bus). Although interface, Zen-like, means everything and nothing, its most general sense is "link" or "connection." PHIGS is a link to graphics programming; a user interface is a connection between person and machine; a bus is a physical connection between a computer and peripherals that routes data from the former to the latter.

Sometimes even the precise designation of a company's product is in doubt. An operating system from Digital Research Corporation not only shows how difficult it can be to standardize a name but also demonstrates the vicissitudes of a volatile industry. Intergalactic Digital Research was started in the early 1970s by a California programmer named Gary Kildall; he later dropped the *Intergalactic* from the name. One of Kildall's creations was the CP/M operating system, which soon took the emerging microcomputer world by storm. CP/M quickly became a standard in the industry, with many microcomputer manufacturers basing their products on it. It also spawned numerous books, one of which sold more than 100,000 copies.

One company that did not adopt CP/M, however, was IBM. Although the mammoth computer company held discussions with Kildall, it ended up working with Microsoft Corporation to develop what became known as DOS, for *disk-operating system*. Kildall complained that DOS was a clone of CP/M, but to no avail.[16] DOS won out, and by the mid-1980s CP/M was moribund, if not finished. (Remember the adage "IBM is not the competition, it's the environment.") Before CP/M evanesced, if you asked a sample of its users what the abbreviation meant, you might have gotten any of the following answers: Control Program/Monitor, Control Program for Microcomputers, Control Program for Microprocessors, Control Program/Microprocessors,[17] or "I don't know."

As is the case with many terms in the computer industry, especially abbreviations and acronyms, their users don't really care what they stand for. Knowing what they are and what they do is important. In-house PR and marketing people, however, are likely to cringe when they witness such designative discrepancies. These communications professionals do their best to promulgate the party line, but that can be a difficult job in a large decentralized company in which the marketing and PR groups can control any material that originates in or passes through their offices, but only a fraction of the total information disseminated by the company. Furthermore, they have almost no control over what appears in the press.

Since its inception, Sun Microsystems has played down the acronymic, perhaps apocryphal, origin of the company. What became the first Sun workstation was developed at the heavily networked Stanford University, but Sun wanted to downplay its university origins in quest of commercial markets. Thus, employees were told, regardless of what they may have heard, that Sun did *not* stand for Stanford University Network, and that the proper designation was Sun, not SUN. Nevertheless, materials that escaped the eyes of marketing and PR often employed the all-caps spelling, as did some of the early marketing material itself. Compounding the confusion was the company's logotype: *sun,* all lowercase.

Another area in which the company failed to prevail was the proper designation of its product models. The company-sanctioned convention was the word Sun, followed by a hyphen, followed by the product series number, followed by a slash, then followed by the model number, as in Sun-3/160. In no formal way was this designation disseminated company-wide, with the result that any and all variations began to appear: SUN3/ 160, Sun 3-160, Sun/3-160, etc.

You Say Tomato, I Say Baseball

Another aspect of the computer industry's Tower of Babel is different lexical strokes for different lexical folks. What you call a *server,* I may call an *engine.* My colleague may refer to a piece of software as an *interface,* while yours may call it an *application*. One user's *tool* may be another's *utility*.

An example of this rubrical confusion is a large device whose purpose is to store large quantities of computer data. Consisting of high-capacity disk drives mounted on a frame, it developed the name *rack*, or the variants *rack mount* or *rack-mounted*. Perhaps because *rack* has unsavory connotations (e.g., a medieval torture device), some people in the industry took to calling the devices *cabinets* even though a cabinet is actually an enclosed rack. Although the tide seems to be turning in favor of the genteel, Latinate *cabinet*—in part because industrial designers are making the things look like space-age furniture—the monosyllabic, Anglo-Saxon *rack* still rings through some corridors. Always in search of ameliorative images, marketing people seem to have dreamed up *cabinet*.

Full of Disk

One of the techniques of word coinage that is common in technobabble is to append the suffix *-ful* to nouns: *stateful,* characterized by states; *diskful [system],* a system having a disk or disks. A problem with these and other concoctions is that they are rarely codified in company style guides. Editorial purists and prigs tend not to admit their existence anyway, so users of these terms are more or less on their own.

When it came to the spelling of *diskful[l],* one computer company demonstrated inconsistency from department to department when it introduced a new computer product in mid-1990. The product data sheet, which preceded the press release, noted that one of the system's features was a "preloaded [operating system] on diskful systems." The press release noted, "When large, diskfull systems are stacked up against competitive desktops."[18]

The spelling of the root word that forms the term meaning "to have a disk" comes from the Latin *discus*, "dish." The first recorded use of the word in English was in 1664 in a figurative sense: "the apparently flat surface or 'face' of the sun, moon, or a planet as it appears to the eye."[19] Nearly 300 years later, the primary meaning of the word is concrete—rigid and fixed in the case of nonremovable hard disks. The *Oxford English Dictionary* gives *disk,* which preceded *disc,* as the preferred spelling—going so far as to say it is "better" than *disc. Oxford* goes on to say that the latter spelling has tended to predominate in certain scientific senses, although not in botany. In contemporary technical senses, *disk* is commonly accepted to mean a magnetic disk (either metal, "hard disk," or mylar, "floppy disk") for the storage of computer data. Disc denotes a phonograph record or an optical CD (compact disc), used to store video, sound, or computer data. These distinctions are de facto, however, and not universally observed. In a June 3, 1990, article in the *San Jose Mercury News*, for example, hard disks were referred to as *discs*. Today, despite the *disk/disc* convention, you will occasionally run across *disc* used in reference to a magnetic computer disk. The difference may become moot in the near future. Optical discs, which are made of plastic and whose data are recorded on them by laser beams, show signs of supplanting magnetic disks. The optical variety are cheaper and more reliable and can hold proportionally more data than their magnetic brethren. As magnetic disks are phased out, *disk* may supplant *disc* as the common spelling for compact discs (CDs) used for computer-data storage.

Fractious Fractions

Computer disk drives come in various "form factors"—the two most common being three and one-half inches and five and one-quarter inches in diameter. The computer industry does not yet have a standard way of denoting disk size. Some people prefer the decimal approach: 3.5 and 5.25; others opt for fractions: 3 1/2 and 5 1/4. Some people spell *inches;* others prefer to use ". And the misplacement of hyphens results in such phrases as "5-1/4 inch rigid disc drive" and "This drive measures 5.25-inches."

Roman as well as Arabic numbers cause confusion in the industry. Even though Roman numerals are rarely used in contemporary culture (some uses being clock faces, building-foundation stones, and the Super Bowl), some computer companies and organizations have chosen to employ them. AT&T named a version of its UNIX operating system "System V." Since the correct pronunciation of the term is "System Five," the marketing-communications director of a UNIX company was committing a gaffe when he routinely referred to it as "System Vee." Yet when Release 4 of System V is noted in its shorthand form, SVR4, the pronunciation becomes "Ess Vee Are Four."

AUGUSTANA UNIVERSITY COLLEGE
LIBRARY

Space Out

Inconsistency concerning the way in which compound nouns are treated is rampant throughout the computer industry. Companies working within the same segment of the industry call their product a *workstation, work station,* or *work-station.* A large computer that handles lots of files is dubbed a *fileserver, file server,* or *file-server.* Certain types of display-screen graphics are, depending on whom you're interfacing with, *bitmapped, bit mapped,* or *bit-mapped.* The list goes on: *real time, real-time, realtime* (all in a nominative sense); *on line, online, on-line* (all in an adverbial sense); *chip set, chipset, chip-set;* and others.

Standardization is likely to remain elusive in many segments of the industry's lexicon. The computer industry is volatile and is likely to continue in that vein as long as technological advances outstrip the capacity of many people to keep up. As the technology-standards wars increase in viciousness, lexical-standardization efforts may continue to fall by the wayside.

5

Techniques of Coinage

Any computer scientist worth their salt can make up anything out of an acronym.
—Adele Goldberg, president of ParcPlace[1]

This chapter examines some of the techniques by which technobabble is coined, such as turning verbs into nouns and vice versa; coining neologisms on the spot to meet a perceived lexical need of the moment; concocting acronyms with equal rapidity and enthusiasm; and adding suffixes such as *-ize* and *-ality* to words with abandon. Perhaps the most notable characteristic of these techniques is expediency. The computer industry moves fast. Many of its frantic denizens are "high energy" types. They have to think fast—although not necessarily coherently—to keep up. This sort of environment is conducive to hasty, reflexive coinages of terms.

The coinages may be reflexive, but most of the mechanisms are now well established in the computer industry. The rule of thumb is that nearly anything goes. Coin a word to fit a singular occasion, and then discard it. Turn practically any part of speech, acronym, name, or process into a noun or verb. Add various suffixes to just about any word to come up with a variant of that word. To paraphrase an industry buzzphrase, "The coinage possibilities are limited only by your imagination."

Neologisms

Neologisms (*new words*) are very important in an industry whose lifeblood is new technologies and products. Keeping up with all the changes requires an ever-increasing vocabulary. The industry produces mainly two kinds of neologisms: those that become a permanent part of the lexicon and those that are coined on the fly to respond to a singular situation. Words in the former category are either unique coinages, such as *modem, trackball, foo, endian,* and *nerd,* or existing words that take on a different meaning when used in a new context, such as *mouse, bug,* and *interface.*[2] Words in the latter category are often solecisms, such as *degradate, implementate,* and *tempestize,* that are spoken quickly in a given situation and as quickly disappear (*implementate* did make it into print in a computer-company product catalog). But once technobabble neologisms have started to appear with regularity, in a variety of publications, they are likely to start appearing in mainstream dictionaries.

Until new words can make their dictionary debuts, however, someone has to define them. A September 1990 press release from a San Rafael, California, company offhandedly employs a neologism it never defines, although its meaning is fairly obvious from context: "a leading developer of *telepresence* [my italics] systems for remotely operated vehicles." The release, by the way, comes from International Telepresence, an ominous-sounding name.

Given the broad definition of *neologism* proposed above, this book, by default, is replete with neologisms; most processes as verbs ("to grep," "to troff"), for example, are neologisms; many acronyms also qualify. Although its coinages are for the most part obscure, the hacker community is responsible for many computer neologisms; for a comprehensive list of such words as *frobnitz, cuspy,* and *bletch,* refer to *The Hacker's Dictionary.* In a sense, the techniques that follow could all be subsumed under a general category of "coining neologisms."

Where, Oh Ware?

The first documented use of the noun *ware*—in the sense of "articles of merchandise or manufacture; the things which a merchant, manufacturer, or pedlar has to sell; goods, commodities"—noted in the *Oxford English Dictionary* occurred in the year 1000. In the millennium since, *ware* has come a long way. In 1200, for example, it meant "pus, matter." In the mid-sixteenth century, it stood for "the privy parts of either sex" (adding a new dimension to "Said Simple Simon to the pieman, let me taste your ware"); more specifically there was *lady ware,* an early combining form. The first documented combination form is *yren ware* (ironware) in 1398. Other such forms that developed included *earthenware, chinaware, silverware,* and *tableware.* Today, notably because of the computer industry, we are familiar with the word mostly in combinations with defining words.

First came *hardware.* From the entrance of the word into English in 1515 until the mid-twentieth century, *hardware* meant merchandise or goods made of metal. When *software* entered the language circa 1962, *hardware* took on the meaning of the electronic or mechanical parts of a computer, as opposed to the programs that ran the computer.

For about twenty years, hardware and software were the extent of computer wares. But early in the 1980s, public-relations and advertising people became intensely *-ware* aware and started to append the suffix to many roots. Words such as *courseware* and *thoughtware* began to show up in ads and the writing of journalists who covered the high-tech beat. In the computer world, *-ware* as a combining form has been adopted liberally to label types of software, concepts, and philosophies. The *-ware* technique ranges from appending the suffix to an existing word to create a new word that has the same meaning as the *ware*less word—*bookware* for *books,* for example—to using *-ware* to form the name of a company or a product line. Peachtree Software of Atlanta marketed a line of programs called Peachware; a California company named Advanced Electronic Designs changed its name to AED Colorware after the success of a line of products of the same name. A Pittsburgh company that specializes in artificial-intelligence products is called NeuralWare.

Here is a sampling of computer wares:

• backware: a term that showed up on Internet and was defined as "stand-alone Mac applications that happen to be particularly friendly with MultiFinder. They run in separate windows, sharing processor time." The explanation went on to indicate that backware applications were "double-clickable."

• Bucketware: a computer-novelty company. Probably derives from "bit bucket," "the place where information goes when it is lost or destroyed.[3]

• Concertware: a music program for the Apple Macintosh computer.

• courseware: educational software; falls under the category of CAI, or computer-aided instruction.[4] (An early recorded use of this term occurs on the cover of Southwestern Publishing's *1983 Microcomputer Courseware & Data Processing Catalog.*)

• Designware: an educational-software company.

• Earthware Computer Services: a computer-game company.

• EduWare: an educational-software company.

• firmware: somewhere between hardware (a piece of equipment) and software (the intangible instructions that cause a computer to perform some action) is firmware, a program encoded in ROM (a physical entity filled with intangible memory) to perform a function that used to be carried out by software or hardware. This ware is "firm" because it is in "read only," or "nonvolatile"—as opposed to "random access," or "volatile"—memory, which is fixed. (Along with many other computer terms, this one entered the language in the mid-1960s.)

• foodware: food (PR people dreamed this one up for invitations to company hospitality suites at computer shows).

• FoundationWare: a software company (not a girdle manufacturer).

• freeware: software that can be obtained at no cost, often over computer bulletin boards.

• gameware: computer games.

• groupware: software used jointly by a group of people with the same objectives or interests. This term arose in the late 1980s as a corollary to so-called workgroup or enterprisewide computing.

• *Hardware:* the name of a 1990 movie about technology run amok in post-nuclear-holocaust America.

• HESware: the name of a line of products from Human Engineered Software.

• ideaware: programs whose purported purpose is to enhance your ratiocinative powers.

• Intelligence Ware: a software company.

• Learningware: a courseware product.

• MetaWare: a California software company.

• Microware: Several companies employ this term in their name (e.g., Interactive Microware, Kensington Microware).

• mindware: similar to thoughtware and ideaware.

• NetWare: networking product from Novell, a Utah-based company.

• OpenWare: trademarked name for a networking product from CMC, a division of Rockwell International. Note the combination of *ware* and the 1980s buzzword *open*.

• PDware: public-domain ware. Similar to freeware and shareware.

• shareware: similar to freeware, except that its providers often request a donation. Shareware is so popular and pervasive that a bimonthly magazine called *Shareware* is devoted to it.[5]

• Underware: a special printer ribbon that uses heat transfer to affix printed images onto T-shirts.

• vaporware: touted products that either do not exist or are weeks or months away from being ready to ship.[6]

• Visionware: a British software company.

• wetware: booze; goes with foodware. This tongue-in-cheek coinage preceded another use for the same term. A group of people who posit the prospect of "artificial life"—"A-lifers," as they are called—refer to carbon-based life forms, such as humans, as *wetware* because of their high water content.[7]

• WormWare: an "operating system extension to UNIX"[8] made by Optical Software Solutions, or OSS.

Once people in high technology had broken free of the limitations of hardware and software, the floodgates were open. The *-ware* technique remains popular, as witnessed by the proliferation of the late 1980s coinage *groupware*. The potential of the *-ware* technique has only begun to be mined, however. Consider the possibilities: "sumware" (math software); "Nohware" (Japanese word-processing program for playwrights); "knowware" (knowledge-base software); "anyware" (a freeware grab bag); "everyware" (a highly integrated program); "wearware" (a wardrobe-selection program); "where?ware" (software for self-actualization); and "wareware" (self-replicating software).

Environments

"'Environment' the Buzz Word During TED2" ran the headline above Denise Caruso's "Inside Silicon Valley" column in the March 4, 1990, edition of the *San Francisco Examiner* (TED stands for Technology, Entertainment, and Design).[9] Although Caruso was writing about the physical environment, the first part of her headline was also applicable to the world of computing. What the computer world needs is an Environmental Protection Agency. Instead of safeguarding the physical environment, however, this agency would protect people from the proliferation of the word *environment* in high-tech environments. The overuse of *environment* is a symptom of a phenomenon that reaches beyond the boundaries—or parameters—of technobabble: the aggrandizement of the commonplace. In the computing environment, such aggrandizement turns offices into "corporate environments," DOS (a computer operating system) into "the DOS environment," a computer program that operates in windows into a "windowing" (note the ersatz gerund) environment, and so forth. The technique is to tack the word *environment* onto a perfectly serviceable word.

A product data sheet from a Silicon Valley corporate environment demonstrates a lack of environmental diffidence; in fewer than 1,000 words, this document yields the following: "distributed computing environment," "distributed environment," "a programmatic interface for the user who wishes to integrate custom applications into the window environment," and "which is optimized for the technical application environment."

The industry has spawned numerous market-research firms, which prognosticate and pontificate about various sectors of the industry. One such outfit, Creative Strategies International, of San Jose, California, predicted in a 1983 press release that "after 1986, sales of integrated software packages will be eclipsed by new operating environment shipments," a phrase that appears to concern the shipment of environments that work. The question here is, What exactly is an operating environment, and how do you ship it?

Verbs into Nouns

As its name suggests, the verbs-into-nouns technique involves changing verbs (usually transitive) into nouns. In this technique, the root meaning of the new noun stays the same. Take, for example, the "noun" *install,* as in "the install usually takes two hours." *Install* is representative of the verb/noun in that a pseudonoun is created when a true noun is pared down to its verbal root. Thus, the noun *installation* becomes "the install." This technique also produces *the announce* in lieu of *the announcement, the disconnect* for *the disconnection, the interconnect* for *the interconnection,* and *the create* for *the creation.* Most of these verb/nouns substitute the verb form of a noun ending in *-tion* for the actual noun.

Documentation and other technical writing is replete with nouns *né* verbs such as *the acquire, the compile,* and *the connect.* Often the technique involves use of the auxiliary verb *to do*—as in "He did a compile." In addition to the verb/nouns listed above, the following "nouns" are among those favored by high-tech types: *the attach, the concatenate, the interrupt, the configure, the evaluate, the debug,* and *the migrate.*

The last term in this list is interesting for a couple of reasons. Whereas the four "nouns" that precede *the debug* are the verb forms of *-tion* nouns, the noun that would correspond to *the debug* would be the gerund *debugging*—as in "The system needs debugging."

Sometimes when a verb becomes a noun, as in *the confirm,* an accent shift occurs. The verb *confirm* is accented on the second syllable; however, the neonoun *the confirm* receives an accent on the first syllable.[10]

The verbs-into-nouns technique probably derives from industry conventions—once again, illustrating that terminology is a reflection of technology. Many nouns that become verbs do so because they are based on software commands or actions—for example, *install* and *compile.* In formal computer writing, such as a system-setup manual, verb-nouns are generally set in a different typeface (often Courier or some other monospaced font) to differentiate them from surrounding text and to signify that the verb-noun means to use the command on which it is based to perform the desired action: "The `install` is straightforward."

What has increasingly happened, however, is that such typographic distinctions have disappeared in a lot of writing about computers, especially in brochures and other "collateral": "The install is straightforward." This development is ironic because, presumably, people reading collateral, or "high level," material are not as familiar with technobabble conventions as are people who read manuals, so it would seem that more conventional English usages would be in order.

A variation on the verbs-into-nouns technique is verbs-into-adjectives. A couple of examples come from the world of computer graphics. Two types of software for artists are so-called paint and draw programs. Names of modes are frequently verbs employed as adjectives: "read mode," "write mode."

Nouns into Verbs

The obverse visage of verbs into nouns is nouns into verbs. PR specialist Doc Searls suggests that nouns used as verbs be called "nerbs." This technique turns nouns into transitive verbs. Again, this technique is not new; many of the verbs we use routinely started out as nouns. The verb *to contact*, for example, began life as a noun; it gained widespread use as a verb in spite of the apocryphal thundering of a New York publisher: "In this house, *contact* is not a verb!"[11]

Despite the protestations of critics, nouns are constantly becoming verbs. "Any noun can be 'verbed,'" asserts author David Roth.[12] And high-technology mavens are not the only group "verbifying" nouns. "Miss Watson," a fat-cat politician commands his secretary in the comic strip "Frank and Ernest," "turn some of these nouns into verbs for me. I want this [a sheaf of papers he holds up] to sound important."[13] The implication here is that, at least in government circles, turning nouns into verbs inflates the perceived importance of an otherwise mundane pronouncement.

The reasons for verbifying nouns in the computer industry are sometimes more prosaic, often prompted by the need for a shorthand method of explaining an action based on a new technology. When the computer mouse, for example, became a commercial product in the early 1980s, *InfoWorld* columnist Doug Clapp needed a way to describe the use of the device, so he wrote, "I predict that executives will never learn to type properly or even to 'mouse' properly."[14]

Clapp, an industry wag, probably had his tongue so far into his cheek that he looked like a food-stuffed rodent, but the technique is illustrative of the need to come up with verbs to explain or talk about phenomena that might otherwise require a small dissertation. Another computer magazine that got in on the nouns-into-verbs act was *MacUser*, with "Versionary lets you specify which applications or folders it should 'version.'"[15] On the other hand, sometimes the need, or desire, to sound important is the sole motivation for transforming nouns into spurious verbs.

Consider the verbal behavior of Steven P. Jobs, cofounder of Apple Computer and a natural master of the nouns-into-verbs technique. In January 1983, Jobs addressed about 2,000 Apple shareholders in an auditorium in Cupertino, California. The purpose of this business-cum-revival meeting was to introduce the company's new Lisa computer, which, rumor had it, had been named after a person. The breathless prose in the Lisa press kit, however, explained that Lisa was an acronym, standing for Locally Integrated Software Architecture. The glossy press kit neglected to explain exactly what "Locally Integrated Software

Architecture" meant.[16] Jobs was ebullient when he proclaimed, "With Lisa, Apple has 'architected' a new standard."[17] He was not the first to "architect" this verb out of a noun, but in the years since he used the term, it has continued to gain currency among computer people as part of the growing list of nouns becoming verbs. Another young industry cheerleader, Scott McNealy of Sun Microsystems, managed to use the neoverb "architect" twice—as well as the nominal form once—in as many sentences in a 1989 interview.[18]

The nouns-into-verbs technique has two variations. The first, as in "to mouse" and "to database," turns nouns that have no acknowledged verbal meanings into verbs. The second, as in "to tempest" (see "-Izing," below), uses nouns that do have verbal forms but employs them in a nonstandard context. The verb *to tempest* has a legitimate lexical meaning, "to raise a tempest in and around," that dates from the fourteenth century. The computerese verb *to tempest,* however, has nothing to do with this meaning.

Many nouns made the transition to verbs in the mid-1960s—a fecund period for the acceptance by dictionary publishers of these verbs-once-nouns. *To interface, to access, to keyboard,* and *to format* all became verbs in the mid-1960s. The latter verb took 124 years to make the transition; *format* entered English as a noun in 1840.

Processes and Products as Nouns and Verbs

A common word-creation technique in high-technology circles is to use a process or activity as a verb or—less frequently—a noun. An example is "to troff." The word *troff* (pronounced *tea-roff*) is a creation from the acronym for "*t*ypeset *ru*n*off.*" troff is a set of UNIX formatting commands, with which a UNIX user can prepare text for typesetting on a laser phototypesetter or printer. UNIX users talk about "troffing this" and "troffing that" because *troff* is a verb in the UNIX community. Pseudoverbs such as *troff* are rife in the computer world, and for a good reason: They make it possible to explain processes concisely, whereas a full-fledged explanation might require a virtual treatise.[19]

The processes-as-verbs technique occurs with great frequency in operating-system environments. For example, another system, CP/M and other operating systems less contorted than UNIX have contributed their own processes as verbs to computerese.[20] A portion of the CP/M operating system called the Peripheral Interchange Program, or PIP, is necessary to transfer a data file from one disk to another. This transfer process is called "PIPing" (pronounced *pipping*). Another CP/M process is called "SYSGENing," from *SYStem GENerator,* which involves PIPing certain special system files from disk to disk in a computer. Both *PIP* and *SYSGEN* can also function as nouns, as in "to do a PIP" and "to do a SYSGEN." Both of these neoverbs also represent the acronyms-as-verbs technique of word coinage. In the DOS world, SYS = SYSGEN. Other DOS acronymic processes as verbs/nouns are REN (rename) and DIR (directory).

Acronyms and Abbreviations

The Department of Defense (DoD) is probably the world's greatest coiner, user, and abuser of acronyms. But the computer industry runs a close second. Both groups deal with innumerable processes and tasks that are logistically, technically, and linguistically complex. It is fitting that these two entities should be so enamored of acronyms, because without the DoD, the computer industry would not exist, or certainly would not exist on the scale that it does today. A side effect of the often cozy relationship between the military and the computer establishments has been a wealth of DoD-generated acronyms and terms such as "smart bomb" and "hardened computer." (See "The Military-Industrial Acronymplex" box for examples of DoD/computer industry acronymic synergy.)

The Military-Industrial Acronymplex

The April 9, 1990, edition of the newsletter *Advanced Military Computing* comprises eight pages. On the first page alone—almost a quarter of which is consumed by the newsletter's logo—are a dozen acronyms/abbreviations:

CLS[21]
DARPA
DOD
IDSS

IEEE
MIPS
NAS
NASA
RFP
RISC
SIMNET
UNICOS

The DoD is one of the largest—if not *the* largest—procurers of computer technology. Many major developments in computing technology—even those that eventually end up in commercial and other arenas—have been funded by the military. A major computer network used by university and computer researchers was called ARPAnet, named after the Advanced Research Projects Agency (ARPA), an electronic arm of the DoD. ARPAnet went on line in 1969. In 1975 ARPA became DARPA, the *D* standing for *Defense;* but the network remained ARPAnet.

Neither the DoD nor the computer industry can exist without acronyms. Given the wealth of convoluted and turgid phrases that abound in computing, a shorthand method of stating and writing them is essential. How would you like to have to spew out the relentless and redundant phrase *extended binary-coded decimal interchange code* every time you wanted to talk about this code "consisting of 256 8-bit characters and used for data representation and transfer." It's so much easier to write EBCDIC or to say "EBB-see-dick." *Beginner's All-purpose Symbolic Instruction Code* becomes *BASIC; COmmon Business-Oriented Language* yields *COBOL;* "what you see is what you get" is shortened to *WYSIWYG,* pronounced "WIZ-ee-wig."

ENIAC was not only an early computer, but it also probably gave the computer industry one of its first acronyms. ENIAC was born in 1946, which means its development started during the war. According to both the Random House unabridged dictionary and *Webster's Ninth New Collegiate Dictionary,* the word *acronym* came into existence in the 1940s, during the development, and shortly before the appearance, of ENIAC.

Both John Ciardi and the team of William and Mary Morris provide extensive discussion of *acronym*, whose origin is the Greek *akros* (tip) plus *onym* (name). Ciardi notes that the *Oxford English Dictionary* has no mention of the word until the 1972 supplement, which places its origin in 1943. He points out, however, that acronymic formations existed before the word used to describe them; the 1930s witnessed the coining of *radar* (radio detecting and ranging) and *Nazi* (*Nationalsozialist*), to name a few early acronyms. "Search as I may I can find no securely attested case of an acronymic word formation in English or American before FDR's New Deal introduced acronymania into Federalese and then into general American." Ciardi goes on to point out that many acronyms today are forced into being to reflect their subject matter.[22] This exercise is especially common in the computer industry.

The Morrises view acronyms as "probably the most interesting and widespread development in our changing language."[23] They write that the earliest acronyms are unknown but indicate that some scholars claim to have located examples in ancient Hebrew scriptures. Although they give no examples, the Morrises claim that nineteenth-century American and British coinages yield acronyms, but their profusion dates from the First World War, with the appearance of Anzac (Australian-New Zealand Army Corps) and WAAC (Women's Army Auxiliary Corps). Like Ciardi, these authors believe that "the full tide of popularity of acronyms in America came with the advent of the New Deal and World War II." Since the Second World War, they note, "no single classification of word coinages has proliferated so rapidly."[24]

"We're inclined to think that the vogue for acronyms, which has recently burdened the language with such lunacies as EGADS [Electronic Ground Automatic Destruct] and MOUSE [Minimum Orbit Unmanned Satellite of Earth], may be petering out. Who with a straight face could possibly invent an acronym that could match the one . . . during Watergate—CREEP, for Committee to Re-Elect the President?"[25] The Morrises' prediction has not come to pass; acronyms are actually on the increase. Unlike the Morrises, Michael Swaine, editor-at-large for *Dr. Dobb's Journal,* suggests that this proliferation may have some hidden benefits. "Acronyms and legitimate techie neologisms point unambiguously to things that the computer industry desperately needs to have pointed to unambiguously and internationally," Swaine believes.

For now, though, the aims remain less lofty. Frequently, the marketing arms of computer companies have to come up with, in Ciardi's words, the "catchy effect . . . to bumble about the phrase or the title of the program or organization from which the acronym is supposed to derive . . . to fit the catchphrase."[26] The marketers have to force the phrase for which the acronym stands into an already conceived acronym that forms a word suggesting the orientation of the acronym. So they name a visually oriented "graphics programming environment" VIEW because the yet-to-be-named acronym suggests a visual state. It is then necessary to reverse-engineer VIEW to come up with Visual/Integrated Environment for Windows.[27] If the reverse-engineering itself is not clever enough, devisers of acronyms sometimes try to add a typographic twist to make the acronym stand out from its thousands of all-caps cousins—as in NeWS (Network/extensible Window System).[28]

Acronyms as Verbs

Although acronyms have functioned effectively as nouns for many decades, once computer people have invented acronyms, they often turn them into verbs, as in the "verb" *to OEM*. OEM is short for *original equipment manufacturer*. According to *Webster's Ninth New Collegiate Dictionary*, an OEM is "one that produces complex equipment (as a computer system) from components usually bought from other manufacturers." As a verb, OEM has a dual meaning. The "other manufacturers" are said "to OEM" their equipment to the OEMs; and the OEMs talk about "OEMing" the manufacturers' equipment. As noted earlier, certain neoverbs—*grep, troff, PIP,* and *SYSGEN*—fall into the categories of processes and acronyms as verbs. Another neoverb in this category is RIP (raster-image processor).[29] The virtual verbs PIP, RIP, and *grep* present orthographic and pronunciation problems within the relative confines of English pronunciation. Although English is notorious for its lack of standard rules of spelling and pronunciation, it does have some conventions, one of which states that when a vowel and a single consonant precede a participial or gerundive ending, the vowel is long if the syllable is stressed, as it is in the verb from which the participle/gerund is formed. The syllable break occurs after the consonant.

Take the verb *snipe* as an example. The *i* is long, and it remains long in *sniping,* which breaks thus: *snip-ing.* To make the vowel short, you have to double the consonant. The syllable break then occurs between the two *p*s: *snip-ping*. This rule almost always holds true: *loping* vs. *lopping, rating* vs. *ratting*, etc.

What to do in the case of the three neoverbs PIP, RIP, and grep? The latter is the least problematical. Because it is already lowercase, you can tack an additional *p* onto it to come up with *grepping*. The added letter in this case is merely a pronunciation device, since the letters *g, r, e,* and *p* each stand for a word. (*Troff* already has the double consonant, so forming a gerund/participle is no problem; but with such lowercase acronyms, is the first letter uppercase if the acronym begins a sentence, as it does in this one?)

RIP and PIP, on the other hand, are rendered more conventionally in all caps. Unless they are lowercased—in which case they can be confused with the real words *rip* and *pip,* although *pip* is a verb only in British slang (meaning "to blackball")—it is difficult to determine how to construct their participial/gerundive forms. PIPing and RIPing are eyesores; PIP-ing and RIP-ing look worse and are even more confusing. Worse yet are PIPping and RIPping or PIPPing and RIPPing. Another possibility is *pip*ing.

The copy department at *MacUser* magazine has opted to handle this situation by simply adding *ing* to the acronym. With this approach, the acronym stands as a discrete unit, which separates it from the *ing* ending for pronunciation purposes. *MacUser*'s solution is not universally applied, however, and readers of computer literature are likely to see all of the methods listed above. They're also likely to see, depending on what they're reading, "ROMed"or "ROM'd"—both ersatz past participles concocted from acronyms.

Acronyms as Roots

As noted, acronyms can serve as the roots of "neogerundives." These portmanteau constructions can also be the roots of neonouns. A print spooler, for example, is a memory buffer in which to store files awaiting output from a printer. The term *print spooler* would seem to be derived from *spool,* in the sense of the buffer's unwinding the files from the queue as they become ready to print. But the root of *spooler* is actually the acronym SPOOL: Simultaneous Peripheral Operations On Line.

Another example of this kind of root structure is MIPS (millions of instructions per second). Since MIPS has effectively become a plural noun, its "singular" form, "MIP," is the root of (MIPper, MIPPER, mipper—take your choice): "a 10-mipper [that is, a computer system running at 10 MIPS]."

Acronyms as Plural Nouns

MIPS is the classic example of an acronym that has become a plural noun, with the S forming the plural of the singular "MIP." Forming a plural adjectival phrase containing MIPS is like forming one with, say, feet: "a 10-foot pole"; thus, "a 10-MIP system." This construction has taken hold even though MIPS is not a noun and even though the phrase "10-MIP system" literally means a system of "10-million-instructions-per," which makes no sense. Per what? Another example of this approach to forming plural acronyms is NURBS, which stands for Non Uniform Rational B-Spline. Still, you may encounter references to, say, ten NURBS and a single NURB, or a "Non Uniform Rational B."

"Nested" Acronyms

In the high-tech world, when one or more of the letters that form an acronym stand for yet another acronym, the result is referred to as a nested acronym, a term that derives from mathematics. In math, a nested set is one that is contained in the previous set. Take, for example, the SLAT-1 networking product from UniNet, a Southern California company. SLAT stands for SCSI Local Area Technology; SCSI is an acronym for Small Computer Systems Interface. Another example of this kind of construction is OAR. As computer-related acronyms go, OAR is short. The *AR* portion of this acronym stands for Analysis Reporting. The *O,* however, stands for Order Module for Accounts Receivable, or OMAR (*module* is a favorite term among computer people; it can mean anything from a physical computing device to something as intangible as a concept). The company that came up with OAR apparently wanted to avoid having to go as far as OMARAR, for Order Module for Accounts Receivable Analysis Reporting. OAR is short, easy to pronounce, and recognizable.[30]

In 1990 IBM announced a new line of RISC (reduced-instruction-set computer) workstations and servers called, respectively, POWERstations and POWERservers. In choosing these designations, IBM was following a pattern set by Sun Microsystems with its SPARCstations and SPARCservers (SPARC stands for Scalable Processor Architecture). The difference was that IBM's acronym was nested; POWER stands for "performance optimization with enhanced RISC." Sun was also busy burying acronyms within acronyms, as noted in the August 1990 issue of the *Sun Observer* in an article about Sun's standardization of the SCSI standard and acronym (Small Computer Systems Interface).[31] Sun's effort was called SCSA, for Sun Common SCSI Architecture. A 1989 press release from Gateway Corp. footnoted the acronym VHDL, explaining that it stood for VHSIC Hardware Description Language, without bothering to explain what VHSIC meant.

Related to nested acronyms are those that combine acronyms with whole words, as in VMEbus. "The term VME stands for Versa Module Eurocard and was first coined in 1981 by the group of manufacturers who defined it. *Bus* is a generic term describing a computer data path."[32] The first revision of the specification was taken from an earlier spec for Motorola's VERSAbus. In 1981, a group of engineers at Motorola Microsystems in West Germany proposed the marriage of the VERSAbus specification and the popular Eurocard packaging format into what they called VERSAbus-E. "A manufacturers group was formed and composed of members from Mostek, Motorola, and Signetics corporations, who later named the new bus VMEbus." A spokeswoman for the VME Industry Trade Association (VITA: *life* in Latin) indicated that VERSA is not an acronym, even though the word's origin in Germany does not suggest any particular meaning for it based on the German language (it may in fact be derived from *versatile*). So VME is apparently not a double nested acronym. The name of the organization that promotes this bus, however, is nested. As noted above, the V in VITA stands for VME. The Latin *versare* means to turn, bend, twist, ply, influence, or agitate.

A related coinage technique is to append the Greek suffixes *mega-* (million) and *giga-* (billion) to an acronym, as in megaflops [or megaFlops or megaFLOPS] (a million floating-point operations per second) or gigaflops (or gigaFlops or gigaFLOPS).

As the denizens of high tech continue to depend on acronyms, they will doubtless create more acronyms within acronyms. It is not farfetched to suppose that eventually a three-letter acronym will emerge whose every letter will stand for a separate acronym. An example would be VAD, for VME ASIC for DOS. A value-added reseller that dealt in VADs would be a VAD VAR.[33]

"Bacronymlash"

"Acronymitis" is a spreading plague in the computer industry—and just about everywhere else—one that cannot be stopped but that can be resisted. "The common measure of computer speed, MIPS, is an acronym for millions of instructions per second," wrote William Bulkeley in his "Technology" column in the *Wall Street Journal.* "But cynical customers joke that it means meaningless indicator of processor speed or even marketing instructions for pushy salespeople."[34]

William Safire's vacation-replacement columnist, Jack Rosenthal, warned of the danger in straining for acronyms. He noted that a *New York Times* editorial once suggested that maybe the time had come "to create, for the name alone, Action Committee to Reform Our Nation's Youth Morals."[35] In the late 1960s, the antithesis of the staid *Times,* the "counterculture" *Realist* magazine, proffered the ultimate acronym: DEAD (dedicated to ending acronymic designations).

More than twenty years later, acronym use is so rampant that it has given rise to "acronymaphobia," according to a humorous column in *UNIX Today.* The subject of this piece, Alan Potts, wakes up one day and responds to his wife's routine question about how he slept: "Never Could Rest. All Tossing and Turning. Sleep Never Arrived." After some more outbursts, such as "Migod, Acronyms Proliferate. Can't Alter Delivery, Can't Alter Mindset. I've Been Mindwiped," his wife takes him to a psychiatrist. The psychiatrist diagnoses Alan as having "acronymaphobia" and tries to cure him but cannot. Finally giving up in frustration, the doctor blurts out: "To Coin a Phrase, I'm Perplexed. I've Simply Done Nothing. It's Terribly Troubling." Alan jumps off the couch and exclaims, "Thanks, Doc, I feel great!" He resumes normal life, "never to be troubled by this strange affliction again." The column concludes that "Acronymaphobia is sweeping the country. Beware. Safe sex is no longer enough. We must now practice safe conversations."[36]

Portmanteau Port

Some of the industry's terms are parts of words that have been moved together to form new words. A *modem,* for example, is a *mo*dulator/*dem*odulator, meaning that it sends out signals over telephone lines and retrieves and interprets them in the same way. A *transputer* is a *trans*action com*puter,* and a *transponder* is a *trans*mitter/res*ponder.* A device that compresses and expands signal is a *compandor. Voxel* is a combination of *vo*lume *el*ement, with the x thrown in for elision. In the same vein, *pixel* means *pi*cture *el*ement. A portmanteau neologism for signifying "computer-controlled communications" is *compunications.* Future possibilities include *pox* (processing box), *workwork* (workgroup network, and *opart,* (operating system for artificial intelligence).

Part of the rationale for acronyms and abbreviations is to have a shorthand method of designating something that would take longer to spell out. Perhaps the ultimate abbreviation is a single letter. The C programming language came after B, which followed BCPL. (UNIX is "written in" C, and so one of its "shells" is called the "C shell.") MIT's X Window System followed on the heels of one developed at Stanford: W.

The Xerox Factor

The Xerox Corporation has gone to great lengths and spent a lot of money to discourage people from using the company name as a verb or noun.[37] Xerox's management wants you to say, "I'm going to photocopy this document" or "I'm going to make a photocopy," rather than "I'm going to xerox this document" or "I'm going to make a xerox." Xerox's motive is understandable: The company wants to protect its registered trademark, just as Kimberly-Clark wants to protect its Kleenex name.

Nevertheless, the examples of Xerox and Kleenex have not dissuaded computer people from taking trademarks in vain. A company called Interleaf produces an eponymous computerized page-layout and typesetting system. Among Interleaf users, to use the product to produce documents is known as "to interleaf"—as opposed to *to interleave* (lowercase *i*), a legitimate verb meaning "to arrange in or as in alternate layers." A variation on this technique is to form a "verb" out of the Apple trademark LaserWriter. The LaserWriter is a laser printer; the pseudoverb is "to laserwrite," meaning to print on a LaserWriter. "'To Claris' someone will become a buzzverb in Silicon Valley, meaning 'To yank the rug out from under anyone whose attitude reminds you of Bart Simpson's,'"[38] wrote Editor Paul Somerson of *MacUser* magazine.

A similar problem, from the point of view of corporate lawyers, is the wanton use of trademarks as nouns. The best way for a company to protect a trademark is to use it as an attributive adjective and somehow coerce others who use the trademark to employ it in a like manner. The legal departments of AT&T, DEC (which prefers Digital Equipment Corporation, by the way), and numerous other companies have done everything from send threatening letters to bring suits against violators, but these actions have not done much to stem the trademarks-as-nouns tide.[39] Some examples: Macintosh, UNIX, 386, Word, WingZ, Claris.

Xerox and Kleenex can be found in a dictionary, which cautions readers that both began as trademarks. As computerese proliferates, it is likely that companies will step up their efforts to ensure the inviolability of their trademarks, which computer people are increasingly using generically, with impunity.[40] Corporate-legal insistence on adjectival use leads to useless nouns and redundancies, such as "MS-DOS operating system," meaning "Microsoft Disk Operating System operating system."

-Izing

A common technique of technobabble concoction is -*izing,* which consists of adding the suffix -*ize* to all or part of a noun or adjective to form a verb. More than a decade ago, Edwin Newman cautioned that excessive use of -*izing* was weakening the language and making for some silly neologisms. Yet, the -*izing* phenomenon has been with us since Elizabethan times. According to *Webster's Ninth New Collegiate Dictionary,* "The suffix -*ize* has been productive in English since the time of Thomas Nashe (1567–1601), who claimed credit for introducing it into English to remedy the surplus of monosyllabic words. Almost any noun or adjective can be made into a verb by adding -*ize* ; many technical terms are coined this way. Nashe noted in 1591 that his coinages in -*ize* were being complained about, and to this day new words in -*ize* are sure to draw critical fire."

Critical fire from Newman and others has not dampened the enthusiasm of people in the computer industry for relying heavily on -*izing;*

prioritize, for example, is a favorite among computer people, as well as those in government and the military. Another favorite is *rasterize,* to render something as a raster image, and *vectorize,* a linear cousin. In the quest for easy-to-produce multilingual software, the industry is on a campaign to *internationalize* and *localize* software products. In a 1984 press release, a company called Comsell managed to squeeze *computerize, technologize,* and *modernize* into a single sentence.

One irony of the heavy use of *-izing* is that its enthusiasts are hardly using the technique "to remedy the surplus of monosyllabic words." Rather, they tend to tack the *-ize* suffix onto words that already have plenty of syllables. The *-ize* suffix is also used to create words on the fly. People in high technology must constantly come up with labels for inchoate technologies and products. It's no wonder that in this environment, *-ize* creations such as the following occur:

The Tempest

Scene: a lunchroom in a nondescript building in Silicon Valley.

Dramatis personae: members of the marketing department of a computer company.

Synopsis: The manager of one of the groups in the marketing organization is addressing the group. He is describing a process called Tempest, which inhibits the emission of detectable radiated data from computers. Devices exist, he explains, that can decipher electronic information from a computer. The Tempest process, he says, is the answer to this security problem.

Early into his discourse, he begins to use *tempest* as a verb, employing the technique of Processes as Verbs, which is explored earlier in this chapter. He talks about "tempesting" and how "to tempest."

A man in the audience is curious: How can a company practically apply the Tempest process to computers? "What do we have to do to 'tempestize' our products?"

The man coined the *-ize* verb *tempestize* to describe a process he had just heard about for the first time. He was not consciously contemplating what he had done, and he got his point across to the group. Structurally, what he had done was to change a noun into a verb and then construct a verb-variant: an *-ize* variant. Although *tempest* is recognized as a verb, the two men who were talking about the Tempest process had used the word *tempest* as a verb, but a verb with a meaning completely different from the accepted meaning: "to raise a tempest in and around."

A computer -*ize* verb that originated in the 1950s and is still in vogue is *initialize,* which, *Webster's Ninth New Collegiate Dictionary* informs us, means: "to set (as a computer program counter) to a starting position or value." Another ancient computer -*ize* verb is, of course, *computerize,* which dates from the mid-to-late 1950s, when computers were just beginning to make inroads into businesses and institutions. Since then, this word has given birth to such -*ize* compounds as *microcomputerize, minicomputerize,* and *supercomputerize.*

-*Izing* has been with us for nearly four centuries, so its prolific use in the computer world is not new. Computer people, especially those in marketing, however, are more prone than other -*izing* practitioners to use the technique on an ad hoc basis. An example is the -*ize* verb meaning "to take a product out of research and development and bring it to market." The verb describing this process is "productize."[41] A related -*ize* verb is "commoditize."

People in the computer and other high-technology milieus are not likely to restrict themselves to adding -*ize* to nouns to make verbs. They are just as likely to tack -*ize* onto an acronym or a brand name. When the marketing people at Sun Microsystems want to add the "Sun look" to a brochure they are producing in conjunction with another firm, they speak of "Sunizing" it. It follows that other companies can IBMize, Unisysize (or would that be Unisize?), DECize, etc., their co-collateral.

All these companies compete globally, with significant presences in Japan. A March 12, 1990, press release from Sun announced that one of its corporate partners had shipped "Japanized Versions of SunWrite, SunPaint, and SunDraw." Another company incorporated the -*ize* suffix into a line of products. Van San Corp. of Southern California offered a variety of padded enclosures for dot-matrix and daisywheel printers that dampened the machines' din. These enclosures were called Quietizers, a registered trademark.

Optimize is a favorite -*ize* verb among computer and government people (for a sampling of some other words for which the industry has -*ize,* see "The -Ize Have It" box). The first secretary of commerce during the Reagan administration, the late Malcolm Baldrige, was so annoyed by the proliferation among civil servants of gobbledygook such as *optimize* that he had Wang Laboratories program word-processing machines in the International Trade Administration to flag this expression—as well as many others such as *maximize* and *untimely death*—and suggest alternatives.[42] No such champion has yet emerged in the computer industry, or the world at large.

The -Ize Have It

acronymize (acronyms themselves can be the basis for *-ize* words, as in PROMize)
modemize
modularize
parameterize
randomize
roboticize
ruggedize

Company Names

The names of computer companies range from the generically, multinationally boring (International Technology Corp.; see "Mix and Match" box for a convenient way to come up with such bland names) to the suggestively innovative (Metaphor, Apple). Some combine Latin or Greek roots with technobabble (e.g., Micrognosis—in this case, the technobabble itself is a Greek root). The biggest name in the business is one of the least exciting and interesting: International Business Machines.

Some names become part of the industry's vocabulary and folklore. Some are consigned to oblivion, although the names of some defunct companies live on because the companies represented a lasting reminder to the industry. Osborne Computer Corp. is one of the best examples. Osborne rose more quickly and burned out faster than just about any other company in the business. So you would not want your company to be "another Osborne."

Mix and Match

Stumped for a name for your company? Just select one item each from columns A, B, and C. In some cases, you could combine parts of words from the first and second columns (e.g., Intertech Solutions).

A	B	C
International	Technology	Corporation
Integrated	Software	Associates
Parallel	Development	Partners
Innovative	Hardware	Solutions
First	Generation	Systems
Worldwide	Enterprise	Configuration
Digital	Functions	Group

As farfetched as the "Mix and Match" process might appear, in 1986 a company called Salinon offered a computer program named Namer. The program's Original Name Generator spat sobriquets onto the screen at the rate of one a minute. If you liked the looks of one, you could save it; otherwise, you could let it go by. Menu categories, one of which was "high-tech," produced names that allegedly fit the bill. If you selected "high-tech," "analytical," "powerful," and "devious-mischievous-harsh," you would get such options as Ceptonym, Cadicon, Nulavak, and Quisicac. The program cost $235 and was employed by such "moniker-meisters" as J. Walter Thompson and Proctor & Gamble.[43]

For many thousand dollars, you could hire the services of NameLab in San Francisco, which has professional linguists on staff. NameLab specializes in combining morphemes to come up with suggestions for catchy company names; naturally, a computer is employed for this task. Most prospects are discarded as nonsensical, but one of the most successful has been Compaq, which suggests a combination of computers or communication and a small package. Incidentally, Compaq is one of the most successful computer companies in history. On the other hand, the MindSet company, whose name was suggested by NameLab, has vanished without a trace.

NameLab cautions against the mix-and-match approach. An example was the undistinguished Digital Transactions, Inc. (DTI).[44] NameLab also stresses that a copycat approach will not necessarily succeed. Apple is a documented success story, but whatever happened to some of the other contenders in the orchard (Pear and Apricot, for example)? Apple sounds nontechnical and "friendly," but so does Rainbow, a disastrous foray by DEC into the personal-computer arena, whose failure owed more to technological blunders than to nomenclature.[45]

NameLab refers to its morpheme meldings as "fusion words." Another term for such blendings is *portmanteau word,* coined, according to the *Oxford English Dictionary,* by Lewis Carroll in the 1880s. Whatever you call them, they are prevalent in the computer industry, especially in the names of companies.

"For all the high-tech companies that pick their names with careful calculation," though, others "select their names over six-packs, in honor of pet wolves, by whim, at random, and in last-minute desperation." At least that was the case when the article that made this statement appeared in early 1984. The article points to several examples of companies extant at the time:

• The Soroc logo looks like a beer-can top because the founders were drinking Coors (of which Soroc is an anagram) while trying to come up with a name.

• Sorcim is *micros* spelled backwards.

• Lobo Systems (*lobo* is "wolf" in Spanish) was named after the founder's pet wolf.

The article also points out that the numerous *X*s—and to a lesser extent *Y*s and *Z*s—that form the names of so many "scientific-sounding companies . . . can induce zzzzzzzzzz, but there is a rational reason for using them. The letters are symbols in Boolean algebra, which is widely used in digital computers."[46]

According to the authors of *Silicon Valley Fever,* company-naming patterns, like technobabble itself, have gone through an evolutionary process. Until 1960 eponyms were the name of the game, with such examples as Hewlett-Packard and Varian. In 1961, Signetics, a combination of *signal network electronics,* signaled a nearly fifteen-year period during which many companies chose names that suggested electronics and technology, with such components as "ecks," "techs," "tecks," and "teks" (example: Avantek for avante garde technology). After 1975, names implying "honesty, truth, and health" were in order: Coherent, Verbatim, North Star, Tandem.[47]

From the internationally nondescript to the linguistically clever to the whimsical, the names of high-technology companies induce, enforce, and reflect technobabble.

Eponyms

The computer industry has immortalized several people by naming everything from programming languages to benchmarks after them.[48] A recent and prosaic example of such eponymous activity is the renaming of a street in San Jose, California, after one of the founders of Apple Computer, Steve Wozniak. Wozniak goes by the sobriquet of "Woz," and Woz Way runs near the relatively new downtown convention center.[49] Wozniak's name also forms part of the eponymous acronym SWIM, for Super Woz Integrated Machine, an ASIC (application-specific integrated circuit).

Other notable eponyms date further back. The Pascal programming language is named after the French philosopher and mathematician Blaise Pascal. A DoD-sanctioned computer language, Ada, derives from Ada Lovelace, daughter of Lord Byron and associate of the inventor of the Analytical Engine, Charles Babbage. Babbage's device was a conceptual forerunner of the computer, and Babbage's, a national chain of software stores, pays tribute to this proto–computer scientist. Boolean algebra is named after nineteenth-century English mathematician George Boole; a twentieth-century software company is named Boole and Babbage.

Alan Turing was the British scientist who helped crack the Enigma code developed by the Nazis. Turing's name became associated with the Turing Test, a technique for assessing claims of intelligence in computers. French mathematician J.B.J. Fourier (1768–1830) has posthumously lent his name to Fourier Analysis, Fourier Series, and Fourier Transform, the latter term illustrating the "transform" of verbs into nouns. A more recent example of an eponym is S.R. Bourne, for whom one of the "shells" of the UNIX operating system is named. The Andrew Window System, developed at Carnegie-Mellon University, is named after one of the institution's founding benefactors, Andrew Carnegie.

Miscellaneous Techniques

Hyphen Based. Like "environmentalizing," *-basing* is an embellishing technique. Computer people tend to cobble it onto words that have no need for the embellishment. For example, a "FORTRAN-based application" means the same thing as a "FORTRAN application" (FORTRAN is a computer language as well as an acronym standing for FORmula TRANslation). A "computer-based task" is, more simply, a "computer task." In both of these cases, the phrase makes equal—and more concise—sense without being *-based.* This technique caught the attention of trademark lawyers at AT&T, who sent out "corrective" correspondence to companies that used the term "UNIX-based" to describe their systems that were indeed based on the UNIX operating system pioneered at AT&T. UNIX, the lawyers warned, is a registered trademark of AT&T and, as such, can be used only in a singular adjectival sense—preferably "the UNIX operating system."

Intensity. On the increase is the technique of adding *-intensive* to words and phrases. Some examples are "compute-intensive," "data-intensive," "keyboard-intensive," "code-intensive," "programming-intensive," and "CPU-intensive." Like one of their predecessors, *labor-intensive,* computer-*intensive* terms mean that, as in the phrases above, a lot of *computation, data, keyboarding,* and *CPU activity* are required for the given applications. A 1989 press release from Omni Solutions (tag line, "Higher Productivity Workgroup Computing") referred to "workload-intensive workstations"—work, work, work!

Participles and Gerunds

Most participles in the computer industry are of the dangling variety: "Programmers write code using keyboards." Gerundives crop up all the time, and the section on acronyms earlier in this chapter deals with acronym-rooted pseudogerunds. Otherwise, technobabble gerundives simply involve adding the *-ing* ending to nouns, common or proper: "modeming," "lasering" (as in outputting on a laser printer), "Winchestering." The only one of these ersatz gerunds that seems to have made it into a dictionary is "windowing," the simultaneous display of one or more portions of one or more files on a screen.

Sufferin' Suffixes

-able, -ability, -ality. These catchall techniques sometimes give computer people a quick out when they have to come up with a term. If an operating system "does windows," it might be said to be "windowable"; a file that can be telecommunicated is "modemable." (Is that pronounced MO-dem-a-ble or mo-DEM-a-ble?) The *-able* suffix shows up frequently on the ends of acronyms: "PROMable," "ROMable," "OEMable."

Anyone has the ability to do it. All you need is the inclination to append the *-ability* suffix to a word or term, as in "cross-callability," the ability to do "cross-calling." The data-communication and networking communities have added to the lexicon *interoperability,* meaning the ability of communications and networking software to operate concurrently with different kinds of computer systems.

Apparently the founders of a New York–based company were so taken with the *-ability* suffix that they incorporated it into the company's name when they incorporated. Datability manufactures servers and boards for various computer systems. Although the name appears to be a melding of *data* and *ability* or *capability,* it suggests the ability to obtain dates.

Representative of the *-ality*-appending technique, *functionality* came into vogue in computing in the late 1970s. It meant—variously, depending on context—"usefulness," "function," "number of functions," and "ability to operate," although it most commonly stood—and continues to stand—for *function*. In 1980 the computer magazine *InfoWorld* even started using *functionality* as a rating category in the magazine's software evaluations. Software reviewers rated a program's functionality from excellent to poor. Since the magazine never defined what it meant by the category, the free-lance product reviewers must have been rating it depending on their interpretation of the word.

In that year, the word *functionality* still did not exist, according to many standard dictionaries. Only with its 1983 edition of the *New Collegiate Dictionary* did *Webster's* admit the word to its lexicon. But the *New Collegiate* never did define the word; it just listed it as a variant of *function*.

To this day, *functionality* still means different things to different computer people and in different computer contexts. What it means etymologically is "being functional." The suffix *-ality* (a combination of *-al* ["of the kind of, pertaining to"] and *-ity* ["concerning state or condition"]) comes from the French *-alité,* which in turn comes from Latin *-alitat-em,* "the quality of being X"—in this case, functional.

-alike. This suffix is appended to just about any part of speech to turn it into a noun having a sense of "being like something else." For example, a workalike is a computer that works similarly to another. An article in the *Sun Observer* referred to SPARCalikes, computers that were like Sun Microsystems' SPARC machines. An educator who read *InfoWorld* wrote about someone who had a job similar to his in a different school district: "Glenn is my jobalike."

-ful, -full. The previous chapter examined the use of this fulsome suffix as an appendage to the word *disk.* It is also added frequently to *state* (stateful[l]: characterized by states) and *swap* (swapful[l]: performing swaps).

-ify. This iffy technique involves adding this suffix to words to form neologisms having the sense of "being created," as in the recently coined *iconify*: "to represent a heretofore [alphanumeric] entity as an icon on a screen."[50] The suffix *-ify* is a variation on *-fy,* a verbal suffix meaning "to make, cause to be, render" or "to become, to be made." It was introduced into loan words from Old French, but it is also used in the formation of new words, usually with a Latin root." *-fy* comes from Old French *fier,* which comes from Latin *ficare,* "to do, make." Note the *usually* in the above definition. *Icon* comes from the Greek. Forming words with *-ify* holds other non-French possibilities. Formations with acronyms: OEMify; with brand names: Macify; with processes: Tempestify.

-ism. This suffix signifies the many dialects, philosophies, and characteristics of the computer industry. You will find "DOSisms," "Macisms," "Compaqisms," and just about any -ism you can imagine or concoct.

This chapter has dealt with many of the common techniques by which technobabble is coined, all of which are part of the overall style of technobabble. Think of chapter 5 as an overview of specific stylistic techniques of technobabble. The next chapter is more like its "grammatical primer."

6

Elements of Style

If you do not understand a particular word in a piece of technical writing, ignore it. The piece will make perfect sense without it.
—Mr. Cooper's Law[1]

The techniques presented in the previous chapter represent more than mechanisms for creating and modifying terminology. They also embody specific elements of the style of technobabble. More generally, technobabble is characterized by anthropomorphic language, excessive use of the passive voice, flash-in-the-pan neologisms, solecisms, synecdoche, euphemism, obfuscation, and mangled metaphors, among other traits. Strunk and White, authors of *The Elements of Style,* a guide to writing clear English prose, would no doubt be appalled, as technobabble violates most of their tenets.

One of the closest things to a primer on technobabble came in the form of a short satirical article by David Roth. In the second paragraph of the article, "William Safire, Eat Your Dictionary: Here Comes TechnoBabble," Roth suggested that technobabble has conventions: "Under the rules of TechnoBabble, it's OK to turn nouns into verbs, verbs into nouns, and to institutionalize words that mean the exact opposite of what you're really trying to say." A "cardinal rule" of TechnoBabble, wrote Roth, is that "any noun can be 'verbed.'" As examples he gives *architect* and *obsolete.* When it comes to adjectives, invention is "only limited by your imagination. Add 'ability' to any word," such as *maintain,* for "maintainability." He notes that "portable" software is not something you carry in your pocket but rather software that is "written in a programming language that makes it easy to adapt, or 'port,' to many different computer systems." Roth cited the mythical B.L. Schematic, "an industrial psychologist at the TechnoStress Institutes in Santa Clara, California," who advises that "even the greenest liberal arts major can elbow up to the cognoscenti by mastering the simple art of hyphenating everything." For office environments, Schematic suggests terms such as "It's on my screen," in response to a query about your participation in a board meeting, or for procrastinators, "I'll keep your input on-line."[2] Most of Roth's other examples have already been noted in this book.

Personification

Probably no other trait so characterizes technobabble as anthropomorphism and personification, attributing human characteristics to hardware and software. (In the male-dominated computer industry, it is routine to hear programs and devices referred to as "he"; I for one have only once seen "she" used to describe computer technology.[3]) Two reasons for this tendency stand out: (1) from their inception, computers have appeared to mimic certain human cerebral traits; as computer technology advances, it increasingly appears to replicate human thought and other processes; and (2) many computer mavens feel more at ease with technology than with people and transfer animate traits to the technology in the process.

Behind this penchant for personification is the long-standing tradition in the industry, dating from the inception of computing, of employing terms that suggest that computers are living entities. The term *memory* as applied to the storage of data goes back to John Von Neumann and the concept of stored programs.[4] Almost since their advent, computers have been called "electronic brains" or "computer brains." Today it is the CPU, rather than the entire machine, that is thought of as the brain. Terms such as *intelligence, logic,* and *virus* further promote the computer-as-human analogy.

Anyone who has used a computer regularly knows how easy it is to be seduced into believing that the machine is thinking—and doing it faster than the person. Computer chess and backgammon games, for example, make nearly instantaneous moves while their human competitors labor over their countermoves. In spite of continual reminders from critics and aficionados alike that, of course, computers are likely to beat us at chess because they are generally better at analyzing numeric probabilities, many people still tend to slip into anthropomorphic language when describing them.

Popular culture—particularly science fiction, a genre viewed as a literary art form by many computer enthusiasts—has done a lot to promote the notion of computers as beings. Starting notably with Czech playwright Karel Capek's 1920 work *R.U.R.,* which gave us the word *robot,* pulp and serious literature and, especially, movies have portrayed computer technology with a human (inter)face. In 1957, for example, Katherine Hepburn and Spencer Tracy played opposite a huge, blinking, thinking IBM mainframe in *Desk Set.* Tracy was an efficiency expert sent in to automate a business. Hepburn and her skeptical colleagues called the machine "electronic brain" and the like. In the 1960s, HAL ran amok in *2001: A Space Odyssey.* This cultural trend culminated in 1977's ludicrous *Demon Seed,* in which a computer imprisons and impregnates Julie Christie. As we approach the millennium, fantasy has given way to serious quests for "virtual reality" and "artificial life." This kind of vivification verbiage is rife in technobabble, yet it does not necessarily extend to the liveliness of the writing used to describe computers.

Passive Voice

One of the ironies of the computer industry is its denizens' heavy reliance on the passive voice. Computers deal with concrete binary calculations: yes or no, on or off, black or white. Except in the case of "fuzzy logic" (see chapter 10), the industry has little room for shades of gray, for interpretation, for assumptions. Yet much of the writing about computer technology is awash in the vague, evasive passive voice.

The tradition of "scientific" writing predisposes people who write about computers to use the passive voice. Examine the articles in any scientific journal, and you will see a preponderant use of the passive. Since the passive voice removes the agent from the action, it is mistakenly perceived as objective, a valued characteristic of the empirical method, and erudite. Our educational system still pushes the notion that scientific and technical writing should employ the passive voice. In the mid-1980s, a software company actually released a "courseware" program to help teach the passive voice to students.

Usually dull and lifeless, the passive voice need not necessarily be confusing, however. In the sentence "The computer's functions are managed by the operating system," the meaning is clear, if not dynamic: The operating system controls the computer's functions. Try to fathom a long paragraph full of technical information, compound sentences, numerous antecedents—as well as the passive voice—and you're likely to get lost. Attempt to plough through reams of these kinds of paragraphs strung together unrelentingly, and your eyes may glaze over, especially when you also have to contemplate the dangling participles that frequently accompany passive constructions: "The function is implemented by activating the startup procedure."

If you are technically knowledgeable, you may well understand what is happening in these passive passages—even though little is clearly spelled out. A lot of people in the industry assume that everyone else knows what they're talking about anyway and so toss off passive constructions, jargon, and other communication that may dumbfound people who are not in the know. Many hard-core computer aficionados are so obsessed with the technology that they feel uncomfortable relating to people—and personify the technology with which they are more at ease in the process. Excessive introspection can breed passivity, which in turn may lead to passive language. Even if excessive use of the passive voice in the computer industry is not insidious or conspiratorial, it can become a bad habit. The passive voice does have a place in writing—to highlight the object of a sentence, for example. Constant, unmodulated use of the active voice runs the risk of becoming static, but at least readers are not confused about who is doing what to whom.

Euphemisms

The kid in a 1990 TV ad turns to the camera and says, "My dad's a plastics-recycling engineer at Dow Chemical. It sounds complicated, but it's really simple." A similar statement about the computer industry would be equally appropriate—both because of the industry's use of grandiose terms for simpler ones and because of its use of euphemistic terminology. The tendency toward euphemism is most apparent in the omnipresent use of the word *engineer*. Nearly everyone in computing, it seems, is an engineer. If you write software or program computers, you are a *software engineer;* if you design computers, you are a *hardware engineer;* if you help market the resulting products, you are a *marketing engineer;* and if you help sell them, you are a *sales engineer.* After the sale, *support engineers* help maintain the products.

Although the computer industry is generous in bestowing the title of engineer, the industry's overuse of the word at least has an etymological rationale (see below). You can step outside the computer industry to find egregiously euphemistic examples of engineering. The most notorious and most often quoted is *sanitary engineer* for *garbage collector.* Another popular one is *domestic engineer* for *housewife.* I recently spied a man in a restaurant wearing blue coveralls, upon which was emblazoned an oval insignia reading *Stationery Engineer.* Did this man manufacture envelopes and letterhead? Curiosity overwhelmed me, so I walked over to him and asked him what exactly a stationery engineer did. Bemused, he informed me that he ran a large engine.

What exactly is an engineer? According to the *Oxford English Dictionary,* the first documented use of the word occurred in 1325 and meant "a constructor of military engines" (this definition is now obsolete). In the computer industry, although nearly everyone is nominally an engineer, what many of these engineers do derives from the verb form meaning "to arrange, manage, or carry through by skillful or artful contrivance,"[5] dating from the 1870s.[6] It was not until the next century that the "euphemizing" of *engineer* started, spurred on by the computer industry.

Here are some of the industry's other notable euphemisms:

knowledge worker: white-collar employee

information professional: someone who works in the computer industry or with computers

information system: fairly vague term meaning, among other things, *computer system*

proactive: reactive; a defensive euphemism masking what amounts to, "We're getting our asses kicked in the market in the area of X; we've got to make up for lost time and try to catch up with our competitors, claiming that we invented X in the process."

consultant: someone who is unemployed

strategic planner: bullshitter with a cushy job

implementation detail: major obstacle to accomplishing a task

customer-support analyst: "best new euphemism for 'salesman' or 'PR hack'" was the response of the jaded editor who encountered this one

These terms are basically innocuous, if not silly. Two insidious euphemisms in the computer industry are "clean room" and "clean industry." Clean rooms are immaculate in terms of the amount of dust they contain. A single mote of airborne contaminant can ruin a silicon wafer, so the air is heavily filtered to prevent contamination of the wafers from which computer chips are made. Clean-room employees, however, are subjected to highly toxic dopants—gases such as arsine and phosphine that affect the electrical properties of semiconductors.

The computer industry itself used to boast that unlike other, older industries, it was "clean." Because no tall smokestacks visibly spewed poison into the air—an image associated with steel plants in the Midwest and chemical factories in New Jersey—the mistaken notion developed that the high-tech industry did not pollute. We now know that high-tech is one of the most polluting of all industries. Silicon Valley has numerous EPA Superfund sites, and cities such as San Jose and Sunnyvale wash tons of heavy metals and other toxics into San Francisco Bay every year. Major computer manufacturers have "environmental engineers" to deal with such issues.

Hightechperbole

The computer industry is ferociously competitive, and it has a lot of PR people and enthusiastic engineers hyping its wares. Common monikers for these proselytes include the religious-sounding "evangelists," "zealots," "fanatics," and "true believers." It is not uncommon for an otherwise staid, straightforward product engineer to bubble rhapsodically when he is touting his own product. This penchant for "positioning" every item of the industry's creation as the greatest thing since sliced silicon wafers permeates the language of the industry. The overuse of terms such as *powerful* and *sophisticated* and the myriad others that are bandied about with abandon has made them all but meaningless.

Another example of hyperbolic, prolix language in the industry is the superlative descriptions of products and technologies. Everything, it seems, is "first," "best," "fastest," "smallest" or "largest" (depending on the traits being touted), "easiest to use," and on and on. This boasting has led to extensive use of terms such as these:

highly: computer technologies are not merely integrated, parallel, or optimized, they are "highly" integrated, parallel, or optimized.

massively: as in "massively parallel computing."

super——:   given the nebulousness of "technotaxonomy" (e.g., mini-computer, microcomputer, personal computer, workstation) and the increasing overlap of the categories, the term *supercomputer* was inevitable, and it actually defines a certain kind of computer—sort of.[7] Now we also have "supermicrocomputers," "superminicomputers," "superwork-stations," and others. You will see these terms spelled out, variously, as a single word, two words, or a hyphenated compound.

very: first there was "large-scale integration (LSI)," then "very large-scale integration (VLSI)." What will be next—very, very large-scale integration (VVLSI)? Shouldn't chip maker LSI Logic at least change its name to VLSI Logic? *Very* is nothing more than a punctuation mark in computer-industry writings, so frequently does it appear.

Logorrhea

When it comes to bloated, verbose, confusing, evasive language, many disciplines are in contention for top honors. Although the computer industry can't come close to matching such champs as the government, the military, the legal profession, and the social sciences, it does its part to use ten words, for example, when three would adequately tell the story.

Use of institutional verbosity, regardless of the institution, springs from a need to deceive or a desire to sound important—or a combination of the two. Many professionals, apparently, fear that their work will not be taken seriously if anyone outside their group can understand it. Linguists, columnists, and commentators of all stripes continually complain about this situation, which will only get worse before it gets any better.

In the computer industry, logorrhea manifests itself in ways that this chapter presents and others in the book have already examined. For a primer on how the industry, all the way from engineering to marketing, turns simple words and phrases into perverse polysyllables, see "Partial Guide to Survival in the Computer Industry" box.

Partial Guide to Survival in the Computer Industry

If you're going to make it in computing, you'll have to be able to sound like the locals. This handy phrase guide gives you some impressive-sounding polysyllabic terms to substitute for more mundane words.

disk, printer, modem, etc.:   peripheral

does: supports, implements, is designed to (support, utilize), functions as, provides support for, has (facilities, capabilities) to, has the capacity to, is designed to support the implementation of

factor: parameter

functions (n.):   functionality, rich set of functions, options, features, abilities, capabilities

improves: maximizes, optimizes, leverages, provides extensions for

makes: generates, is designed to (make, produce, etc.)

many: (vast, wide) array

method: methodology

price: price point

programmer: software engineer, software developer

set up: configure

supports: provides support for, supports the (design, implementation, development, etc.) of, provides support for the (design, implementation, development, etc.) of

use (n.):   usage, utilization

uses: supports, implements, utilizes, makes use of

varied: heterogeneous

version: implementation, generation

On the other hand, a single polysyllabic word such as *interoperability* (eight syllables) is a shorthand method of saying that a system or a group of systems can work with other, disparate system(s). In this case, what appears at first glance to be a polysyllabic neologism is actually an abbreviated method of stating something potentially much more wordy. But the quest for brevity is hardly widespread in the industry.

Conventional wisdom has it that computer documentation is often verbose but that press releases are written in a compact, factual style. Not necessarily. Although probably not the longest lead sentence in the history of computer-industry PR, this one from Plexus Computers contained sixty-six words:

In a move that will add a rich base of applications packages to its UNIX™-based line of commercial and business computer systems, Plexus Computers, Inc., a leading manufacturer of 16- and 32-bit supermicrocomputers, today announced agreements with three software manufacturers to distribute "bridge software" products that allow Plexus users to run software written for Digital Equipment Corporation (DEC^R), Wang, and Basic Four minicomputer systems.

The following single-sentence paragraph from a computer magazine is a mere forty-four words, but what a fulsome forty-four: "More than the fact that the Lisa is being sold by Apple Computer, which already had a tremendous personal-computer market base, what the Lisa represents is a minimal critical technological mass that will provide the basis for this new generation of software."

Technobabble, unlike the unambiguous, on/off digital world it chronicles, is often convoluted and Byzantine. Perhaps because that digital world has become so complicated—with several-hundred-thousand-line code increasingly common—the lexicon has followed suit. Although binary devices and calculations are conceptually simple, ever-more-complex code means more variables that have to be defined, more algorithms that have to be created. The need to define so many levels of complexity may account in part for the unnecessarily complex language that so often emanates from the computer industry.

Elliptical Obfuscation

In reading the papers, product brochures, and other such literature of the computer industry, you might reasonably reach the conclusion that the industry's wares either never made it out of an R&D lab or did nothing more than fulfill some ancillary service function. Computer products, it seems, do not really "do" anything. Most "were designed" to accomplish a task but apparently never actually perform it. Often they are not even designed to do anything other than perform some nebulous kind of "support" function. Infrequently will you encounter a straight-out declaration that a certain product actually does something. Instead of "This computer runs at 25 MHz," you are likely to find "This computer is designed to run at 25 MHz," leaving you with the conclusion that the design was not realized and that the computer does not, in fact, meet its objective. Perhaps the computer "has a window system"? More likely it "supports the implementation of a windowing environment" or (more simply?) "supports a windowing environment."

Why does the industry beat around the bus, the board, and the chip? Computer-industry critic Theodore Roszak sees insidious motives behind the deception: "In our popular culture today, the discussion of computers and information is awash with commercially motivated exaggerations and the opportunistic mystifications of the computer science establishment. The hucksters and hackers have polluted our understanding of information technology with loose metaphors, facile comparisons, and a good deal of out-and-out obfuscation."[8] A less demonic reason may relate to an inferiority complex harkening back to the early days of computing, when computers were unreliable in operation. Another likely reason is that the industry is still heavily influenced by research for its own sake, with no need to deliver products.

The vague phrase "is designed to" obviates any claim of responsibility for how a product actually performs. In the early days of any new technology, products are likely to have imperfections. Before integrated circuits and miniaturization,[9] computers were destined (not designed) to malfunction, because they were composed of miles of wire and heat-generating relays and tubes. Today's computer products are even more likely than their predecessors were to have bugs, because the intensely competitive environment in which they are produced often forces manufacturers to get products out the door before they are truly ready to go into production. The frantic pace of technological advance compels companies to continually attempt to one-up their competition. The frenzy leads companies to preannounce products or, worse, to tout products that either will never make it out of development or will not be ready for years after the first announcement. Companies have even been known to introduce bogus products just to stir up interest in the company. In their technical papers, engineers may attempt to imply that embryonic technologies over which they are still laboring are complete. Business and marketing types tend to be consciously duplicitous, whereas engineers are more likely to want to outengineer their competitors. When a real product finally is ready for rollout, it is almost inevitable that some part of the demo will bomb.

With the Damoclean threat of failure constantly hanging over their head, it is little wonder that people in the industry are loath to make straightforward claims about what their products can do. Obfuscatory phrases such as "is designed to" leave an out in the event of malfunctioning or nonfunctioning technology. (This attitude may also help explain the industry's use of the word *functionality,* meaning "being functional" or "ability to function" in place of *function.*)

Another reason for the seeming focus on design rather than function is that some big companies in the industry have deep enough pockets to fund research for its own sake: For them, getting products out into the market is not an issue. A couple of examples are AT&T's Bell Labs and Xerox PARC (Palo Alto Research Center). Although other companies have evolved technologies developed at these research institutes into products, commercial success has not motivated the technologies' development. They may have been designed to do certain things; whether they eventually did them was not the primary concern of the researchers. In the rarified realm of research, realizing a functional product may be dismissed as an "implementation detail."

Redundancies and Oxymorons

Redundancy is a notable trait of technobabble. The term "new innovation," for example, shows up with great frequency. Another frequently encountered redundancy is "[RAM, ROM, DRAM, SRAM, etc.] memory." Since the M in these acronyms already stands for memory, *ROM memory,* for example, means "read-only memory memory." Other acronymic tautologies include "RISC computer" (the C in RISC stands for *computer*), "SPARC architecture" (the *ARC* in SPARC already denotes architecture), "the COBOL language" (the *L* in COBOL means *language*), and TCP/IP protocol (spelled out, this mouthful stands for *Transmission Control Protocol/Internet Protocol protocol*).

Acronymic redundancy results because people in the industry use acronyms as if they were common nouns and often forget in the process— or never knew in the first place—what the acronyms stand for. A good example is the use of the acronym MIPS (millions of instructions per second) as the "plural" of the mythical singular noun MIP. It also results, as noted earlier, from corporate legal departments' insistence on using trademarks adjectivally, which produces such redundant phrases as "SPARC architecture" and "DOS operating system."

A reader of *InfoWorld* once took issue with the term *software program(s)*, which appeared with regularity in headlines and text. "As a computer programmer and consultant," he wrote in a letter to the magazine, "it seems to me that software and programs are synonymous in the context of computers and data processing. My mind equates 'software programs' to something like 'hardware circuits' or 'automobile cars.'" Perhaps redundancy is not such a sin in the computer industry. As an *InfoWorld* product reviewer once noted glowingly of a piece of software, "The manual was concise, yet it leads you through the system with only a small amount of repetition."

Whereas redundancies are useless repetitions, oxymorons (from Greek roots meaning "sharp-dull") are seeming or actual contradictions. The granddaddy of technology-related oxymorons is the well-known and humorous *military intelligence*. Although oxymorons are not as rife in the computer industry as they doubtless are in the Catch-22 world of the military, they do crop up from time to time. A newcomer to the complex UNIX operating system might readily conclude that the term "easy UNIX" is an oxymoron. Acronymic terms such as Advanced BIOS (Basic Input/Output System) and Advanced BASIC (Beginner's All-purpose Symbolic Instruction Code) appear to be contradictions in terms—as does the designation Personal Mainframe, a desktop workstation from Opus Systems.

Gender-Specific Language

Although gender-specific language is hardly restricted to the computer industry, the industry, because of its dogged insistence on the use of stilted singular constructions such as "the user," is particularly susceptible to it.

The gender-specific-language problem has its roots in the disintegration of classical rules of English grammar and an earnest, although misguided, attempt to eliminate "sexism" from language. The reasoning behind the latter phenomenon is easy to summarize: The phrase *the user*, for example, is singular, which means it should take a singular third-person pronoun, the choices being *he* or *she* (*it* is inanimate).[10] Male-dominated Western culture has chosen to emphasize the masculine, which has meant that *he* is the grammatically correct choice, unless the reference is clearly, in context, to a female. Adamant antisexist forces insist that to make constructions such as "The user must first turn on the computer, and then X must attempt to use it" gender neutral, the pronoun *they* must fill the X spot, although *the user* is singular and *they* is plural. Feminists aside, a burgeoning tendency—a result of the abovementioned grammatical degeneration—is to mix singular and plural in the third person. In such constructions as "the company ... they ...," Anglophilia appears to have infiltrated American English. (The British consider *the government,* for example, to be a plural noun because more than a single person makes up a governing body.)

No such rationale exists for the singular/plural third-person mix in American English. Writers such as Richard Bolles detail the horrors of gender-specificity. In his classic job-search manual, *What Color Is Your Parachute?,* Bolles argues that one "must" employ *they* with both plural and singular antecedents ("Anyone using this beach after 5 P.M. does so at their own risk.").[11]

In the 1970s, some feminists suggested that the solution to the problem was to come up with a gender-neutral pronoun that indicated either men or women. One suggestion was s/he. Another was to invert the letters of *it* to form *ti* (pronounced "tee"). Those ideas got about as far as Esperanto has.

The furor is unwarranted, because a clean, simple method for dealing with this "problem" exists within the confines of standard American English. Numerous people, it seems, have forgotten about the third-person plural. Take the sentence above: "The user must first turn on the computer, and then X must attempt to use it." To avoid substituting either *he* or *they* for X in this sentence, simply render the sentence in the plural: "Users must first turn on the computer, and then they must attempt to use it." This solution is so simple, so clean—why doesn't everyone in the computer industry take this approach in his communication? (Make that "Why don't people in the computer industry take this approach in their communication?")

The reason seems to go back to why so many people in the computer industry insist on employing the passive voice. It "sounds" erudite, dispassionate, and authoritative. The *user* (or *operator, programmer, developer,* whatever) has a patina of objectivity. It seems to suggest a Platonic ideal of a user, as opposed to a possibly motley crew of users.

The irony in this situation is fairly obvious. Technobabble is becoming an increasingly populist phenomenon, so democratic constructions should be welcome. As a whole, though, the computer industry continues to insist on singular constructions, which then throw industry communicators into the choice of using gender-specific language or gender-solecistic concoctions such as "the user . . . they. . . ."

The foregoing situations are grammatical at base. Another gender-related aspect of technobabble is an offshoot of the rampant anthropomorphism in the industry. Anthropomorphism is everywhere, not just in computing. Sailors call their ships "she"; weaponry is referred to in the feminine; bluesman B.B. King named his guitar Lucille; until protests mounted, hurricanes always had women's names. Seamen and soldiers were forcibly separated from the company of women and named their ships and weapons after women to remind themselves of what they were missing. But hard-core hackers in the nearly all-male computer industry set *themselves* away from female companionship. This neo-Spartanism may account for the tendency to favor masculine monikers. Only four exceptions come readily to mind. The bread and butter of Commodore's product line is the Amiga ("female friend" in Spanish). The Ada programming language is named after Augusta Ada Byron, daughter of Lord Byron.[12] A strange man named Alan Rogers, who claimed to be able to contact God through his TRS-80 computer, referred to the machine as "she." As already noted, *Lisa* was twisted into an acronym. Otherwise, it is essentially "he" and "this guy."

On the other hand, some aspects of technobabble are matriarchal. The main circuit board of a computer is the *motherboard*. Smaller boards that plug into it are *daughterboards*. In the realm of dominant and subservient software processes, however, a unisexual *parent* process dictates to a *child*. Whether computers are designated as men or as women, anthropomorphism is the operating technique. As 1990 came to a close, transsexual writer Jan Morris spoke on the "City Arts and Lectures Series" on San Francisco FM station KQED. Morris talked about the differences between men and women. "A woman is more of a computer," said Morris, and "a man is more of a car."

Numerotomania

In spite of their operations' frequent resemblance to human activities, contemporary computers still essentially "crunch numbers." Binary digits are the lifeblood of hardware and software. Not surprisingly, people who work with computers tend to be intrigued with numbers—although not necessarily uniformly, as chapter 4 has noted ("Fractious Fractions"). Outside of software code, the numbers mania shows up most noticeably in the technical documents and product-revision cycles of the industry. Version 3 of an operating system is released. Then it is finessed ever so slightly to become version 3.1. Another tweak and the system becomes version 3.1.1, and so on until version 3.2 comes along.

The hierarchical manner in which computer manuals and papers are produced is a numerologist's delight. Here is what the table of contents of a manual might look like, minus heads, subheads, and subsubheads:

1
1.1
1.1.1
1.1.2
1.1.3
1.1.4
1.2
1.2.1
1.2.2
1.3
1.3.1
1.3.1.1
1.3.1.2
1.3.2

Another numbers game in the industry is to place a superscript 2 or 3 after a letter in an acronym to indicate that the letter appears two or three times. For example, A^3 might stand for Advanced Algorithm Associates. SMI^2LE does stand for Space Migration, Intelligence Increase and Life Extension.

Copulate or Closed (Compounding the Problem)

Chronicling, as it does, a thoroughly modern phenomenon, technobabble tends to eschew hyphens (often erroneously referred to as *dashes* in the computer industry) in compound attributive adjectives, those that precede nouns. By encouraging this practice, technobabble is following the contemporary trend toward elimination of hyphens in these adjectival instances. *Time* magazine, for example, tends not to hyphenate compound adjectives.[13] This line of contextualist thinking states that hyphens are necessary in compound attributive adjectives only to clear up confusion. In the term *operating system code,* for example, the context makes it clear that the phrase *operating system* is a unit modifying *code.* Addition of a hyphen (operating-system code) is unnecessary, according to contextualist advocates.

The traditionalist counterpoint to this argument is, Who is the arbiter of context? Simply adding a hyphen to every compound attributive adjective eliminates the need to ponder context and makes for a quantifiable rule, unlike in the arbitrary hyphen-for-context approach. In some cases, the lack of hyphenation makes for some confusing, amusing phrases, such as *operating system software.* Although most computer users understand that what is meant here is software that makes up the operating system, in light of software's—especially system software's—tendency to be bug-ridden, the term can be construed as meaning "system software that works."

The following terms represent the hyphenation problem inherent in the compound-laden language of the computer industry: *real-time, multi-user, broad-band, time-sharing, daisy-wheel, stand-alone.* As form follows function, so noun follows adjective. All six of these compounds, with the possible exception of multi-user, can serve as nouns. In the computer industry, you will encounter three orthographic variations on each of the terms—whether they are employed as nouns or as adjectives: (1) two words separated by a space, (2) hyphenated compound, (3) single word. What you will not encounter is consistency of use from company to company, or even within a single company. The tendency, in fact, is toward anarchy rather than toward mere elimination of hyphens in many of the scores, possibly hundreds, of compound constructions that fill the computing lexicon.

To eliminate confusion and inconsistency, the computer industry might best strive to close up compound attributive adjectives whenever possible—for example, *realtime* system, *multiuser* system, *broadband* network, *timesharing* philosophy, *daisywheel* printer, and *standalone* computer.

Another view was expressed by a client of a woman who worked in an advertising agency. According to the woman, "I once had a client who insisted that *standalone* appear as two words in all his literature. He was positive that if people saw it as a single word, they would pronounce it to rhyme with [the Italian pronunciation of] *provolone.*" As with "object-oriented relational-database-system environment" versus "object-oriented relational database," succinct phrasing and/or tight editing are even better solutions.

Tools of the Trade as Shapers of Style

Technobabble is both a direct and an indirect reflection of the *Weltanschauung* it chronicles. The fast-moving world of computers is volatile, and so is the language that describes this world. Curiously engineers who meticulously test and verify every line of code in a program often give short shrift to carefully checking written documents.

Furthermore, true believers in computer technology are often seduced into thinking that this technology holds potential solutions to all problems, and that same misguided optimism shows up in the style and conventions of technobabble. Spelling checkers (or "spell checkers," as they are often known in the verbs-into-nouns computer industry) are a good example of a technology that instills false confidence (see "Too Bees Oar Knot Two Bes" box). Although these tools have become more sophisticated over the years, they all perform the same essential function: checking the words in a given file against a software "dictionary," which is based on a standard dictionary. Most checkers allow you to add nonstandard words to the dictionary—product names, for example—that are likely to crop up again and again in your particular field.

As far as they go, spelling checkers are useful adjuncts to proofreading. They will flag *thier* when you mean *their* and *tis* when you mean *its,* perhaps catching a mistake that a proofreader might have missed. But if you happen to be one of those people who does not know the difference between *their* and *there,* between *its* and *it's,* a spelling checker will be worthless.[14] It will not alert you to a use of *their* when you meant *there,* because *their* is spelled correctly—even if it is used in the wrong context. Unfortunately, spelling checkers cannot compensate for lack of basic grammatical and orthographic knowledge.[15]

Too Bees Oar Knot Two Bes Adjoining in *Technobabble?*

In its newsletter, the Silicon Valley branch of the Society of Technical Communicators pointed out the homophonic dilemma inherent in spelling checkers. A sample:

> Who wood have guest
> The Spell Chequer wood super seed
> The assent of the editor
> Who was once a mane figure?
>
> In deed did it altar
> His work lode's coarse.
> Once, awl sought his council;
> Now nun prophet from hymn.[16]

Some software companies have taken spelling checkers a step forward to produce grammar checkers. In addition to noting spelling mistakes, these programs point out such problems as inconsistency in voice, frequent repetition of words, redundancies, and the like. Some even flag double words ("this is the the place"), a constant potential problem with "cut and paste" editing.

One example is Writer's Workbench, a set of programs developed by and for programmers at AT&T's Bell Labs. Workbench checks spelling, punctuation, rules of grammar, and word use in the "composition stage" of writing. In the "proofing stage," the programs allegedly "can perform the necessary spelling checking, verification and correction of errors usually done by human proofreaders. Because this stage is computerized, however, the programs can further eliminate the human factor that can sometimes lead to even more mistakes." In the third stage, "textual analysis," the Workbench programs "can gear the text toward specific levels of audiences, according to the grade levels."[17]

A writer for the *Wall Street Journal* subjected the Declaration of Independence to Writer's Workbench, and the program suggested that this seminal document might read better if the introductory phrase "When in the course of human events" were reduced to "when." The program indicated that the sentences in the first paragraph, at an average of forty-five words each, should each be half that length.[18]

The *Journal* article quoted people who thought that Writer's Workbench and similar programs were boons to writers because they helped instill habits of concision and such. On the other hand, a Boston University journalism instructor said, "I would never let a computer edit me."

Because the program can be tailored to flag overused words in particular disciplines and because it was developed at a technology company, Workbench, when used in any computer milieu, should, of course, be set up to halt at *support, environment, designed, interactive, powerful, provide(s), offer(s), implementation, functionality, platform,* and all the other overused and misused words that populate writing about computers.

Regardless of the benefits or drawbacks of Writer's Workbench and other programs, such as Nspell, Right Writer, Correct Grammar, and Grammatik, the reason for their existence is clear and rational. The word-alternative component of the document-formatting package FrameMaker, however, is nothing short of bizarre. The built-in spelling checker flags words not contained in its canned dictionary and suggests lists of alternatives. The lists in the box "You Say Tomato, I Say Baseball" suggest that the programmer(s) who wrote the "alternatives" code lost sight of the objective, with the result being pure babble.

You Say Tomato, I Say Baseball (Reprise)

The FrameMaker program flagged these words, among others (usually technobabble, but not always), in a document and suggested the following alternatives:

cdrom: caldron, cutworm, cauldron, coder, chagrin, codger, cadres, children, coders, cadger, coddler, cotter, colder, coterie, codgers

filesystem: fleshiest, filthiest

heron: herein, hereof, heroin, hereon, heroine, Huron, herring, hernia, hearing, herniae, horny, Orion, hiring, horn, harm, Reno *pathname:*   place-name, pythons, pithiness, pythonless, abashment, pathway, playthings

Xerox: thorax, serge, sorts, zeroed, surges, surtax, sorties, assents, assorts, throats, circus, threads, threats, X-rayed, serrate

xhost: host, theist, sought, cyst, zest, aghast, thought

That this program would even bother singling out the common computer term *filesystem* points out yet another problem with these tools, namely the way in which they are programmed. Is it possible that the programmers are sufficiently unaware of such computerese to put it into the programs' dictionaries? The Nspell program, for example, routinely halts at *workstation, login,* and other staples of technobabble.

Writer's Workbench and the demented FrameMaker aside, a problem that continues to plague computer composition is hyphenation at the end of lines. Thad Spinola, a language columnist for the *Peninsula Times Tribune,* once posed the questions, "Ever hear of Count Ercharges? Or Franci Scans? How about Uns Miling? You know Uns. He was in that German war thriller." Spinola pointed out in his column that although these constructions appear to be people's names, they are, in fact, "words mangled by computers unable to hyphenate properly. I am told that computers *can* hyphenate correctly, but only if they are programmed to do so." He suggested that a solution to this problem would be to print everything ragged right, avoiding hyphenation altogether. "A better solution," Spinola concluded, "would be for computers to learn to spell. They do work for *us,* don't they?"[19] Spinola was writing in 1982, and computer hyphenation has improved since then. But as sophisticated as grammar, hyphenation, and spelling programs may be, they cannot replace careful rereading and editing of written documents.

Word-processing programs, which gave rise to spelling checkers and the like, are a mixed blessing. They make writing easy—sometimes too easy. Type the wrong word, and you can merely back up and change it. Need to move a paragraph from one location to another? Simply cut and paste. A problem with this ease is technological seduction. For many writers, "word processing" has replaced the longer, more tedious process of writing: outlining, drafting, revising. It is easy to reach the conclusion that word-processing and similar products are solutions rather than mere tools.

According to a University of Delaware writing teacher, not only these kinds of software tools but also the brand of computer used can have an effect on writing style. Marcia Peoples Halio studied the sentences of writers who employed IBM PCs and those who used Macintosh computers. Halio concluded that the PC writers used longer sentences than did the Mac writers, and on the Kincaid Scale (a "measure of readability"), the PC people wrote at the twelfth-grade level, whereas the Mac scribblers were only at eighth-grade level.[20] Although the results of this informal study are more interesting than meaningful, it could be that because Macs are so easy to use relative to PCs, Mac writers can crank out copy more facilely, overlooking self-editing in the process. Unfortunately, for the purposes of this book, Halios looked only at sentence complexity, grammar, and punctuation. She did not apply a technobabble quotient to the respective writings.

Grammatical Gaffes

Many of the industry's words are used in unorthodox ways. Perhaps the reason is because the computer industry is fundamentally a numbers game, even though some strings of numbers are referred to as "words." The following sections illustrate some of the more common problems that crop up in technobabble.

Misplaced Elements

The two major areas here are dangling or misplaced participles and human-machine confusion. The former often accompany passive constructions, such as "The interface is implemented by clicking the dialog box" or "The process is accomplished using the transfer utility." In these two instances, the meaning of the sentences is clear, even though the structure is wrong. Meanings are difficult to determine, however, when several possible antecedents precede the dangling participle, as in "The hardware, applications, and utilities are invoked when running the operating system." Sometimes the participial phrase simply appears in the wrong place, as this example illustrates: "Today's users need computers to perform tasks running spreadsheet, word-processing, and database programs."

Sentences such as the following point out the tendency among some people in the industry to equate humans with computers and vice versa: "When Heivjak demonstrated the word processor, the speech synthesizer verbalized each letter, word, or sentence, depending on which speech mode he was in." "PDA Engineering and McDonnell Douglas announced that a jointly developed interface that integrates McDonnell Douglas's Unigraphics modeling software with PDA Engineering's PATRAN analysis software has begun first customer shipments." According to the box in which AutoSave II is packaged, "Once installed and configured, you're set." This tendency causes writers on computer topics to write sentences such as this: "Once triggered, the user may display, scroll, disassemble, and, if desired, print the information contained in the event buffer."

A Tense Situation

Politicians often misuse conditional tenses: "I would have the record state," "I would say that that is appropriate." Why? Because deception and evasion are the currency of politicians and the conditional tense makes such deceptions and evasion easier.

In the computer industry, the future tense is always cropping up for no apparent reason: "The PXA will record and display each step of the users [sic] code, both foreground and background";[21] "When you click the mouse, a menu will appear on the screen." Why? The reason may relate to uncertainty about product functionality. Use the future tense, and you leave yourself an out in the event that the menu *does not* appear.

Solecisms

From "very unique" to "implementate," solecisms and malapropisms are rife in the computer industry. Many of these gaffes involve spelling errors, such as this one in a flier for a conference: "trillion byte lazar memory."[22] Sometimes the problem is a combination of spelling and semantic uncertainty, as in the use of *interphase* ("the interval between the end of one mitotic or meiotic division and the beginning of another") for *interface*.

This combination is compounded when nonstandardization enters the mix. Many people in the computer industry know what *mnemonic* means—both in a general and an industry sense. But many do not know how to pronounce it, voicing it "new-MON-ic." Perhaps while gasping for breath, some misspell it "pneumonic," while others go for "mneumonic." (A Pennsylvania manufacturer of light pens and digitizing tablets—sort of electronic drawing boards—is called Numonics.) It is fortunate for the computer industry that its companies employ a lot of full-time and contract editors.

Das Kapital

In reading material produced by the computer industry, you might begin to think that you had encountered a translation of German in which the translator forgot that common nouns in English start with a lowercase letter (all German nouns start with a capital letter). In the computer industry, it seems that every other noun is a proper one.

Some people in the industry, however, are not content to stop at capitalizing the first letter of all nouns. They have a need to capitalize every letter. The all-caps syndrome is most common in the names of companies and products. If every company were as generic-sounding as, say, "International Technology Associates," these outfits would not be able to differentiate themselves. One attempt at differentiation is to spell the company name in capital letters. Another is to apply typographic twists in which part of the name is capitalized: MicroFOCUS. Extreme examples of this approach are NeXT and NeWS.

Constructions such as *NeWS* raise a question about acronyms: Should each letter or letter combination be capitalized? Should, for example, the computer language that rhymes with *snowball* be spelled COBOL or Cobol? Furthermore, when the language's name is spelled out, should the parts of the name that spell the acronym be highlighted—with uppercase letters (COmmon Business Oriented Language) or with italics (*c*ommon *b*usiness *o*riented *l*anguage)? The commonly accepted practice is to make the letters that form the acronym uppercase. But this approach poses an aesthetic problem. Imagine a computer trade magazine that has about 200 pages per issue, 90 of which are editorial. Excluding artwork, each page has about 600 words. Given the glut of acronyms in the computer industry, figure that each page will average ten or more acronyms because commonly used ones will recur frequently. NOW imagine the appearance of THE typography if EVERY acronym on the PAGE is SET in capital letters—or worse, if several all-caps acronyms are strung together, as in this triad from a GE press release: "The MIMS MFG SOMS System. . . ."

As the previous sentence shows, reading these pages will be somewhat like navigating peaks and valleys with your eyes. For this reason, some computer-magazine and book editors have decided to make only the first letter of each acronym uppercase. The visual effect is more pleasing.

Another type of eyesore that can confront readers of computer publications is represented by the acronym XDR, for eXternal Data Representation. Mercifully, most printed materials in which this construction appears have opted for either External Data Representation—which should rightly be EDR, but apparently *X* sounds more "technical"—or simply external data representation. Another example of this approach is PAX—Parallel Architecture EXtended, according to an Alliant/Intel press release of October 1989, but Parallel Architecture eXtended, according to an Alliant release half a year later.

Random Word Generation

Jokes about so-called random word generation are common in the computer industry, and with good reason. A lot of the prose emanating from the industry does appear to consist of arbitrarily arranged words and phrases, as in this press release prepared by a high-flying and respected PR outfit in the mid-1980s: "Pyramid's 90X supermini is a UNIX-based, enabling it to serve as a host to the approximated 80 UNIX-based microcomputers." These fragments culled from the industry's literature also illustrate randomness: "evidently complete key business manipulation capacity method," "primarily distinguished optional contingency philosophy control power environment."

About the same time the Pyramid-power release arrived in editors' mailboxes, an *InfoWorld* reader sent in a page from the documentation for a product called DELIGHT. The reader had highlighted a passage on the page: "DELIGHT is an interactive optimization-based computer aided-design system which was designed to provide a friendly and flexible environment for designers working in a multitude of disciplines." Next to this passage, the reader had written, "This sentence obviously generated by a buzz-phrase generator."

Perhaps the ultimate exercise in random word generation was a 1984 book called *The Policeman's Beard Is Half Constructed*. "The First Book Ever Written by a Computer," touted the blurb on the cover. The computer's name was Racter, short for Raconteur. Undoubtedly an exercise in programming virtuosity, this "computer writing" consisted mainly of surrealistic gibberish. "It is crazy 'thinking,' I grant you, but 'thinking' that is expressed in perfect English," wrote Racter's programmer, Bill Chamberlain, in the book's introduction. The accompanying press release called the book "a bizarre and fantastic journey into the mind of a machine . . . all written in the deranged, yet utterly correct language of Racter . . . the most highly developed [and probably the only, making the superlative superfluous] artificial writer in prose synthesis today. . . . According to Chamberlain, "Racter needs no input once it is running." Neither did HAL. An example of Racter's prose synthesis: "Tomatoes from England and lettuce from Canada are eaten by cosmologists from Russia. . . . My fatherland is France, and I trot coldly while bolting some lobster on the highway to my counsellor [*sic*]." So much for "perfect English"—of the American variety, one must assume, since Chamberlain makes no mention of appeasing British orthographers.

The World According to Computer-Industry Bloopers

The following gaffes actually occurred; citations have been left out to protect the guilty from embarrassment. The sources of these amusing bloopers range from unedited manuscripts to passages that made it into print in both books and magazines.

The first version resides the entire compiler into memory at once.

Especially valuable for minimizing confusion for user unsophisticates, I also am growing to appreciate this convenience.

It lets you keep your recipes on multiple disks, which is a big help, especially if you are running on a computer with low-capacity disks.

following the 1947 development of the geranium transistor.

Long a problem plaguing the industry, the new disk prevents copies of a program in an operable form.

It is rather hard to eliminate erroneous employees once they have been entered.

Execution of the actual computational portions of the program requires virtually no operation.

Of course the greatest piece of technology in the IBM PC can never be copycatted.

a palate of 4096 colors to choose from.

discreet hardware.

Most of the older computers are used by people that can program themselves.

Often one looks at the program from his or her perspective and not necessarily from the shoes of the end user.

For some reason not yet clear to me, I had to jumper pin 5 to pin 6 to get a high.

A spreadsheet program does more than just use the metaphor of the spreadsheet; he communicates a model of the spreadsheet to its users.

Don't expect Money Minder's reports to jive with your bank statement, however.

The factory has also moved into factory-assembled microcomputers.

The compliments would not sop; even our most begrudging "computerphobe" friends expressed enthusiasm.

. . . editorial department has an immediate opening for a copy editor. Duties include editing copy for grammer.

Most of my missing features came from examining Script.

Other companies are going for the juggler in terms of . . . the struggle to carve out market share.

There are other inconveniences attached to this system.

Figure 3.9. The carnage-return routine.

Nomadic Functions [*Monadic* meant].

Large military systems . . . will need their usual hoards of programmers.

Programmers and systems analysts are only occasionally literate. Their's is a different skill.

Buffer = area set aside to receive rewards. [*records* meant].

The MT-180 printer basically is a maintenance free unit, however periodical cleaning ensures the maximum life span.

Instead of pouring through volumes of legal text, researchers simply call up the data base.

High-blown promise of MIS.

Computer Humor

Some would say that the term "computer humor" is an oxymoron,[23] and frequently that is the case. The prototypical computer joke may well be "What do you get when you cross a computer with a gorilla?" Answer: "A hairy reasoner." Another such witticism is "How many programmers does it take to screw in a light bulb?" Answer: "None. That's a hardware problem."

Because computers are inherently not very funny, the most common type of computer humor involves wordplay—most often puns—that often borders on the "pathological," according to Karla Jennings, author of *The Devouring Fungus*. "Computerites," as Jennings calls the machines' mavens, are "shameless about puns." She notes that the DEC VAX has produced a bumper crop of puns, including "The VAX of Life" and Ernie CoVAX (the name of the first VAX 11/780 in the engineering department at the University of California at Berkeley). Other machine monikers have been Kim NoVAX, VAX Populi, VAXimilian Schell, Sandy KouVAX, and VAXine (a Rutgers machine used for medical diagnosis).[24]

Illustrated Computer Dictionary

The August 26, 1990, installment of the comic strip "Eureka" featured a short illustrated computer lexicon.[25]

input: what goes into a computer (The picture shows a big, boxy mainframe chewing on a paper tape.)

data: what computers lose (Picture: caption balloon reading "Oops" emanating from a computer.)

file: where it gets lost (Picture: crumpled piece of paper tape next to computer.)

bit: a small piece of data (Picture: computer "chewing" on a piece of paper tape.)

byte: a slightly larger small piece of data (Picture: computer "chewing" on a slightly larger piece of paper tape.)

number-crunching: what computers do to data (Picture: computer gobbling with gusto.)

process: how they digest data (Picture: bloated computer burping.)

output: what they spit out (Picture: computer spitting piece of paper tape into full trash can labeled "garbage.")

Many of the anthropomorphic and homonymic terms of technobabble (e.g., *byte, nibble, nybble*) were coined with tongue in cheek. In the late 1970s, a Silicon Valley entrepreneur formed a small software company called The Software Works. In mid-1984 he was selling special ribbons for Apple ImageWriter dot-matrix printers that enabled image transfers to T-shirts. He called the product Underware. Another self-employed programmer has his company name, Canta Forda Computer Laboratory, listed on a business card featuring a Mexican motif. A California company that produces a version of the Lisp (List Processing) Language is named Franz. Then there was the rumored merger of Fairchild Semiconductor and Honeywell, which would have resulted in Fairwell Honeychild. Most computer humor, in fact, is based on exploiting the connotations and double entendres of technobabble. This example of computer humor based on wordplay appeared on a computer network:

In the nightmare I'm back at the University of Mars, and the exam in computer science starts in 20 seconds. But there must be some mistake. I'm a poetry major, and I've never been in this class before. Suddenly the professor appears: It's Art Fleming, and I'm on "Jeopardy."

"The answer is," Mr. Fleming begins, "they changed the architecture to get the EMC as a square of the clock frequency for 80386 processors at 16-plus megahertz, and to get switchless setup and faster I/O data transfer with burst capability. What is the question?"

Panic strikes me as the clock ticks away. "I . . . be . . . um. . . ."

"That's right, IBM!" Mr. Fleming says. And now for the bonus round. The answer is SDLC, LAN, LU 6.2, X.25, Asynch, Netbios, Token Ring, VT100."

"How do you expect me to communicate with you crazy people?" I scream.

"That's right!" shouts Mr. Fleming. "Don Pardo, tell him what he's won."

"Congratulations," Mr. Pardo says. "You win a license for OS/2EE1.1 with Presentation Manager and a lifetime supply of all the jargon we use in the computer industry."

Probably the most ambitious computer-humor project based on technobabble wordplay is *The Binary Bible of Saint $ilicon,* which features scripture such as "Promised LAN," "Rasterfarians," and "Hackolyte." Other examples of computer humor are noted throughout this book. Mainstream entertainers such as George Carlin are beginning to work technobabble into their routines.[26] A short-lived radio humor program in the early 1980s had routines about "pasty-faced wonks" living on "Disk Drive."

Humorous or serious, a slim volume called *The Elements of Technobabble Style* probably is not on the horizon any time soon. Many consultants serving the computer industry devote much of their time to improving communication—both internally and to the outside world. As more and more people communicate in and try to decipher technobabble, editorial consultants and presentations such as "Demythifying Technobabble" will assume greater importance.[27]

7

Sex, Drug, and Holy Paroles

Sit on my interface.
—Quip circulated by Silicon Valley oral tradition

One of the salient points of this book has been that technobabble has transcended its origins to be applied to human interaction: Fragments of programming code become "he," and the brain becomes a "computer." Because computers often appear to replicate human thought processes, this connotative role reversal is not surprising. Technobabble is fraught with other, noncomputer, connotations, many of which are in the realms of sex and religion. Ironically, popular culture has tended to portray hard-core computer enthusiasts as virtually virginal—even asexual—with their passion reserved for consoles and code.

It is common to hear technophiles boast about storage capacities, MIPS, and other measures of technological potency with a rapture usually reserved for quantifying sexual prowess. On a less "sexular" plane, "true believers" and "zealots" "evangelize" for technologies and products with religious fervor. Perhaps the binary nature of computer technology helps impart the prevalence of double entendre to technobabble.

Getting Up and Getting High [Tech]

The hero of the 1983 film *WarGames* was more interested in cracking code than in input/output with his girlfriend. The apocalyptic result of unbridled computer lust was demonstrated in a low-budget 1982 horror flick called *Evilspeak,* in which an introverted, reviled military-academy student retreated to the solace provided by his Apple II computer. He and a satanic program eventually wreaked havoc on the academy. Nineteen eighty-four saw the first entry in the *Revenge of the Nerds* film series.

A more overt display of computer concupiscence came from one "Ray Fifo," who, in a parody of the Frank/Moon Zappa tune "Valley Girl," chanted a high-tech torch song to a computer. Fifo was the central character in a 1983 novelty book called *Silicon Valley Guy,* which was replete with such "technosexual" innuendo as "I'm out there direct-accessing cute little programs at peak transfer rate," "I get there and she [a computer program named Julie[1]] is ON LINE. I mean, like she's wearing all this software. I'm calculating the access time to her front-end processor."[2] On a more serious plane, *Psychology Today* magazine ran an article in the August 1980 issue called "The Hacker Papers," which portrayed a group of Stanford University hackers as obsessive-compulsive loners. In *The Second Self,* MIT psychologist/sociologist Sherry Turkle analyzed hackers at her university and found many of the same traits. Turkle noted that excessive use of computer jargon tends to alienate those who are not obsessed with computers. "I try not to use it in mixed company," explained one student, but Turkle concluded, "The hacker is lost in the jargon of his machine and its programs."[3]

An image still prevails of computer types as unwashed, unkempt sociopaths who spend days in front of glowing terminals, eschewing human contact and washing down sugar-laden snacks and Chinese food with tepid caffeinated beverages. Maybe author Steve Levy was wrong, however, when he wrote, "Computing was more *important* than getting involved in a romantic relationship. It was a question of priorities. Hacking had replaced sex in their lives."[4]

Theirs had been a master-slave relationship. She was a hardware freak; he got off on software. They would take turns hacking and thrashing, but tonight, they planned to couple. They had readied the male-female connector. But there was a problem. He had only a floppy, and she wanted it hard. They were incompatible; they couldn't interface. He couldn't get it up and running in her system: He couldn't enter her. And if he didn't finish the code in time, he wouldn't be able to penetrate new users.

"No input/output tonight," she scoffed impatiently.

"I feel like I've been doped," he lamented as he remembered all the junk he'd done. He had to admit—he was a heavy user. Maybe that was why he had crashed. Did he need a hit?

He looked longingly at her backplane slots and the slot of her quivering drive. Would she go down? Would she give him a head crash? To emphasize his point, he really wanted to give her a bang.

She craved his tool, but she didn't want him to rape her system. "This calls for hands-on!" she exclaimed, exasperated. She ran over to him and grabbed his joystick.[5]

A "sexplication de texte" of the preceding passage seems to indicate that it is about sadomasochism, impotence, fetishism, and assault, among other sexual phenomena. Of course, it is merely a partial list of the computer jargon that connotes sex—both mainstream and exotic. Other terms in this category include *snarf, dump, pop, hung, grovel, dike, bum, back end,* and *end user.*

Take a look at the third paragraph in the passage above. To a technotyro it might appear to concern drug use ... *dope, junk, user, crash, hit* (see "Corporeal Computerese" box for explanations of some of these terms). In reality, the drug of choice among marathon hackers is caffeine, most often in the form of Diet Pepsi or Diet Coke—sitting in front of a terminal does not burn too many calories, after all. According to computer-industry philosopher Bill Joy, though, "[Virtual reality] is drugs for the computer generation."[6] "Many people have compared virtual reality to an LSD trip without the drugs," wrote *San Jose Mercury News* columnist Rory O'Connor.[7] And Grateful Dead guitarist Jerry Garcia allegedly commented, "They made LSD illegal; what are they going to do with this [virtual reality]?"[8]

Corporeal Computerese

bang (n.) the exclamation point (!)

couple (v.) join together—two pieces of code, for example

crash (v., n.) abruptly stop functioning. If, for example, the read/write head of a disk drive hits the surface of the spinning disk, the result is a head crash

dope (v.) to treat silicon with dopant—usually a toxic gas such as arsine or phosphine—to alter its electrical properties

dump (v., n.) Similar in sense to *download*. To move the contents of, for example, a graphics file to some sort of output device. A dump is the result of such an action. A screen dump is a printed, film-recorded, or tape-archived version of an image on a screen. Derives from *core dump*, the process of emptying the contents of a core-memory computer

floppy (n., adj.) with reference to disk media, flexible mylar instead of rigid metal

go down (v. phrase)   crash

hard (adj.)   not floppy

head crash (n. phrase)   the read head of a disk drive coming into physical contact with the disk and ruining it

hit (n.)   an access of cache memory

joystick (n.)   action-manipulating tool for some computer games; originally the lever used to pilot an airplane

junk (n.)   bad code

male-female connector (n. phrase)   an electrical connection in which one protuberant part slides into a receptacle

master-slave (adj.)   relationship between, say, a computer ("master") and a connected dumb terminal ("slave")

rape (v.)   to permanently destroy a program

slot (n.)   receptacle for a board

The passage below makes a wider interpretation of the sexual connotations of computer jargon. It is excerpted from a "posting" on Usenet, a network of UNIX users.

Micro was a real-time* operator and dedicated multi-user.* His broad-band* protocol made it easy for him to interface with numerous input/output devices, even if it meant time-sharing.* One evening he arrived home just as the sun was crashing, and had parked his motorola 68000 in the main drive (he had missed the 5100 bus that morning), when he noticed an elegant piece of liveware admiring his daisy wheels* in his garden. He thought to himself, "She looks user-friendly. I'll see if she'd like an update tonight."

Mini was her name. He browsed over to her casually, admiring the power of her twin 32-bit floating-point processors and inquired, "How are you, honeywell?" "Yes, I am well," she responded, batting her optical fibers engagingly and smoothing her console over her curvilinear functions. Micro settled for a straight-line approximation. "I'm stand-alone* tonight," he said. "How about computing a vector to my base address? I'll output a byte to eat, and maybe we could get offset later on."

They sat down. Mini was in conversational mode and expanded on ambiguous arguments while Micro gave occasional acknowledgments, although in reality he was analyzing the shortest and least critical path to her entry point.

Suddenly she was up and stripping off her parity bits to reveal the full functionality of her operating-system software. "Let's get basic, you ram," she said. Micro was loaded by this stage, but his hardware policing module had a processor of its own and was in danger of overflowing its output buffer, a hang-up that Micro had consulted his analyst about. "Core" was all she could say as she prepared to log him off.

Micro soon recovered, however, when Mini went down on the DEC and opened her divide files to reveal her data set was ready. He accessed his fully packed root device and was just about to start pushing into her CPU stack, when she attempted an escape sequence.

"Computers," she thought as she compiled herself. "All they ever think of is hex."

*All of these terms could be closed up to form single words, as noted in the previous chapter.

The February 3, 1991, installment of the comic strip "Zippy," entitled "Behind the Polka-Dotted Door," expressed a similar situation. In the first four of the five panels, Zippy and his wife, who are unseen, exchange this dialogue:

Wife: Oh, Zippy! Let me hold the mouse! Which one is the hot key?
Zippy: First load th' floppy disk, darling. . . .
Wife: Can I call up orphan control via remote access?
Zippy: Not without expansion slots, silly!!
Wife: Do you have desktop potential?
Zippy: Take a byte!!

In the final panel, in which both parties have emerged from behind the door (Zippy with a large lipstick mark on his forehead), Zippy laments, "Uh-oh! I dumped my memory! Could this mean a head crash!" "Not to worry, Zippykins," his wife comforts him, "I'm equipped with surge protection."

This Micro and Mini anecdote employs a variety of technical terms as puns that are replete with sexual suggestion. It is not necessary to play word games, however, to find examples of technobabble's sexual connotations. All you have to do is hang around in places frequented by people in the computer industry. (In Silicon Valley, in fact, about *all* you're likely to hear people talking about in restaurants is computers.) One such example was overheard at Scott's Seafood restaurant in San Jose. Several men were apparently discussing the acquisition of computer equipment for colleagues. One of the speakers said, "We're trying to get a bigger hard disk for her box."

On the other hand, as in the earlier examples, often the sexual wordplay and jokes are intentional. And sometimes they go beyond being the work of people merely amusing themselves. The weekly trade tabloid *Computerworld* is one of the most venerable and surely the most profitable journals serving (or "servicing," as they say, suggestively, in the industry) the computer industry. For several years, *Computerworld* ran a slogan contest. Entries selected were printed on buttons, which were distributed to attendees at computer shows. The theme of the buttons often ran to sexual double entendre, as evinced by this list of some of the buttons:

- Byte My Baud
- Kiss My Bits
- Dad's a UNIX, Mother's Board
- Floppy Now, Hard Later
- Ma Bell Runs a Baudy House

In 1984, Sybex Books, a Berkeley, California, publisher specializing in computer books, issued a novelty item entitled *Mother Goose Your Computer: A Grownup's Garden of Silicon Satire.*[9] The illustrated book was filled with parodies of Mother Goose rhymes, including the following:

In San Jose, Cal,
down Silicon Val,
there's a fine interfacer, sweet Silicon Sal.
Her big eight-inch floppies and baud rate disclose
that she shall have business wherever she goes.

Diddle-diddle dumpling, my son John
went to bed with his Wang turned on.
One floppy off and one hard on,
diddle-diddle dumpling, my son John.

Like the religious implications of computer jargon noted below, the sexual ones are mostly amusing—or attempt to be. But they are not always successful. "The Macintosh Guide to Dating and Marriage" in *The Macintosh Way* by Guy Kawasaki is one such example. Although this chapter is silly and annoyingly cute, purporting as it does to advise men and women in the computer business how to court, it at least reveals still more sexual connotations of computer terminology. Kawasaki couched his advice in sexual/anthropomorphic/mechanistic phrases. For men, he has six points; among them,

- "Position yourself as a tool."
- "Treat your date like she's the only platform in the world."
- "Maintain an open architecture. . . . Don't close the system until the proper configuration is reached."
- "Never ignore your installed base (i.e., your old girlfriends). . . . They can . . . introduce you to more women."

For women, he posits the following question in one of the many "exercises" throughout the book: "Which opening line do you think would work best with a Macintosh man?: Would you unzap my parameter RAM? Want to see my PICT files sometime? My disk is fragmented. Do you know where I can get SUM?"[10]

An account executive with a PR firm must have realized the lubricious relationship between those in the industry and their technology. In pitching a client to *InfoWorld*, the executive wrote, "[My client] is a software publisher with a number of distinguishing features: They [*sic*] perceive computer software as needing to be simple, hot, and deep."

Uncover Stories

Europeans are generally considered to be more sexually liberated than Americans. Whereas the former tend to be open about sex, the latter, influenced by Puritan roots, tend to repress sexual desires and to suppress open sexual expression. Perhaps more than in other cultures, America compensates for repression with tawdry titillation. Bare breasts on European beaches are a common sight, but in America advertising is often more prurient than pornography. Magazine covers and advertisements bear out this notion.

In 1979 the first commercially available "computer porn" game appeared. Called Interlude, it featured a series of provocative, double-entendre questions that, if answered correctly, led the player on to ever-more-explicit descriptions of sexual fantasies. Because this was in the days of primitive graphics for personal computers, the program had no pictures—only descriptions (not very interactive).[11] The Interlude ad, however, showed a provocatively posed, scantily clad woman and offered suggestive prose couched in computerese. Magazines that ran the ad were bombarded with critical letters, and some publications pulled it. Around the same time, the German computer magazine *Chip* ran a cover that featured a nude woman amidst various pieces of computer equipment.

The nude juxtaposed with the hardware actually served to emphasize the magazine's technical content.

In 1984 Commodore, a Pennsylvania-based personal-computer maker, was trying to figure out how to sell its products to women in Germany. The solution, Commodore decided, was to run an ad with a full-frontal-nude shot of a male music student. In English, nouns are genderless, but in German, they can be masculine, feminine, or neuter. It turns out that both German words for computer (*der Computer, der Rechner*) are masculine.[12] (If English nouns had gender, those denoting technology would no doubt be masculine.) The Commodore ad ran not in a computer magazine but in the German edition of *Cosmopolitan*. Headlined "Why the Weaker Sex Needs a Commodore Computer," the ad begins, "Weil er . . ." (technically "Because it. . . ," but because *er* is the nominative masculine third-person pronoun, the ad suggests the following): "Because he will manage addresses, data, and appointments. And make himself useful in many other ways. Because he, the Commodore home computer, costs little and is easy to handle. And because he will give you more time to let yourself be weak."[13] So much for feminist advances in German advertising.

Six years later, indicating that sexism was still alive and well in the computer industry, *MacUser* magazine's July 1990 cover sported a blatantly provocative illustration that related in the most tangential manner to the cover story. Electronic mail was the topic, and the cover art was a close-up of a woman's tongue protruding through glossed red lips and licking a stamp bearing the legend "E-mail."

Getting Serviced

The verb *service* has several meanings. For example, the U.S. government services a burgeoning debt, and mechanics service cars. In a sexual sense, the most common meanings of the word concern mating a male animal with a female or a gigolo's engaging in sex with a woman for a fee. The computer industry employs *service* in a way that bolsters these connotations. "We don't service computers, we service people," declared the headline in an ad from a computer-peripherals manufacturer. Any concupiscent members of the *InfoWorld* staff must have been confused in 1983 when they read in *Magazine* (a publishing-industry trade journal), "Started in 1980 to service the owners of desktop computers,

[*InfoWorld*] has enthusiastic admirers."[14] A less amusing and suggestive approach would be to substitute the word *serve* for *service*.

An employee of a Silicon Valley computer company wondered about getting serviced when he received an e-mail message from his system administrator. The latter announced that he was going to set the former up with a password that would enable him to perform a "remote login" from a home terminal to one of the company's internal computer systems. "I'm going to enter you tonight," was the message. The employee's response was, "Do you think this guy's trying to hit on me?"

Gimme That Realtime Religion

In the 1970s, a matchbook advertisement informed readers how to get information about the "Church of Monday Night Football." Numerous social critics and commentators have observed that in our increasingly secular world, substitutes for religion arise. Everything from sports to television viewing has been singled out as a substitute. If this X-phenomenon-as-religion has any validity, computer technology was the paramount secular religion of the 1980s, although its roots go back further, at least twenty years, according to writer Gerald Youngblood. "I have [been in the microcomputer business for more than twenty years] and learned that it is full of 'religions,' each having its own creed and following. There are DOS mainstreamers, networking gurus, UNIX zealots, and OS/2 stargazers. Include in this list PC fundamentalists, Mac charismatics, mainframe and mini high priests, workstation new-agers, and a myriad of other permutations."[15]

Whatever the permutation, the religion of computing was a dualistic faith, founded, as it was, not on a rock but on a chip of silicon that shunted around binary digits. Among the most fervid of the faithful were true believers in the UNIX operating system. Many computer products and entities have advocates, proselytes, and acolytes, but perhaps none has enthusiasts as devoted as the believers in UNIX (a possible exception is the followers of the Forth programming language[16]).

UNIX was developed in the late 1960s at AT&T's Bell Laboratories by Dennis Ritchie and Ken Thompson, two deities who might be said to have created the "Unixverse." UNIX quickly took hold in the university hacker community. Hacker-created startup companies adopted it because it was inexpensive to license—obviating the need to develop a proprietary operating system—and easy to modify and extend in its functionality.

UNIX's primary enhancer was Bill Joy at the University of California at Berkeley, a hotbed of UNIX activity. Joy eventually became the operating system's leading proselyte. He was so revered in the UNIX community that people—usually with tongue in cheek—started to refer to him as a god. "I've just given a presentation with Bill Joy. Do you want to kiss my hand?" a software engineer once archly inquired. More serious in their reverence were Japanese UNIX users, who sometimes made pilgrimages to Silicon Valley to sit at the feet of the master or request his autograph. Largely because of Joy, UNIX has become *the* operating system of the 1990s.[17]

Another important UNIX advocate is Usenix, an organization that puts on a yearly convention dedicated to developments in the operating system. In the 1986 call for papers, conference promoters requested presentations on the "theology of UNIX."

Finally, the UNIX scripture includes this 1987 e-mail posting:

I would like to discuss my own secular belief, being that this is a free network. I would like to introduce a new religion, Unixtarian. This religion is founded on the belief that when you die you will enter a virtual address for eternity or until the scheduler crashes. In this case, there is a rollback procedure that will place you in a spool queue where you will wait for a new virtual address. Now this religion is based on three great quotes:

"Let the command language be terse." (Thompson 25:1)
"Let the programming language be terse." (Ritchie 23:4)
"Let there be paging." (Joy 45:1)[18]

UNIX, Forth, and other such computer "religions" and their "scriptures" are mostly tongue-in-cheek and secondary to the business of computing. But one person has made a business out of computers as religion. Jeffrey Armstrong of Santa Cruz, California, bills himself as "Saint $ilicon." Well known in Silicon Valley, Armstrong entertains audiences at trade shows and computer-related events. He often reads from the "Binary Bible,"[19] which contains such high-tech homilies as "The Programmer's Prayer." Although Armstrong's "bible" is not likely to be "placed by the GUIdeons in mode tel[ecomm]s," as the pun-crazed author might put it, he claims to have sold 7,000 copies of his self-published book.[20]

In sometimes clever, sometimes groaning word play, Armstrong has taken nearly every computer term and placed it into a religious context. He bills himself as the "founder of C.H.I.P., the Church of Heuristic Information Processing, the world's first computer religion . . . the world's first user-friendly religion." Other examples of Armstrong's computers-as-religion prose:

- "hacknowledgments" at the beginning of the book
- "Divine Diskpensation"
- a section on "Zen Bootism"
- "cathoderal"
- "The 23rd PROM," which goes, in part:

> The motherboard holds my software
> I shall not want . . .
> She restores my scroll . . .
> And yea, though I
> Commute to the Valley
> Each day, I fear no evil.

- A paean to memory—"Hail memory, full of space. . . ."

Industry pundits, observers, and punsters are not the only ones who have picked up on the theological implications of computer jargon. The industry itself promulgates religious imagery. A case in point is so-called evangelists, company employees whose function is to whip up enthusiasm for the company's products among third-party developers. The practice appears to have started at Apple Computer in the early 1980s. One of Apple's primary proselytizers was Guy Kawasaki, whose business card actually read "Software Evangelist." Since then, Apple has bestowed the title of evangelist on various product and technology advocates, and the terms *evangelist* and *evangelize* are fairly common throughout the computer business.

Kawasaki eventually left Apple to found a company called ACIUS and write *The Macintosh Way*—a sort of high-tech Tao replete with pretentious prose and portentous exercises (maybe he should have entitled the book *Macintaosh*). Kawasaki's book has a chapter called "Evangelism," in which he writes, "A Macintosh Way company doesn't sell, it evangelizes." One of the chapter's subheadings is "Spreading Your Gospel," and earlier in the book appears a Sistine Chapel–inspired illustration of a naked man with Asian features, about to touch the mouse of a Macintosh computer.[21] So much for subtlety.

Like Saint $ilicon, Kawasaki has made a one-man industry out of exploiting the computer/religion metaphor. He writes an "evangelism" column for *MacUser*. Never one to keep his ego in check, Kawasaki once wrote about a revelation, "There are a lot of people who know a lot more about evangelism than I do." Kawasaki had this epiphany at the Billy Graham School of Evangelism in Albany, New York, which Kawasaki attended because he is writing a book about evangelism (presumably the computer variety). He had to admit that even though he had always considered himself a master evangelist, he was a "fish out of water" at the Graham school. "For example, when the instructors said, 'Let's read X passage together,' everyone opened their Bibles directly to the passage. It's called DBA (Direct Bible Access)."[22] The rest of the column prattles on about how people in the computer industry could learn a lot from Christian evangelists, making frequent comparisons between belief in God and belief in timely product shipments. Kawasaki concludes that he learned a lot about evangelism and that "a good evangelist never rests"— not even on the seventh day, given the propensity for workaholism in the very secular computer industry.

Other areas of pop culture have picked up on the religious fervor with which some people view computer technology. A 1984 book entitled *Digital Deli* carries an essay called "The Religion of Computers," complete with "The 10111'rd Psalm," which begins: "The computer is my taskmaster; I need not think."[23] Rocker/social critic Warren Zevon has satirized everything from politics to anomie since the mid-1970s. Zevon's 1989 *Transverse City* album contains a song called "Networking," the last part of which prominently features an organ playing what sounds like a hymn. The accompanying lyrics go

There's a prayer each night that I always pray:
Let the data guide me through every day.
And every pulse and every code—
Deliver me from the bypass mode.[24]

Zevon is parodying mentalities such as that of Kawasaki, who, amid the silliness and self-aggrandizement, put some sort of religious faith in a secular phenomenon. On terra firma, the Macintosh computer (and its predecessor, the Lisa) revolutionized, on a large scale, the way people interacted with computers. Although the user interface of the "Mac" was based on technology developed at Xerox's Palo Alto Research Center,

Apple brought it into the mainstream. Prior to the advent of the Macintosh, computer users had to direct the functions and actions of their machines with complex and cumbersome keyboard commands. With the Macintosh, users could simply point to and move cute little pictograms on the screen by using a device called a mouse. These cute little "objects" are referred to as icons.[25]

The word *icon* comes from the Greek *eikón*, likeness, image, figure. In the Eastern Church, an icon is "a representation of some sacred personage, as Christ, or a saint or angel, painted usually on a wood surface and venerated itself as sacred."[26] If you have ever used a command-driven computer, with its often cryptic and convoluted strings of characters, the arrival of an object-oriented user interface might be enough to make you raise your voice in prayer and venerate this simplified approach to computing.

Word-watcher William Safire credits or blames, depending on your perspective, computer users for causing *icon* to frequently supplant *symbol* and *metaphor*. "In this time of symbol fascination, *icon* is being worked harder by people who have tired of using *metaphor* as a voguish substitute for *paradigm, model, archetype, standard,* or *beau idéal.*" Safire notes that computer icons are sometimes "cunningly related to a subject; a command to delete a file may be symbolized by a little wastebasket."[27] He suggests that the root of such icons is in semiotics, the relationship of signs in language.[28] "In this ever-flagging field of study, very hot now in Eastern colleges, an icon is a sign chosen to stand for its object because it looks like, or triggers an association with, the thing it represents."[29] In the computer industry, icons trigger neologisms as well as associations. To render a computer application or process into an icon on a screen is to "iconify" it. Diehard keyboard-command users of computers must surely be known as iconoclasts.

If your computer background is more catholic, you may want to commune with hosts (computers, such as servers, that store files and data for use by other systems) and wafers (the thin slabs of silicon of which chips are made). In any case, you should be wary of possession by a daemon, which *The Hacker's Dictionary* defines as "a program that is not invoked explicitly, but lies dormant waiting for one or more conditions to occur." Gary Hethcoat, one of the many contributors to this book, defines *daemon* as "a long-lived process that typically, although not necessarily, performs system services. The only plausible explanation I've heard for this one is that these are 'devil's helpers,' the devil being the kernel." The kernel is the central part of the UNIX operating system. As further evidence of daemonism, UNIX has a command called *chmod 666.*

Hethcoat is not the only person in the industry to suggest satanic associations. At the 1990 SunExpo trade show, as at all other computer shows, people at various booths dispensed promotional items. One such company was Virginia-based Visix.[30] Visitors to this company's booth could get a T-shirt bearing the legend "Visix—Software from Hell" in an infernal setting featuring licking flames and a devil with a pitchfork. University of California, Berkeley, computer scientist David Patterson has made reference to "levels of benchmark hell."

On a more serious note, in 1984, Harper & Row published a book by Bernard Bangley, a Presbyterian minister. The book, called *Bible Basic: Bible Games for Personal Computers,* was an attempt to teach Bible stories as well as the BASIC programming language. *Bible Basic* featured chapters such as "Bible Quiz Code," "Memory Verses," and "Psychic Computer." A California company called MetaWare bills itself as a "Christ-centered company." The Jehovah's Witnesses have created MEPS (Multilanguage Electronic Phototypesetting System). And a California company called Moses Computers has a networking product called ChosenLAN.

Scriptures

"Ideally a translation of the Bible should be like a computer translation—like translating COBOL to BASIC."—an assistant professor of Greek at Oklahoma State University

"Windows Users Get Religion; Backers See beyond the Pretty Face"—headline in a computer-magazine-publishing-company newsletter

"In Pursuit of the Relational Grail"—headline on a market-research-company press release.

"It is by learning the options of the program that I have encountered its grace."—line from a software-product review

"[Manzi's] speech to introduce Lotus' new software for the NeXT machine was laced with religious overtones. 'This product raises several very large theological questions,' Manzi said. . . . Later, Manzi said Lotus had developed the new program 'because God wanted us to. . . .' I have to confess I feel like John the Baptist."[31]

"Technology that enables you to mouse-click your way to heaven."—Scott McNealy, CEO of Sun Microsystems, at a Xerox product introduction with which Sun was involved as a Xerox partner

"Offerings."—press releases and brochures everywhere. Means *products,* not *contributions*

"Path"—the route, often circuitous, to a file, directory, etc.

As noted in this chapter, technobabble is replete with religious, sexual, and pharmacological connotations—intentional and otherwise. It has other connotations as well, most notably anthropomorphic ones, as noted in other chapters of this book. Let us exit this section with a network benediction:

The Computer Person's Prayer

Our program, who[32] art in Memory,
 Hello be thy name.
Thy Operating System come,
 thy commands be done,
 at the Printer as they are on the Screen.
Give us this day our daily data,
 and forgive us our I/O Errors as we forgive those
 whose Logic Circuits are faulty.
Lead us not into Frustration,
 and deliver us from Power Surges.
For thine is the Algorithm,
 The Application,
 and the Solution,
 looping forever and ever.
Return.

Combining the sexual and religious connotations of technobabble was the name of a now-defunct company: Loving Grace Cybernetics.

Other Connotations

Although sex, drugs, and religion seem to account for the majority of extracomputer connotations of technobabble, they are not the only realms represented.

Death and Mayhem

If you spend enough time around computers, you are bound to do—or hear or read about their being done—one or more of the following:

- *Execute* a program
- *Abort* a process
- *Hit* the Return key or have your cache *take a hit*
- Have your system *die* on you
- *Terminate* a process (sometimes "with extreme prejudice")
- Encounter a *brain-dead* programming job
- *Kill* a process
- *Bomb* a program
- *Fork* a child (Slaughter of the Innocents? No, a UNIX process.)
- *Thrash* a program
- *Punch* or *pound* a key

Physical Fitness and Hygiene

To listen to some descriptions of computers and programs, you might think you were hearing about body building:

- A robust program or system (*Robust* is common in the industry to describe everything from hardware to software, although it seems to be applied more often to the latter. It is most often a euphemism for "incredibly complicated" or "requires a huge amount of memory.")
- A powerful program (*Powerful* is an overused and essentially meaning-less piece of industry hyperbole.)
- Clean code (*Clean* means relatively bug-free; UNIX has a utility program called "lint" for cleaning up code.)
- Computer jocks (A jock is a proficient programmer or hardware engineer.)
- A flexible programming style (*Flexible* is a euphemism for "not impossibly rigid.")
- An extensible window system (*Extensible* entities leave room for improvement.)

Automobiles

It seems that one of the first success symbols manifested by people in the computer business—everyone from engineers to marketers—is flashy, fast, expensive cars. Porsches appear to be favorites. When one successful Silicon Valley company went public, its president expressed his hope that a lot of Porches [*sic*] would not start to show up in the parking lots when employees started cashing in their stock options. In keeping with this vehicular obsession, some of the terms employed to describe computer performance suggest hype lifted from a car brochure: *hot, blazingly fast, screaming, powerful.* Carrera, a Porsche model, was the code name for one company's product.

Since the mid-1980s, the term *turbo* has been popular as a component of product names. Digital Equipment Corporation has a bus called TurboChannel. Borland International developed a souped-up version of the Pascal programming language called Turbo Pascal. (Some said it was "Blaiseingly" fast.) Another California firm, Hewlett-Packard, sells a "graphics subsystem" (meaning a board added to an HP computer to improve graphics performance) called TurboVRX.

Agriculture

While family farms were going bust in the 1980s, the computer industry was cultivating some agricultural terms. A "disk farm," for example, is a large assemblage of disks in a common location, employed for storing vast amounts of data. Similarly, a "microprocessor farm" is many microprocessors in a single location. These terms most likely derive from industrial uses of the word *farm*, such as *tank farm*, a tract of land in which oil-storage tanks seem to grow out of the ground.

The word *grow* itself is quite popular in computer circles, and it is most often employed unconventionally. Instead of hoping to make their businesses grow, computer-industry people talk of "growing their businesses." Some of my colleagues and I once heard someone use the phrase "grow clients in the CAD environment." To illustrate the phrase, one of the colleagues drew a landscape representing the so-called CAD environment. Out of the ground sprouted the heads of "clients." Many computer programs have "tree" structures that grow from "roots," in which different elements "branch out" hierarchically.

Preparation of Commodities

What with all the farming and growth going on in the industry, computers are left to process the resulting cornucopia. They process data, transactions, documents, words, outlines, and thoughts. Data processing is a general term referring to the jockeying of computer information. *Data* is such a bland and all-encompassing word in computing that *processing* seems a perfect complement for it. Online transaction processing (OLTP) is the province of banks and financial institutions. Compound-document

"This Guy" Syndrome

The following excerpts are from a long essay by Edsger Dijkstra that appeared in *Communications of the ACM* (Association for Computing Machinery). Dijkstra is considered to be the "first professional programmer" and the "father of structured programming."[35]

My next linguistical suggestion is to fight the "if-this-guy-wants-to-talk-to-that-guy" syndrome. Never refer to parts of programs or pieces of equipment in an anthropomorphic terminology, nor allow your students to do so." [Dijkstra then goes on to suggest that instructors institute fines for violations.] "By the end of the first semester . . . you will have collected enough money for two scholarships . . . . The anthropomorphic metaphor . . . is an enormous handicap for every computing community that has adopted it. I have now encountered programs wanting things, knowing things, expecting things, believing things, etc. . . . In computing science, the anthropomorphic metaphor should be banned.[36]

processing is the production of manuals and other large sets of documentation. But one of the connotatively least appealing kinds of computer processing is so-called word processing, a term that reduces the craft of writing to the mere arrangement of words.

Related computer programs are "outline processors," with which you can randomly rearrange sections of outlines to possibly find a more logical or appealing order for the outline's elements. More ambitious versions of these products are pretentiously billed as "idea processors" or "thought processors."

With the unpleasant implications of processing, as well as other undesirable aspects of life in Silicon Valley in mind, a group of San Francisco writers created a magazine called *Processed World.*[33]

Anthropomorphism and Vice Versa

As the previous chapter suggested, the computer industry outpaces all others in the area of anthropomorphic language. Computers seem almost human in many ways, so an inevitable result of that similarity is that much of the language describing computers seems to refer to humans. Consider the following by-no-means-exhaustive list of terms that are rooted in mind and body:

anticipate: used in reference to software programmed to react to an event or occurrence *aware:* used in reference to software programmed to react to an event or occurrence

behave: operate—if a program works without problems, it is "well behaved"

brain: a computer's central processing unit (CPU). Once large electromechanical components of computers, CPUs are now contained on a single chip of silicon.

child: a child process is subservient to a parent process

clever: a clever program is one that accomplishes a tricky task or uses a small amount of code to do a lot

convince: "I can contribute to your goof anthology," wrote a reader of *InfoWorld* in response to a request for gaffes. The reader pointed to an article in the magazine in which the author wrote, "Some computers are unconvinced about automation's benefits."

dumb: the opposite of intelligent. A dumb terminal, for example, is a mere conduit to the intelligence of, say, a computer.

he: computer mavens often refer to machines, software, processes, and screen objects as living entities; synonym: *this guy*

forgive, forgiving: programmed or constructed to work around some errors and problems

guy: an object on screen, a piece of code, a computer, etc.

handshaking: two devices working together

intelligent, intelligence: an intelligent device is one that can perform processes on its own. Some of these devices, modems, printers, and peripherals of all stripes, as well as buildings, have intelligence.

interpret: to process a computer instruction

intuitive: essentially means "easy to figure out"—as in an "intuitive interface"

know: used in reference to software programmed to react to an event or occurrence

live: synonymous with reside; also an antonym for *die* ("The system lives.")

memory: location for data storage, generally on a chip made for the purpose. Can be "dynamic," in which case the data vanishes when the computer is turned off, or "static," in which case the data remains in the storage location. In a cover story on memory of the human variety, *Newsweek* magazine reported that "neurobiologists are trying to chart the hardware of memory, the network of nerve cells—neurons—within the brain whose activity and changes constitute the actual physical basis for memory . . . the mind can store an estimated 100 trillion bits of information—compared with which a computer's mere billions are virtually amnesiac . . . psychologists are probing the software of memory."[34]

neural: as in *neural network*, a collection of microprocessors arrayed to suggest the arrangement of neurons in the brain

parent: a process or entity that rules a child

reside: to be located on ("That function resides on the server.")

sleep: to stop functioning for a defined period or until some event triggers an "awakening"

smart: intelligent. A "smart house" is one whose functions (heating, lighting, etc.) are computer-controlled; a "smart bomb" is one with a computer guidance system that helps it find its target.

talk to: communicate electronically

The other side of the anthropomorphism coin is mechanism, describing people in terms of technological phenomena. "People are thinking of themselves in computational terms," wrote psychologist Sherry Turkle. "These people are not just using computer jargon as a manner of speaking. Their language carries an implicit psychology that equates the processes that take place in people to those that take place in machines."[37] Here are a few such descriptions:

bandwidth: "the smallest range of frequencies constituting a band, within which a particular signal can be transmitted without distortion." At least that is how the Random House unabridged dictionary defines *bandwidth.* Anthropomorphically—the way it is increasingly used—it refers to a person's ability to keep multiple thoughts simultaneously in mind ("He doesn't have enough bandwidth to deal with all those concepts.")

competition, the: term for the human brain in the "artificial life" community[38]

cycle: the technical definition for this noun is "the smallest interval of time required to complete an operation in a computer."[39] Increasingly, *cycle* is showing up in the speech of people affiliated with the computer business to refer to their personal time—as in "I won't be able to do that; I'm out of cycles." As a verb, it means to repeat in cycles.

hardwired: permanent, built-in. By employing this term, Jean-Louis Gassée, former product-development leader at Apple, managed in one quick stroke to capture the essence of anthropomorphism and mechanization: "People are not hardwired for data; computers are not good at pattern recognition."[40]

in sync: to employ an earlier technological metaphor, "on the same wavelength," as in "We're in sync on the product-release timetable." *In sync* derives from the synchronization of, say, disks.

integrated: organized; having one's "act together"

interrupt-driven: frantic

multiprocess, -task: do more than one thing at once

on-; off-line: involved in communication of some sort; not involved in communication or in private discussions, outside of a larger group

screen, on my: on my list of things to deal with

swap out: to stop interacting with someone; derives from the way processors and software put processes "on hold" while they deal with other processes[41]

Using e-mail, a hardware engineer summed up the penchant for mechanism: "I think it's funny and sad how we use impersonal terms from computer terminology to talk to each other. It seems that the people around me have incorporated our work terminology into their personal conversations—and they don't even realize it." Conversely, MIT's Joseph Weizenbaum sees "nothing wrong with viewing man as an information processor"—as long as the reference is in a specific computer context, as opposed to serving as an encompassing metaphor. Weizenbaum also makes a contextual case for computers as "behaving" entities.[42]

Terminal Chapter Mode

The editor of *Embedded Systems Programming,* a monthly magazine devoted to "embedded systems,"[43] summed up many of the connotations of technobabble in his October 1990 editorial, entitled "Version Notes." Tyler Sperry introduced this issue by writing, "We hope you find this new, improved version to be even more user-friendly than previous versions." The remainder of the editorial was rendered almost entirely in techno–double entendre, for example:

Regular use of this product should make your applications run faster and cleaner without those unsightly code patches and munged[44] overlays found in other magazines. . . . As you might expect, this new version is marked by a number of enhancements or (as they're more commonly referred to) "bug fixes." For example, some readers had requested faster response time from the main editor module. . . . The Sperry module is still interrupt-driven and given to stack overflow errors, but at least the behavior is well-documented. . . . At the time of this release we should have solved the hardware problems with our support BBS. Our sysop, George Walsh, has survived the initial installation procedure and miscellaneous hardware failures.

8

Apocrypha and Folklore

The anarchic computer in the 1968 film *2001: A Space Odyssey* was named HAL, not because it exhibited *hard-array logic* but because the letters *H, A,* and *L,* respectively, precede the letters IBM.[1]
—Movie and computer folklore

Computer jargon derives from a variety of sources, as previous chapters have noted. Chapter 3 stressed the importance of the oral tradition in the perpetuation and propagation of technobabble. Oral tradition—and its technological variants such as networking and e-mail—is often a vehicle for sustaining folklore and myth, both of which are sufficiently prevalent in the computer industry to have already spawned at least three books on the subject.[2] All of these books cover in passing apocryphal and documented origins of certain computer terms.

This chapter deals more comprehensively with a handful of terms, most of which appear to have come from some proto–Indo-European language or to have sprung from the pages of Lewis Carroll. The speculations on the origins of these mostly monosyllabic *mots* are amusing and often fanciful.

biff and Other Unixsyllables

biff (note the lowercase *b*) is a UNIX command. Among UNIX's conventions and quirks, its vocabulary is all lowercase, prompting the thought that perhaps e.e. cummings was a proto-UNIX hacker.[3] Not only is the UNIX lexicon designated in lowercase but it is also largely unisyllabic, with many of the words having the appearance of grunts: *awk, sed, diff, troff, vi, grep,* and, of course, *biff.*

The biff command enables a UNIX user to monitor incoming e-mail. I am sitting at my workstation and I want to know every time I get an e-mail message (and I am not using an iconic user interface, such as mailtool, which has a little representation of a mailbox whose flag goes up every time a message arrives). If I "invoke" the biff command, incoming messages pop up in the window. Typing **biff n** turns off this facility.

According to *Life with UNIX,* the University of California, Berkeley, programmer who wrote the biff program was unable to come up with a short simple name for the program. Rumor has it that a dog, Biff, who frequented the building where the programmer worked, always barked when the mailman arrived, so the program writer named his creation after the dog.

The *awk* programming language is an eponymous abbreviation, standing for its authors, Aho, Weinberger, and Kernighan,[4] although Bill Tuthill, a former columnist for *UNIX World,* suggests that "the name is probably also an abbreviated indictment of the language's syntax."[5]

Other UNIX terms have more prosaic, mainly abbreviation-oriented, origins. *grep* is an acronym for which the precise meaning is in the eye of the beholder. Whatever *grep* denotes, it is a method for locating words or strings of characters in files. "Although Celtic influence on the UNIX system predominates over Hebraic," notes Tuthill, "*greptz* means 'belch' in Yiddish. Output from the grep program looks remarkably similar"— although to what, Tuthill does not specify.[6]

The word *UNIX,* whose pronunciation is homophonous with *eunuchs,* appears at first glance to be an acronym. Unlike its lexicon, it is written in uppercase letters. But it is not an acronym. "In contrast to an earlier operating system, Multics,[7] Brian Kernighan [a UNIX pioneer] coined the word to indicate that UNIX is simpler and more unified." The most commonly accepted theory as to UNIX's origin is that the word is a pun on *eunuchs* and that it stands for "castrated Multics," or "Multics without balls. Although AT&T [where UNIX was invented, at Bell Laboratories in New Jersey] will not officially admit this, 'UNIX' also describes the sex lives of certain programmers in New Jersey."[8]

Bug

If your computer crashes, a bug may be to blame. A bug is a *glitch*—a problem or malfunction—not something a company wants to boast about in its products. As is often the case, though, euphemism comes to the rescue. According to Guy Kawasaki in *The Macintosh Way,* his erstwhile company, ACIUS, calls bugs "anomalies"; the Claris company refers to them as "unexpected results"; at Microsoft Corp., they are "wrongful terminations"; and at Apple, bugs go under the ameliorative rubric of "undocumented features."

Concerning the origin of these unexpected anomalies, the story goes that U.S. Navy Captain Grace Hopper, a pioneer in computer science and developer of the COBOL language, once had a dead Mark II computer on her hands. She finally tracked down the problem: A moth had become jammed in the computer's circuitry—thus the term *bug.* (The moth is preserved in one of Hopper's logbooks, which is in the Naval Surface Weapons Center in Dahlgren, Virginia, but is slated to take up residence in The Smithsonian Institution.) By extension, the process of fixing software or hardware problems has become *debugging;* a *bug fix* solves the problem.

Bugs are unwanted, unforeseen problems. A related but more malevolent and premeditated problem is *viruses:* software-debasing or -destroying entities planted intentionally to wreak havoc on computers and programs. A term for a certain type of these destructive creations is *worms.*

Technotrivia

The 1990 second annual "Computer Bowl" was a fund-raising trivia contest that pitted East Coast and West Coast industry heavyweights against each other. Contestants had to answer these, among other, questions:

1. Name three famous personal computers introduced during the summer of 1977.

2. Which of the following was not the name of a computer during the 1950s? Leprechaun, Mobidic, Babbage, or Maniac?

3. When using a computer you might use a spooler. The word *spool* is an

acronym. What do the letters stand for?

4. At least three computer companies were named after their founders, but the founder no longer works for the company. Can you name these companies?

Answers: (1) The TRS-80, Commodore PET, and Apple II. (2) Babbage. (3) Simultaneous Peripheral Operations On Line. (4) Shugart, Amdahl, Cray.

Code (and Other) Names

The computer industry, like many others, devises code names for products that are under development. Code names serve as common, informal nomenclature until the company comes up with the product's formal name just before it is announced, and they also help confuse the competition and stimulate press curiosity. Peter Quinn, engineering manager for Apple's Apple IIc, said that a company executive once decided to employ obscene code names to discourage the media from using them. One example was LF, for Little Fucker.[9]

Jef Raskin, a former Apple manager, wrote, "My goal [in choosing the code name Macintosh] was to minimize information leakage by choosing internal project names that 'evoke inappropriate images.' An industrial spy can learn little from names arbitrarily chosen from a list of a hundred varieties of Apples. 'Macintosh' tells nothing, and thus serves its purpose."[10] Sometimes, as in this case, the code name sticks and becomes the product's commercial designation, but code names are most often too cute, tongue-in-cheek, or nondescriptive to remain with the product.

Until the arrival of the personal computer in the 1970s, the industry's products usually had numeric designations such as PDP-11, System 370, and the like. Microcomputers, as they were first called—because they were based on microprocessors and to nomenclatively differentiate them from timesharing minicomputers—were *personal*. You could have your own computer system sitting on your very own desk and do whatever you wanted with it—within the considerable limitations of those early systems. Because these little machines were personal and not locked away in some climate-controlled room, they needed names that were more personable. Although some of the companies that entered this new business continued to use numeric names (Imsai 8800, TRS-80), others looked to the cosmos: Altair, North Star. Or to necromancy: Sorcerer.

Another early entry in the personal-computer arena went on to become one of the most successful computer companies of all time. Apple Computer was named, as the story goes, because its two cofounders, Steve Jobs and Steve Wozniak, couldn't come up with anything else. Furthermore, they were part of the hacker counterculture,[11] and Apple seemed sufficiently like a nonsequitur. Also, Jobs reportedly was a fructarian at the time. In light of its approach to naming itself, Apple makes for an amusing study in code naming.

When Apple introduced its Apple IIGS product, the company's own engineers got confused, because during the course of its development, the IIGS had at least seven different code names: IIX, Brooklyn, Golden Gate, Rambo, Gumby, Cortland, and Phoenix.[12] At the product-announcement press conference, different engineers used different names to refer to the new product.

Code names were an obsession, recalled Wayne Rosing, director of the Apple II group in the spring of 1985, when "It seemed like we had a code name a week"—none of which stuck. The code name for the Macintosh did stay nearly intact, winning out over names of other varieties of apple. But the development team had to change the spelling from McIntosh to Macintosh to avoid a trademark conflict with McIntosh amplifiers.

The code name Lisa remained, in part because, as Rosing recalled, the company came close to naming the product Applause. That burgeoning idea was blocked, however, when an engineer walked into a meeting one day and threw a package of Applause condoms down onto the table. A more pragmatic factor in determining the Lisa's name was that the industrial engineers had tooled just enough space on the computer for a four-letter name.[13]

Most personal-computer code names reveal a playful nature. Even staid IBM used such monikers as Peanut, Popcorn, and Rover. According to a former employee of Atari, an engineering manager once code-named a custom chip TIA for Television Interface Adapter. When the marketing people got wind of the name, they interpreted it as a woman's name, rather than a TLA (three-letter acronym) and proceeded to code-name every consumer product after women. Some of the names the marketers came up with for chips, games, and systems were Debbie, Paula, Fran, Candy, Colleen, Pam, and Nancy.

Opposing this naming approach was Jef Raskin at Apple. "When I created the Macintosh project at Apple, I wanted to break what seemed to me to be a sexist [Apple] habit of giving projects female names."[14] Raskin's imperative and the practice he opposed run counter to the common industry practice of calling nearly everything from code to processes to machines "he." At the code-name level, women's names may have predominated at Apple—and possibly at other companies—but such feminization rarely appears in computing's lexicon.

Glitch

At least five sources suggest essentially the same origin of *glitch:* It comes from the German *glitschen,* to slip or slide, which gave rise to the Yiddish *glitsch,* a slippery area.[15] In computer parlance, a *glitch* is an error, a malfunction, a *bug.* What, more specifically, do these five sources have to say about this slippery word?

The Random House unabridged dictionary is not definitive about the word's origin, indicating that it is "perhaps" from *glitschen* and *glitsch.* It suggests 1960–65 as the period for the word's origin and notes that the word can also be a transitive verb: "to cause a glitch in." Compares it to *bug,* with which it is synonymous.

Webster's Ninth New Collegiate Dictionary is more specific about date of origin: 1962. It indicates that *glitch* is akin to Old High German *glitan,* to glide.

The Hacker's Dictionary states that "the word almost certainly comes from Yiddish." This source gives no indication of when *glitch* originated but does define it as a noun, as well as a verb having two meanings, the first of which is "to commit a glitch." A second, unrelated, definition of *glitch* as a verb is "to scroll a display screen," with text jerking or "glitching" every five seconds or so.

John Ciardi, in his *Good Words to You,* is unequivocal about *glitch's* origin: from Yiddish *glitch* from German *glitschen,* to slip, slide (implies "and fall"). According to Ciardi, *glitch* has been common in American slang since the late nineteenth century. He cites *The Joys of Yiddish* by Leo Rosten, who defines the word as: "1. to slide, to skid; 2. a risky undertaking (that risks a fall); 3. not kosher, also a shady business. Ciardi says that all of these senses have carried over into American slang with the exception of number 3. If Ciardi is right, dictionary editors who give the 1960s as the origin of the term are surely looking at it only from the computer perspective. Ciardi discounts the proposition of some computer "clickers" that *glitch* is an acronym for Gremlin Loose In The Computer Hut. None of these people could give him precedent for "hut" as "programming center." He says, "The fact is that these boys and girls, more given to formulas than to language [with the exception of computer languages, of course], amuse themselves by compiling 'dictionaries' for the computer to print out, and that they have been frivolously inventive in this acronym, as in many other terms, failing to recognize that *glitch* is precomputer American slang."

The authors of *The Dictionary of Word and Phrase Origins* first encountered the term in 1965, while they were talking with technicians about the computerized typesetting of the original *American Heritage Dictionary*. They note archly that this was also the time they encountered *input* (a word that has been around since the eighteenth century) as a synonym for manuscript. They suggest that although computer "whizkids" may have been quick to pick up on *glitch,* U.S. astronauts were the first to give it general circulation. They cite John Glenn, who wrote in 1962, "Another term we adopted to describe some of our problems was 'glitch.'" Glenn claimed that *glitch* was "a sudden spike or change in voltage in an electrical circuit which takes place when the circuit has a new load put on it." Both the Random House unabridged dictionary and *Webster's Ninth New Collegiate Dictionary* corroborate Glenn's meaning, giving it as one of several definitions for the word.

Kludge

Here is a word that at first glance you might expect to find in a rhyming dictionary as a prospect for pairing with *budge, sludge, grudge, nudge,* and *judge.* Actually you would have to look under *stooge,* because the word is pronounced "klooge," and it signifies something that might be crafted by Moe, Larry, and Curly. A kludge is a jury-rigged piece of equipment or a temporary solution to a problem; to produce such a solution is "to kludge" the solution.

Concerning the word's spelling, John Singer, an engineer from Boulder, Colorado, and an *InfoWorld* reader, wrote, "I propose the formation of

The Society of Engineers in Favor of the Rationalization of the Spelling of Kluge. . . . C'mon, people, let's do it well for once. Engineers have a very poor reputation as users of English; let us band together and dispell [*sic*] this!"

Webster's Ninth New Collegiate Dictionary claims that the origin of the word is unknown; the Random House unabridged dictionary lists *kludge* as an "expressive formation." But an anonymous reader of *InfoWorld* pointed out in 1982 that "as used in computing, *kludge* was coined by Jackson Granholm in an article, 'How to Design a Kludge' in *Datamation* [February 1962]." Bolstering that theory was Dennis Hamilton of Penfield, New York, who wrote, "I first encountered this term in *Datamation* in articles about the Kludge Komputer Kompany. This send-up, published ca. 1959–1963, involved Jackson Granholm and doubtless others."[16] Like the anonymous reader above, Jack Rochester and John Gance pinpoint the year as 1962 in their 1983 book *The Naked Computer* and cite *Datamation* as their proof. But unlike these other kludge theorists, Rochester and Gance do not claim that a *Datamation* writer actually invented the word. According to the *Naked* authors, *Datamation* merely noted that the word was coined to mean "an ill-assorted collection of poorly matching parts forming a distressing whole." Ironically, Rochester and Gance note, *Datamation*'s first editor was named Charles Kluge.

Both the anonymous reader and Hamilton had responded to a query I had placed earlier in *InfoWorld*—namely, what do you believe is the origin of the word *kludge*? As with other computer jargon (see *nerd* below), origins are uncertain and theories abound. The purpose of my *kludge* (not kludged, I hope) exercise in *InfoWorld* was to unscientifically determine just how widespread the theories might be concerning the origin of this word.

To begin with, three of the respondents to the "survey" disputed the early-1960s theory of origin. They claimed that it has been around since at least 1956 and possibly longer. "While I cannot supply a derivation of the referenced word, the term 'kluge' was in common use in Southern California electronics/aerospace companies in *1956,*" wrote Leonard Anderson of Sun Valley, California. "This was noticed when I moved to Los Angeles to work for Hughes Aircraft Company (HAC) in that year. 'Kluge' (without the d) was seen in at least two memos internal to HAC."[17] Andersen also disputed a strictly computer-industry origin. "Kluge, as still used, refers to something temporary or jury-rigged in electronics or mechanics to make it work long enough for evaluation. There was insufficient software in the mid-fifties to warrant justification of origin from computer work. . . . *Datamation* was an interesting magazine, but mere publication does not place the stamp of authority on a subject."

John M'Carthy of Washington, D.C., agreed. "The term 'kludge' did not originate in the computer business. [It] was coined to describe the monster command and control display device assembled with baling wire in 1956 by Bernie Kravitz at General Electric's Heavy Military Equipment Division in Syracuse, New York. At that time Bernie created a two-story-high color display that refracted light through thin oil films on rotating disks. This house-sized unit was dubbed Kravitz's Large Unwieldy Giant Enigma. Please note that there was no *d* in kludge at that time."[18]

David Krauss of Los Altos, California, shared the skepticism of Andersen and M'Carthy. "I find all of the definitive theories claiming origins in the 1960s or 1970s to be very weak. I first encountered the term in use in 1957 in Phoenix, Arizona. I heard it used frequently by one Mr. Garth Ghering and his associates, electronics technicians with the U.S. Geological Survey. Their manner of usage gave me the impression that it was not a new term even at that time. Although these were very sophis ticated technicians working regularly with analog computers, I doubt they had more than a theoretical knowledge of digital circuitry and most certainly had engaged in no programming activity as we know it today."

None of my correspondents hazarded a guess as to the etymology of *kludge*. Neither does the Random House unabridged dictionary, which lists it as an "expressive coinage" from 1960 to 1965. Another possibility is that it is onomatopoetic in origin. Not so, claimed the majority of survey respondents, who believed that the word derived from the German *klug,* clever. This response from Tom Linders of Bruckmuhl, West Germany, set the tone for the German-origin theory. "The origin of the word *kludge* is from the German word *klug* [pronounced 'klook'] meaning intelligent, clever, smart, cunning, shrewd (per the *New Cassell's German Dictionary,* 1965)." A plausible enough explanation, but Linders went on to add this anecdote: "It was brought to America by the World War II Germans who came to Huntsville, Alabama." Tom Pittman, a longtime observer of the computer industry, agreed with Linders: "*Kludge* is a corruption of the German word *kluge* [*sic*], meaning 'clever.'" Pittman continued, putting the word into a computer context, "In the early days of computers, it took a very clever programmer to fit a program into the space or time constraints imposed by the first computers; the term was a compliment. Of course, such a tightly packed program was totally unmodifiable, and as maintenance became a higher priority, kludges fell into disfavor. Consequently, the term broadened to include any programming style that is disapproved or unstructured. A 'kludgemeister' is a person who is expert at packing the bits into programs for every higher performance, never maintainability."

"Semantically, I have no problem [with the German-origin theory]," wrote Peter Lincoln of Honolulu, Hawaii, "because kludges are typically quick repairs to software that bypass formal maintenance procedures with a bit of cleverness and élan." The obvious problem, noted Lincoln, is the spelling. "Why spell it as if it rhymes with *sludge* and then rhyme it with *huge*? I favor the spelling k-l-u-g-e."

A German-origin theory that missed the *boot* was presented by John Marshall of Narbeth, Pennsylvania: "*Kludge,* I suspect, comes from an 'Englishing' of a German word for boot (as in 'foot gear' or 'to give the boot to'). A German general/field marshall surnamed Kluge had his name punned on this way. . . . the implication of a rough, quick, heavyhanded (-footed?) fix rather than a careful, reasoned solution with the German pun lead me to fault—er, credit—the German language for *kludge.*" This argument is undercut by the lexical fact that the German word for boot is *Stiefel.*

German was not the only language suggested as the inspiration for *kludge.* Devlin Gualtieri of Morristown, New Jersey, believed he had found a classical origin: "After exhaustive study (a two-minute scan of my Classical Greek Dictionary), I have concluded that the word *kludge* stems from the Greek word κλυδων, meaning 'a wave, billow, or surge,' as a contraction of the classical metaphor κλυδων κακων, meaning 'a flood of ills.'" Whereas it was Greek to Gualtieri, Robert Harris of Corona, California, made a case for Latin: "Although the word is probably a spontaneous neologism that would be impossible to track, such an answer is not very learned. So, if you want to impress your friends, here is a possible etymological derivation: From *klaudo,* in Latin, *claudere,* to close, include, dump together; from *klud* or in Germanic, *hluta,* lot, portion, lottery, chance; from Indo-European *kleu,* hook, peg (as in 'hooked together')." Russian is the language of origin, according to William Remington of Wilmington, Delaware. Remington wrote that the Russian word ключ means key or wrench and is pronounced "clyooch."

Other readers made nonlinguistic suggestions, such as this one from ID72245,711 on the CompuServe network: "Back around 1970, while at MIT, I was told that *kludge* originally was the last name of the creator of a piece of graphics hardware that did three-dimensional hardware transformations in real time. . . . The use of the word *kludge* had less of a negative connotation then. It tended to mean something that worked amazingly well. . . . A later 'definition' that we adopted was, 'A kludge is a crock that works.'"

While the footwear theory above does not hold water, the following—presented in slightly different versions by both Gertrude Reagan of Palo Alto, California, and H.W. Verseput of Kalamazoo, Michigan—is waterborn. Briefly, it goes like this: During World War II, a new man reported for service onboard a ship and announced that he was a "kludgemaker." He said to make kludges, he required heavy equipment such as a crane and torches. He then proceeded to fabricate a large, unrecognizable object, which he jettisoned overboard—either by virtue of his own strength or with the crane. When it hit the water, it made a sound: *ka-looge.*

Finally, computer-magazine pioneer Wayne Green claimed that *kludge* derived from klieg lights in the early days of television. These lights, said Green, were "real kludges."

Lisa (Acronym or Eponym?)

Apple's Lisa computer was the precursor of the popular Macintosh. Although the name was spelled with only the *L* uppercase, Apple claimed that it was an acronym standing for Locally Integrated Software Architecture—whatever that meant. By locally integrated orthographic convention, however, the name should have been designated Locally integrated software architecture. Another theory making the rounds about the origin of Lisa was that the computer was named after the illegitimate daughter of Steve Jobs,[19] one of the cofounders of Apple. Jobs et al. then had to "reverse-engineer" the abbreviation out of the name—a common practice in the naming of products (as in [Sun]View, which became [Sun]Visually Integrated Environment for Windows). Some wag in the computer industry, commenting on the industry's obsession with abbreviations, suggested that what Lisa really stood for was "let's invent some acronym."

Nerd

In mid-1990 television viewers were inundated with ads for the Saturn automobile from General Motors. In one of the spots, a kid speculated on what he might face when he moved to Smyrna, Tennessee, site of the Saturn manufacturing plant, where his father had just landed a job. In the process of convincing himself that the move would be a good one, the kid voiced a concern: "All the kids might be nerds or something."

Nerd is a word whose spelling—to say nothing of its origin—is not fixed. An alternate spelling is *nurd,* and several nondictionary theories of *nerd's* nativity have been suggested. The Random House unabridged dictionary notes that the term entered the American English language between 1960 and 1965 and that it is an "obscurely derived expressive formation." *Webster's Ninth New Collegiate Dictionary* is more specific, placing the date of first use in 1965 and stating flatly that the origin is unknown. *Webster's Ninth* defines the word simply as "an unpleasant, unattractive, or insignificant person." Random House puts it into its most common context: "an intelligent but single-minded person obsessed with a nonsocial hobby or pursuit; a *computer nerd.*"

The prototypical nerd is Jerry Lewis in such films as the 1963 *The Nutty Professor* (note the date—right in the middle of 1960 and 1965—and the resemblance of *nutty* to *nurdy*). In this film and others, Lewis played characters who embodied the character traits that later films—most notably the *Revenge of the Nerds* series—spelled out specifically: whiny voice, klutziness, antisocial behavior, haberdasheral horrors, deformed dentition, nervousness around girls.

In light of the well-publicized and perverse Gallic veneration of Lewis and his work, I will note my own nerd-origin theory that suggests the word is an alteration of the French *merde,* shit. In another fecal vein is the proposal (by computer-industry observer and prolific columnist John C. Dvorak) that it is a combination of the Yiddish *nebbish,* "a timid, meek, or ineffectual person," and *turd.* Another francophone possibility is that the word comes from *nœud,* a word with many meanings, one of which, in a computer context, is *node*—as in a node on a network; such a node, especially a diskless node, occupies a subservient position on the net. This French word is pronounced approximately like a New Englander's pronunciation of *nerd*, "nuud." *Nœud* can also mean *knot* or *snag*, each of which is a *glitch* of sorts. Yet another linguistic theory (also my own) is that the word is a shortening of the already contracted construction *ne'er-do-well*.

A mid-1980s article in the *San Francisco Chronicle* claimed that the word had originated twenty years earlier among California surfers. Interestingly, *surf* and *nurd* do share assonant properties; in 1964, a "one-hit wonder" group called the Trashmen recorded a popular, nonsensical single called "Surfin' Bird," which rhymes with *nerd*.

John C. Dvorak has said that all these theories are wrong. According to him, *nerd* derives from a Dr. Seuss character of that name. A search of the Seuss œuvre unearthed a nerd in *If I Ran the Zoo*.[20] Dvorak has chronology on his side: *If I Ran the Zoo* was published in 1950, well before the dates suggested in the preceding postulations. But the demeanor of Seuss's nerd is wrong. With his baleful stare, he looks more like a defiant, genetically altered eagle (a Surfer Bird, perhaps) than the visual stereotype of a nerd.[21]

Although *nerd* used to have strictly pejorative connotations and denotations, the 1980s saw a fundamental shift in nerd consciousness. In 1982, for example, *California* magazine ran a cover story about those funny guys in high school who wore high-water pants and pocket protectors and never went out with girls.[22] Those same guys were now fabulously wealthy, having started successful computer companies. The feature artwork for the article showed a nicely coiffed computer guy with horn-rimmed glasses, sitting in a designer chair, surrounded by beautiful, adoring women. Even though the nerds in *Revenge of the Nerds* were portrayed in unflattering physical terms, one of them got the girl, and they eventually vanquished their fraternity tormentors (a triumph of the geeks over the Greeks).[23]

The cover story of the April 9, 1990, issue of *Newsweek* was entitled "Not Just for Nerds: How to Teach Science to Our Kids." "The nation needs its nerds," proclaimed the article. "Maybe we all better become nerds." The subtitle of a *Baltimore Sun* article, "Rise of the Neonerd," was "The Geek Is Becoming Kinda Hip."[24] According to the article, by Mary Corey, *nerd* originated in the 1950s as a successor to *geek,* which, Corey claims, first surfaced in the early 1920s. In the 1960s, it was *dork,* which segued into *dweeb* in the 1980s. Corey concluded that "the nerd begins in the 1950s as a victim and he rises in the '80s to be a hero," citing such "neonerds" as Elvis Costello and David Byrne of Talking Heads. She also writes about Mike MacDonald, "a former scientific computer programmer and self-proclaimed 'outcast.'" MacDonald started a company in Illinois called Rent-A-Nerd, which dispatches "dorky-looking characters" to parties and other such functions.[25]

In contrast to the above "nerdvana," a late-1980s ad campaign for the Domino's pizza chain was based on a theme of avoiding "The Noid," a pizza-chilling cretin whose name and appearance may have been derived from a Brooklynese pronunciation of *nerd*. In the February 24, 1991, "The Far Side" by cartoonist Gary Larson, a mother and father cross a road with their three children while a car with a male and a female occupant is stopped, waiting for them. "Oh, look Roger!" remarks the woman, "Nerds! . . . And some little nerdlings!"

RISC

When you come up with the acronym RISC (reduced-instruction-set computer, or computing), you have to be ready to take a few jibes; RISC, after all, is pronounced "risk."[26] RISC is the opposite of CISC (complex-instruction-set computer, or computing). The former approach to computing aims to accomplish computing tasks by using the smallest number of instructions possible. It also seems to be the wave of the future in computing.

RISC was developed in large part at IBM. Eventually, the field split into two camps, one centered at Stanford University under the leadership of John Hennesey, who had been involved with the IBM development efforts, and one at University of California, Berkeley, under David Patterson.

According to *UNIX World,* IBM coined the acronym. Patterson has said that many people think he invented it but that it was actually the creation of Carlos Séguin at Berkeley. The computer industry considered the technology a gamble, so Séguin concocted an acronymic pun. Ex post facto, Patterson says, his colleague Séguin came up with CISC.[27]

Belying its wobbly beginnings, RISC appears to be de rigueur for the 1990s. Nearly every major computer company either bases all its products on RISC or offers a RISC line. One all-RISC company, Sun, and a "MIPS solution" firm, DEC, exhibit friendly as well as serious rivalry. A story goes that people at Sun stopped referring to DEC's RISC as SPIM[28] (because of something called "reverse byte order") when DEC denizens pointed out what Sun's SPARC spells backwards.[29]

Winchester

One of the respondents to the "kludge survey," Warren Michelsen of Page, Arizona, noted that "several theories as to the origin of *kludge* . . . revealed . . . a number of different opinions." Michelsen was also curious about the term Winchester disk, "as in hard disk . . . I have read several different explanations. All had in common the 30-30 link. One had it as 30 megabytes and 30 tracks. Another, which was just presented in *InfoWorld* by Kathy Chin, is 30 megabytes and 30-millisecond seek time. I know I've heard at least one other 30-30 combination, but I cannot remember what it was."

It may have been the one suggested by the Random House unabridged dictionary, which pegs the origin of the term at 1970–75. According to *Random House,* it was originally an IBM code name. A Winchester disk is a permanently mounted hard disk, and the designation for a device that held two such disks of 30 megabytes each was 3030, the same as the model number of the famous Winchester rifle.

Some Winchester-disk companies are located in San Jose, California, where computer disks were first developed. San Jose is also the location of the Winchester Mystery House, a sprawling structure with secret doors and stairs going nowhere, surrounded by Silicon Valley's sprawl. The house's eccentric owner, Mrs. Winchester, who apparently believed she would not die as long as she continued building, was the widow of D.F. Winchester, the rifle's manufacturer.

Winchester and the other terms examined in this chapter constitute some of the apocrypha and folklore of the computer industry. What they help demonstrate is that not every entry in the computer's lexicon is merely a dry acronym, a logorrheic turn of phrase, or a solecism. They are often amusing and evocative.

9

The Tyranny of User Friendliness

Story Machine has pleasant color animation, which is the highlight of the program. It never failed to happily reinforce the students' efforts.
—From a product evaluation submitted to *InfoWorld* magazine[1]

This book has repeatedly stressed the relationship between the evolution of computer technology and its attendant lexicon. Anyone who has used computers continuously over the past ten or more years has had demonstrable proof that computing has in many ways become more—in the parlance—user-friendly, even though computers and their software have become increasingly complex. One reason working with computers has become friendly is the computers themselves, which have gone from being hulking monoliths hidden from view in locked rooms to being tiny silicon mites tucked away in virtually everything we touch. Computers—in the form of microprocessors—are embedded in cars, toasters, elevators, cameras . . . just about everything. You can't see them, but they're in there—running fuel-injection systems, powering credit-card–size calculators, and performing numerous other functions we now take for granted.

In some cases, computers have gone beyond friendliness to outright congeniality. In a chatty, annoying, intrusive way, conversational cars inform us that our doors aren't shut or our seat belts aren't fastened; elocuting elevators tell us what floor we're on; kibbitzing cameras remind us to open their shutters, switch to flash, or change film; chatting cash registers "recite" the price of items. A lot of this data chatter has a generic, disembodied, synthesized sound.

And what about "voicemail," that ultimate in technotyranny?—especially the multilayered, hierarchical, aural-maze variety that keeps you on the line with a ludicrous litany of choices: "If you want to speak to an editor [assume you have called the offices of a magazine], press 1; if you have a question about your subscription, press 2; if you desire advertising information, press 3," ad nauseum. So you press 1: "If you wish to speak to a senior editor, press 1; if you wish to speak to a copy editor, press 2. . . ." You press 1 again: "If you are using a touch-tone phone, please use the buttons to spell the last name of the person you are trying to reach." You attempt that and get the wrong person. If you have a "rotary dial" phone, you just have to hang on and hope for the best. The final insult: "If you wish to speak to an operator, press zero." You press that symbolic digit, and the phone rings for an eternity until, completely frustrated, you give up—five minutes after placing the original call. As Lewis Beale, a writer for the Knight-Ridder News Service, put it, "[The New Rude] pitch you helplessly into their labyrinthine telephone voicemail."[2] *Los Angeles Times* columnist Michael Shrage calls voicemail a "Roach Motel."[3]

A new form of technological tyranny has been unleashed: the tyranny of user friendliness. In the realm of technobabble, its most noticeable manifestation is the display icons that appear on the Macintosh computer. To begin with, you boot up the computer, and its screen presents you with a tiny representation of the Macintosh with a "smiley face." (You half expect the words "Have a nice datum" to appear.) That's bad enough, the smiley face being perhaps the most cloying, saccharine, and—distressingly—enduring symbol of our age. Then you get into transactional—not transaction—processing. You decide to search for a word in a file and start your search about midway through the file. The search program reaches the end, and then you get a representation of a person on the screen with a dialogue balloon emanating from its mouth. "End of document reached. Continue searching from the beginning?" inquires the balloon. You have a choice of selecting "OK" or canceling the search. Fine—cute, but fine. You're "dialoging" with the machine. But when you have no choice but to answer "OK" to messages such as "An application can't be found for this document" or "A system error has occurred," it ceases to be cute. *Irritating* is a more apt description of the situation. Then again, maybe annoying, cute icons were to be expected in a product whose creation was driven by a grown man—a company chairman—who punctuated his speeches to company shareholders with expressions such as "Neat!" and "Insanely great!"

Smiley faces and their ilk have also showed up in ASCII characters. It is not uncommon for terminally cheery types in the computer industry to sign off on their e-mail messages with this: (:-). Turn the string of characters sideways, and you see a representation of "The Smiley." Four other examples of this deep expression of sentiments are

The Wink (;-)
The Shock (:o)
The Sorrow (:()
The Sarcasm (:/)[4]

No doubt some technically astute people have programmed these ideograms into function keys and distributed them over networks. One can only hope they don't start showing up in commercial products.

Computers Are Your Friends

In the early 1980s, a company "backgrounder" for Human Edge Software Corp. claimed, "Personal computers have been called friendly, but never a *friend*." That may have been true then, but a few years later, Commodore introduced the Amiga, a computer whose name lets you know that it is your pal. The Ami word-processing program, from Samna Corp., is your "pen pal." But the "granddaddy" of technobabble phrases that sprang from the tyranny of user friendliness is the anthropomorphic *user-friendly* itself.[5] This compound adjective, which can be either attributive or predicative, is used in conjunction with computer products and technologies to imply that they are easy to use ("This is a user-friendly system"; "This system is user-friendly"). But friendly for whom? For what class of users? According to the Random House unabridged dictionary, the term first cropped up in the early 1980s, although it appeared earlier. Random House defines it as meaning "easy to use, operate, understand, etc.," suggesting that it is an offshoot of the affable advent of *personal* computers. It was, however, a sometimes cruel phrase to novices at computing, because early personal computers were far from easy to use. Among this group, it gave rise to the counterterm *user hostile*.

Ironically, now that many computers and much software have truly become easier to use, the term *user-friendly* has evanesced; instead you are more likely to be confronted by cute little icons beaming at you from a screen. The term is still around, though—employed most commonly today by marketing departments of companies whose products are still difficult for a neophyte to learn to use: for example, UNIX-workstation manufacturers. The problem with putting a friendly interfacial façade on UNIX is that the iconic methods of interaction merely manifest the complexities of the operating system.

So what does *user-friendly* really mean? Semantically, the term is a little dubious, particularly since some of its users hyphenate it and some do not. Does it refer to a cordial computer user or to a computer that is easy for a user to employ? It has the latter meaning, of course, and a more clear definition is "easy to use."

Here is what *The Hacker's Dictionary* has to say about users of computers:

Basically, there are two classes of people who work with a program: there are implementors (*hackers*) and users (*losers*). The users are looked down on by the hackers to a mild degree because they don't understand the full ramifications of the system in all its glory. (The few users who do are known as *real winners*.)

The term is a relative one: A consummate hacker may be a user with respect to some program he himself does not hack. . . . there is some overlap between the two terms; the subtle distinction must be resolved by context.

It is true that users ask questions (of necessity). Sometimes they are thoughtful or deep. Very often they are annoying or downright stupid, apparently because the user failed to think for two seconds or look in the documentation before bothering the maintainer.[6]

Here's another complimentary comment: "One who asks silly questions. See *luser*." "Luser" is defined as "a user who is probably also a *loser*," the two words being pronounced identically. A loser is "an unexpectedly bad situation, program, or person."[7]

It seems that even though hackers wanted to free computing power from the confines of the priesthood, they still looked down on the technically benighted. It is likely that the term *user-friendly* was coined by hackers as a sarcastic comment about people below them in expertise. Since *user* already had disparaging connotations, tacking *friendly* onto it amplified the derogation. Then something happened that illustrates some of the methods by which technobabble proliferates. Marketing types got wind of the term and didn't catch on to its negative implications. Part of their job was to convince people that their company's products were easier to use than they really were, and here was a term whose use was becoming widespread and that seemed to fit the bill. "Unfortunately, the term *friendly* does not seem to have any objective meaning," wrote book and software author Paul Heckel.[8] "Too frequently it is a term a vendor uses to describe a software product, the same way a soap manufacturer uses the phrase 'new and improved.' It communicates positive associations to the customer more than real substance."[9] Here are some examples that lack "objective meaning":

• From a Kaypro (a company close to extinction at the time this book was written) press release in the early 1980s: "To enhance user friendliness, Kaypro is also bundling *dBase II for the First-Time User*, a new training book published by Ashton-Tate. InfoStar is also included in this bundle."[10]

• From Vivid Software Corporation (September 1984 press release): "The Facility Manager is a user friendly software package developed to help facilities personnel manage their systems furniture, free standing furniture and fixed wall office space. The Facility Manager is fully integrated with a data base management system to allow easy, but controlled access to inventory." (To have been "reader-friendly," Vivid, an apparently defunct company, could have added a few hyphens to this compound-phrase-laden release.)

• In what seemed an oxymoron, a software company called Quick Brown Fox had as its tag line "Friendly Professional Computer Software."

• Apparently tiring of the industry cliché *hands on*, a Marlboro, Massachusetts, company called Data Translation issued a press release for "data-acquisition modules" that featured "'hands-off' calibration and operation." The modules were also billed as being user-friendly. If so, they were in contrast to the release's opaque, hands-off (i.e., passive) prose.

Once people in computer marketing latch onto a term, they often thrash it to death, which is nearly the case with user-friendly, although, as noted above, it still hangs in there. When the hackers who coined the term see it applied to noncordial UNIX, they must be laughing all the way to the data bank. The term has even escaped beyond the bounds of the computer industry—as noted in an article entitled "Home Design Gets User-Friendly."[11]

In mid-1990 General Motors was running a TV ad for the Chevrolet Corsica in which the vehicle's interior was referred to as "user friendly." A few months later, ads for GM's Pontiac TranSport touted the same sort of internal vehicular environment. As the end of the year approached, Toyota was pushing "easy-to-park, user-friendly cars." So pervasive has this term become that it even slips into news reports. A notably inappropriate example of such use occurred on the November 8, 1990, National Public Radio news program "Morning Edition." A reporter who was doing a story on battered-women's shelters in San Francisco observed that "some battered-women's shelters aren't very user-friendly." A San Francisco local-TV reporter noted during the cold wave that swept through Northern California in late December 1990 that the unseasonable weather was "user-unfriendly."

In a column meant to point out the potential difficulty of getting a home computer running, *Baltimore Evening Sun* writer Kevin Cowherd focused on the importance of the computer's blending in with its surroundings: "Oh, you can talk all you want about . . . user-friendliness, etc. . . . but if the computer doesn't blend with the rest of the décor—if, for example, it clashes violently with the Bud Light sign in the window—it seems to me you'll have problems from the get-go."[12] In a twist on the tyrannical term, a headline writer titled the column "In His Own Way, a Most Computer-Friendly User."

Reflecting on the tyranny of computer cordiality, an *InfoWorld* reader wrote, "User-friendly, yuck. Why not 'user-obnoxious' or 'user-combative'? Most of us hate overly friendly people; why should we feel different about a machine? All this friendliness is boring as hell." Also expressing annoyance with the lexical equivalent of smiley faces, another reader wrote, "[*InfoWorld*'s "Computer Illiteracy" column] has convinced me never to read again a journal that even remotely refers to 'user-friendly' [or] computer literate . . . in any way, shape, or form." Still another reader wrote, "It would seem that *user friendly* should fall in the same category as *interface* [that is, taking on extraindustry connotations]. However, I came across a legitimate use for the phrase when I spoke to an official of a large management-recruiting firm. I was told that many companies are seeking data-processing people who are 'user-friendly'—that is, people who can interface with, or perhaps even talk to, the computer illiterates that run most companies."

A one-man industry of friendliness tyranny of the 1980s was Peter McWilliams, author of *The Personal Computer Book* and *The McWilliams*

II Word Processor Instruction Manual. In an attempt to be nonthreatening to newcomers to computers, the former book assailed them with cute, cloying, self-deprecating introductions to computers. The latter book was a series of photos and public-domain engravings retouched to include the "McWilliams II Word Processor," a pencil. (Retouched nineteenth-century engravings were a design cliché in the computer industry in the 1980s.) McWilliams even published a series of articles in *Playboy.* The first, which ran in the October 1983 issue, was called "Fear of Interfacing: A User-Friendly Computer Primer." "Face It—You're Techno-Illiterate!!!" screamed one of the blurbs on the opening illustration. In spite of itself, the article did have a couple of interesting things to say about technobabble. On its proliferation: "People use computer terms they aren't quite sure about and are never corrected because people they're talking to aren't quite sure about them either." On its becoming a singular mode of communication: "conversational computerese, an idiom intricate enough to qualify as the world's 297th language." On the importance of sounding knowledgeable: "After reading this article, you'll be able to trade jargon with some of the best computer salespeople in town." McWilliams and his ilk, with pronouncements such as the preceding, help explain the evolution of technobabble as a pop phenomenon.

In his book, McWilliams kicks off chapter 2 in the friendly mode of first-person plural, with a double redundancy in one sentence: "This chapter will provide a general overview of a personal computer's component parts . . . As we go along, I will also introduce you—as painlessly as possible—to that collection of jargon, technical terms, and buzz words known as **Computerese.** There's nothing to be intimidated about here either. The people who created computerese are far less intelligent than you . . . considering the mishmash of acronyms, tortured conjunctions, and fractured idioms, it's obvious they are far less intelligent than *anyone.*" If McWilliams was referring to marketing people, he might be right. If he meant pioneers such as Alan Turing, John Von Neumann, and Steve Wozniak, however, one might take issue with the statement.

With his curly hair and nonstop self-promotion, McWilliams was the Richard Simmons of computing. Both dropped from public view in the latter half of the 1980s but staged comebacks in 1990—Simmons tormenting cable viewers with ads for his "Sweating to the Oldies" video and

McWilliams with his "completely revised and updated for the 1990s" *Personal Computer Book,* which contained the same photos of terminals and the like that were already antiquated when the book was first published in the early 1980s. The friendliness faction may have found its apotheosis in a Florida Ph.D. in systems engineering, who early in 1983 was pitching to computer magazines a column called "The Computer Room." "'The Computer Room' is the Dear Abbey [*sic*] and Joyce Brothers of microcomputers."

Getting Personal

In 1981, the microcomputer got personal—thanks to that most impersonal of companies, Big Blue (a.k.a. IBM). That was the year IBM introduced its Personal Computer—something of a surprise from the giant outfit that specialized in million-dollar mainframes. No doubt much to the chagrin of IBM's trademark lawyers, the term *personal computer* quickly became generic. IBM designated the first machine in its small-computer line the PC in 1981, and that abbreviation also rapidly attained generic status. Today when someone talks or writes about a PC, the abbreviation can refer to any personal computer—from an IBM machine to one made by Apple to one of the many Asian IBM knockoffs. (The IBM PC model itself has since been discontinued, although millions of them are still in use.)

Personal computer was a friendly-sounding alternative to the technical term *microcomputer.* The friendly phrase added a personal touch to an industry noted for its impersonal nature. Initially, the term suggested an intimate, one-on-one relationship between user and machine—no big machine in a back room somewhere; no timesharing, in which users had to wait for their turn to exploit a small portion of a minicomputer's resources. The personal computer was all the user's (an interface right in your face).

The *personal* epithet became popular in the titles of computer magazines. *Personal Computing,* which ceased publication in mid-1990 after ten years of existence, was the first publication to use it. A plethora of publications with *PC* in the title proliferated: *PC, PC World, PC Computing, PC Tech Journal, PC Resource.*

By the end of the 1980s, a lot of PCs were connected through local-area networks (LANs). The majority of these machines had been purchased by businesses for word processing and other office-automation tasks. They were not so personal anymore because they were often being shared among a group of people working on the same projects. Because the huge market optimistically projected for home PCs never materialized and because computer manufacturers and sellers were much more interested in the volume sales represented by corporate purchases, the term *personal computer* started to have a slightly hollow ring. Terms such as *networked PCs* were coined to describe this new state of affairs, but it took a master of the techno–sound byte [*sic*] to come up with the next-generation term for these interoperating personal computers.

Steve Jobs, founder of NeXT, is credited with devising the term "interpersonal computer." The word *interpersonal* dovetails nicely with such other then-recent coinages as *workgroup computing* and *enterprise-wide computing*, but until then, the word *interpersonal* had mainly psychological or human-relationship connotations. Perhaps Jobs had his tongue firmly in cheek when in late 1989 he came up with this moniker, which sounds like a sendup of *personal computer*. (In a 1981 anti-IBM print ad, Jobs had claimed credit for Apple's invention of the personal computer, though not of the term itself.)

Denise Caruso, a technology columnist for the *San Francisco Examiner,* acknowledges that the term *interpersonal computing* "smacks of buzzword-itis," but she goes on to write that "at its core is the noble and most attainable goal of making human-to-human communication both easy and effective by using state-of the-art networking technology and software."[13]

It may have been a case of "buzzword-itis"; it may have been in pursuit of the lofty goal expounded by Caruso, but in July 1990, Sun Microsystems, which at the time was becoming populated in some departments with refugees from Apple, named its newest workstation product SPARCstation IPC. Although the company did its best to downplay the interpretation, the term was generally accepted to stand for Interpersonal Computer—a seemingly perfect fit for Sun's emphasis on "easy workgroup computing."[14]

Meanwhile Apple was helping underwrite the formation of a startup firm, staffed by Apple alumni who had designed the Macintosh, called

General Magic. Inside sources described the product on which General Magic was working as "a lightweight, low-cost machine that [would] let users send and receive pictures, letters, documents, and other messages by way of a specially built network."[15] A spokesperson for General Magic would not elaborate on the project, but an official Apple press release referred to the device as a "personal intelligent communicator," a sufficiently vague phrase. It could as well have applied to Ronald Reagan, were it not for the second word. Around the same time, Wavefront Technologies, of Santa Barbara, California, announced a new "scientific visualization" product. Not as complex or powerful as the Advanced Visualizer, the Personal Visualizer, which sounded like some self-fulfillment gimmick, was aimed at less-demanding tasks.

Home Is Where the Hard [Disk] Is

In the early 1980s, predictions started to appear about so-called home computers. These predictions ranged from the reasonable (people would start to buy the machines for simple accounting and writing projects) to the outlandish (by 1990, half the households in America would have computers in them).

Well-meaning educators reacted to the optimistic assessments and launched campaigns aimed at increasing use of computers by kids. They were quickly joined by less well-meaning advertisers. In the well-meaning camp were such educational pioneers as MIT's Seymour Papert, inventor of the LOGO programming language. In the malevolent camp were some manufacturers and their ad agencies, including Coleco (the toy company that tried to get into the business with its Adam computer, now defunct) and Commodore. Using shameless, pandering commercials, these firms attempted to frighten parents into buying the firms' computers for their kids. The message was as bogus as it was blatant: "Don't buy Johnny one of our machines, and he'll be left out; he'll be left behind; he'll be a failure in school—and in life."

The ads did have an effect. Lots of people went out and bought "home computers," most of which promptly began to gather dust or were used by the kids for playing games. One of the main reasons people who bought these machines never used them was that they could not understand the documentation. In 1983 *InfoWorld* magazine ran a cover story about the unused-home-computer situation. The cover photograph pictured a puzzled man sitting in front of a closet stuffed with the usual domestic detritus such as tennis rackets and board games; also prominently featured was a home computer.

What exactly is a home computer? Part of the reason for the failure of the Adam and the PCjr, IBM's disastrous foray in the putative home market, was that this market did not really exist except in the minds of misguided forecasters and manufacturers. Unless you consider Nintendo machines to be computers, the number of homes that have computers in use is small relative to the population. True, the home-computer market *is* potentially huge, but only in the sense that the Grand Canyon is a potentially huge swimming pool. (As of late 1990, the "installed base" of Nintendo machines in the U.S. was reported to be more than 30,000,000 "units." Although these game machines have dubious educational potential of the sort envisioned by Papert and others, they are part of an introduction of computer technology and its lexicon to budding technophiles.)

Computer Literacy

Promoting mass familiarity with computers was an admirable idea, but *computer literacy,* the term employed to describe this ideal goal, quickly devolved into a buzzword. Coined in the late 1970s, the phrase was quite popular by the early 1980s. Although still around, it is now moribund, largely because it was so overused in the early part of the decade.

Because most people in the industry consider themselves to be "computer literate," the industry essentially disregarded the term. It appeared most frequently in mainstream publications or in marketing mumbo-jumbo from agencies and PR firms that had a vested interest in pushing the concept. Industry critic Theodore Roszak called computer literacy a "chimera." Here is a sample from the computer-literacy glut of the early 1980s:

"New Poor: Computer Illiterates"—headline in *USA Today* article, which cited a Harris poll that concluded, "Computers are . . . separating the USA into classes of information-rich and information-poor."[16]

"Computer Literacy: Is It Worth the Effort?"—headline for a *Personal Software* article, which was billed as a "buyer's guide to computer literacy."[17]

"'Computer Literacy' and Test Patterns"—headline in the *Wall Street Journal,* circa 1983. The article equates the hysteria of the time about so-called computer literacy with that of the swine-flu epidemic: "While the swine-flu hysterics at least had the public's well being in mind, today's computer-literacy snakeoil salesmen are in it essentially out of greed."[18]

"Press Conference Introduces 'People-Literate' Computers"—headline on a November 9, 1983, press release for a Dun & Bradstreet business-computer system. The writer reversed the order of the words in the term to indicate that it is people, not computers, who are literate.

"The Master of the Game Takes a Byte Out of Computer Illiteracy"—headline for a Prentice Hall press release for *Ken Uston's Illustrated Guides.*[19]

"Prentice Hall Cuts Price of Computer Literacy"—headline on March 1984 press release about a series of workbooks.

"Become 'Computer Literate' This Winter"—headline on promo piece for "Dvorak's Instant Expert Series."[20]

"Free Computer Literacy Catalog"—headline on press release from MicroMedia, an educational-software company.

"KQED Fights Computer Illiteracy with the 'Academy on Computers'"—headline on press release for a twelve-week televised computer course in early 1984.

"Computer Literacy: A Gentle Introduction to Computers"—headline on a flier for an introduction-to-computers seminar. "No jargon spoken here," proclaimed the flier.

"We're Making Computer Literacy as Easy as A, B, C"—headline for full-page ad in the January 19, 1984, edition of the *Wall Street Journal.* The ad was for McGraw-Hill's textbooks for computer courses.

Computer Literacy Survival Kit—title of a McGraw-Hill "textbook and diskette."[21]

"Eradicating the Scourge of Computer Illiteracy"—headline in *World Press Review.* "There is always money in scaring people to death," the article began, noting the unscrupulous tactics of companies such as Commodore. "The big scare this season is computers. Computer literacy," the article concluded, "is the foot odor of the 1980s."[22]

"Computer Literacy: Where to Begin"—headline in *Perspective for Teachers of the Hearing Impaired.* This thoughtful article, which starts with the anthropomorphic lead "Computers are getting smarter everyday [*sic*]," notes that "in education, this push to teach every student something about computers tends to be lumped under the buzzword 'computer literacy.' [Educators'] definitions of computer literacy run all the way from basic skills needed to play Pac Man [an early, popular computer game] to the conviction that all students need to know whole programming languages."[23]

In 1988 the *Atlantic Monthly* carried an article, "The Literate Computer,"[24] which was not about the early-1980s notion but rather about computers as writers' tools. And in 1990, a newsletter about the overused and unclearly defined word *media* carried an article about "media literacy."[25]

The computer-literacy crowd may have been well meaning at first, but the term, as suggested by the "Test Patterns" article above, soon became part of the arsenal of scare tactics aimed at convincing parents and educators that if their children and charges were not users they would be losers. Not long after computers became warm and friendly and personal, a dark side of all the congeniality appeared. As already noted, computer companies, ad agencies, and others perverted the altruistic, if naive, motives of some computer-education pioneers. What was once called the pseudoscientific-sounding *computer-aided instruction* was supplanted by the vague *computer literacy*.

As the "Is It Worth the Effort?" article in *Personal Software* appropriately noted, "If you ask ten different people what Computer Literacy means, you'll get ten different answers"—a valid claim for much computer-industry jargon. (For more on the nebulousness of the term, see "Comp. Lit." box .)

Comp. Lit.

In 1983 an *InfoWorld* reader supplied the following thoughts on the term *computer literacy*:

If *computer literacy* has a meaning as broad and all-encompassing as Thom and Glenn tell me, then a synonym would have to be equally broad (or vague). Both Thom and Glenn tell me that computer literacy means literally to be educated in computer use and terminology, which includes knowing about software and hardware, knowing how the machine works and how programs work, and being able to write programs (at least simple ones). It can also include learning programming languages. There are, apparently, varying levels of what is called computer literacy. A secretary who learns how to use a word-processing machine cannot be said to be computer literate. However, a programmer who knows little or nothing about hardware is said to be computer literate. So, it is a vague and confusing term. Computer literacy, taken on a concrete level, sounds like computers are literate like educated humans are.

Here are some synonyms:

computer proficiency
computer familiarity
computer knowledge
computer education
computer usage
computer skill(s)
computer awareness
computer cognizance
computer study
computer perception
computer comprehension
computer appreciation
computer consciousness

In 1984 book publisher William Kaufmann issued a title that played on the connotation of computer literacy as having something to do with literature, that is serious writing as opposed to the usual meaning of the word *literature* in the industry: brochures, data sheets, white papers, and the like. *Sing a Song of Software* was billed as "verse and images for the computer-literate." The poems had titles such as "COBOLitany," "Where Do the Overflows Go?," and "I Am Pascal." The titles of some of the book's computer-generated illustrations were technobabble puns: "Fiche and Chips" and "Fenestration." More interesting than the book itself, from a technobabble viewpoint, was its self-important preface:

Said Wordsworth: "Poetry is the spontaneous overflow of powerful feelings." Do computers have feelings? Computer people certainly do; and the sometimes nerve-jangling but often funny world they inhabit cries out for poetic description. . . . Marie Gilchrist has written that "the life of poetry lies in the spontaneous fusion of hitherto unrelated words." Words like UART, gigabyte, and algorithm, perhaps. If such words are not part of your working vocabulary, the Glossary which follows the poems will help you translate the verse and will facilitate your communications with those special computer people in your life.

The book's "Mini-Glossary" was a compendium of terms found in the poems, an example of which follows. The preface contained the quaint early-1980s terms "electronic cottage," which eventually gave way to "smart home."

Coexistence

I sing the machine with no moving parts,
Capacitive keyboard, I/O through UARTs.
Main memory has no mechanical risks;
Bulk storage in bubbles eliminates disks.

The processor's solid state switches don't click,
No gears, cogs, or levers to rattle or tick.
The CRT output is silent and still;
No movement betrays this numerical mill.

But what can it *do*, this motionless brain?
It might calculate, reckon, and puzzle in vain.
If no action ensues at the end of a thought,
The point of the thinking might easily be lost.

The machine without motion must finally demand,
As it grows more aware that it lacks arm and hand,
An effector to give its thoughts body and force,
And what will it choose? Why, a person, of course![26]

Touchy-Feely Computing

Tactile tyranny entered the personal realm in 1983 when Hewlett-Packard introduced its HP 150 computer and attempted to popularize the term *touch-screen* in the process.[27] The user interface for this machine was digital—literally. To manipulate elements and objects on the computer's touch-sensitive screen, users had to remove a hand from the keyboard and put their fingers on the objects.

The HP 150 TV ad campaign showed a monarch butterfly alighting on the screen and changing one of the menus by its gossamer touch. Allegedly HP spent about $30,000 just to get the butterfly to land on the right spot. The computer was an example of technology for its own sake (a common occurrence in the industry), and the 150 bombed—as did "touch technology" for personal computers. But the term made its way to Southern California, a major touchy-feely center. An Escondido company of the early 1980s was named Touch Technologies. One of its products was a "courseware authoring system." (In the software business, as in other fields, one does not write, one "authors.")

Touchy-feelyism was the centerpiece of an early-1980s ad for The Source, an online information service owned by the Reader's Digest Association and located inside the Washington, D.C., Beltway. "The New Togetherness Technology" was the ad's 100-point headline. The pitchman for this warm and fuzzy commercial was then-senator Howard Baker, sporting a cardigan and sitting in front of his CRT hearth. Baker used The Source to keep in touch with his son Derek, who was pictured sitting close to an EMR (electromagnetic radiation)-emitting display and holding his infant son on his lap about a foot from the screen.

The ultimate in touchy-feely computing is "virtual reality," the modern-day equivalent of the "feelies."[28] Employing hundreds of thousands of dollars' worth of computer equipment, companies such as VPL of Redwood City, California, can put you into simulated settings reminiscent of Wonderland and other fantasylands. By donning a computerized mask and glove, you can immerse yourself in a "virtual environment." You can reach for and manipulate "objects" by grabbing them with the glove. This technology in search of practical applications has already added such terms as "data glove," "artificial reality," and "virtual environment" to technobabble's lexicon.

Computerphobia

Apprehension about the uses and abuses of computer technology preceded the emergence of terms such as *user-friendly* and *computer literacy*. In fact, these apprehensions were largely responsible for the coining of such terms. Well-meaning people with faith in the power of technology to solve all—or at least many—of the world's problems first had to convince the masses that the computers were not malevolent machines, keeping tabs on them and trying to extract taxes from long-dead relatives. Less well-meaning people wanted to sell computers—in many cases to people who did not need them—and manipulated language and emotions accordingly.

Both altruistic and manipulative methods for overcoming computerphobia peaked in the mid-1980s. These methods seemed to bring out a need for bad puns—not that there was any lack of them already. In March 1984, for example, Howard Sams & Company released a book entitled *Computers Won't Byte*, which was pitched at "beginners interested in the machines for home and small-business use." The cloying photo that accompanied the press release showed a stuffed toy kitten sitting on a keyboard. The previous year had seen publication of *Byting Back, A Compendium of Techno-Whimsy*. This cartoon book featured an illustrated and predictable "glossary" of such technobabble as *byte, chip, data dump*, and *user friendly*. Nineteen eighty-three also brought the technobabble-influenced and pun-laden *The Official Computer Hater's Handbook* by D.J. Arneson.

As the 1990s begin, the majority of people in the United States still do not knowingly use computers. Many are no doubt skeptical about or even afraid of them. Even people who use them all the time have reservations—about everything from their impingement on privacy to their use in weapons of mass destruction. Those reservations, however, do not keep many of these people from wallowing in technobabble. Putting a friendly, euphemistic spin on the lingo helps make it all a little more palatable.

10
NOW-THEN

The "gigabit age" is coming—soon.
—Teaser from a newspaper article about future computer technologies[1]

Anyone who lives in urban America—particularly in high-technology areas such as Silicon Valley; Route 128 around Boston; Austin, Dallas, and Houston, Texas; Research Triangle, North Carolina; and the Los Angeles–San Diego megalopolis; as well as in university towns such as Ann Arbor, Michigan, and Bloomington, Indiana—may think that technobabble is as much a part of the American landscape as are McDonald's restaurants. If you are surrounded by people who are talking constantly about *interfacing, networking, enterprisewide workgroup computing,* and *I/O devices,* your view may become somewhat myopic. Although millions of people do routinely use technobabble as a major component of their daily communication—to describe both computer systems and human interaction—millions more do not. At least not yet.

If technobabble were as prevalent as computers themselves, everybody would be speaking it. Most people who use computers are not even aware that they are employing them. The computers are "embedded" in devices and products people use to do their jobs or to entertain and inform themselves. Technobabble is still largely embedded in the speech and writing of a few million people associated with the industry, universities, and research centers. But in less than half a century, it has gone from being the province of a select few to the lexical currency of a large and growing minority. Technobabble is escaping into the general populace. Movies, TV programs, and compact discs are called *software.* Fifty million Nintendo game players now have a passing familiarity with some of technobabble's terms. Computer terms such as *user-friendly* are increasingly heard in news reports and advertising. Vehicles for popular culture, such as movies, are even doing their bit to embed technobabble into the collective consciousness.

As technobabble spreads, an inevitable question arises: What are its effects on language? At one extreme, purists assert that technobabble is a degrading and corrupting influence, yet another nail in the coffin of language—along with bureaucratese, military doublespeak, legalese, and all the other bloated and euphemistic professional argots that thwart clear communication and understanding. A strident expression of this belief came from Steve Lopez, who created the "Valspeak" contest (see chapter 3), in a *PC* magazine article entitled "Brave New Words." "Technodrivel is upon us. Silicon Valspeak—high technology's low-quality jargon—is destroying the English language. And some say it's here to stay." Lopez referred to the language destroyers who employ Valspeak as "technobabblers."[2]

The middle ground is staked out by people of a more observational bent who are interested in documenting the effects of technobabble on language. This group takes a more neutral view of the subject. At the other extreme are people who welcome linguistic changes such as those wrought by technobabble, arguing that these changes are what keep a language "living." Some in this camp suggest that much of technobabble—especially acronyms stripped of their abbreviational denotations and used as words unto themselves—become language- and culture-neutral, thereby contributing to the creation of an international language for the Global Village. A group of what might be called professional pragmatists argue that technobabble is necessary, even desirable, as a means by which professionals can quickly and efficiently exchange information.

All these opinions have some validity. As with any argot, technobabble is malevolent when it is employed to hoodwink, mislead, or obfuscate. Attempting to hide bugs, flaunting vaporware, directing attention away from corporate mismanagement, soft-pedaling layoffs—in these and other instances, technobabble is employed to gloss over problems or to falsely raise expectations. More often in the computer industry, though, the intent in using technobabble is less sinister than it is a manifestation of a tendency to call a spade not a spade, but rather a "wood- and steel-based hardware module designed to support the implementation of earth-excavating processes." Why call a disk a mere disk when you can label it a "peripheral" or, even better, a "mass-storage subsystem." Why use the boring word *product* when you can use *solution* (a meaningless word in most industry contexts, as no problem is raised that needs solving).

To paraphrase Billy Crystal's "Fernando" character, in the computer industry, it is often better to sound good than to be precise. In an effort to appear more important than it really is (and it really is important), the computer industry has fallen victim to the habits of polysyllabic palaver and euphemism. The industry's neologisms, "izifications," and solecisms do not pose a major threat to our language. Technobabble's real victim could well be the industry itself, which is in danger of sliding into the same semantic swamp in which wallow lawyers, civil servants, military officers, sociologists, and politicians. "Modemize" and "to mouse" are breaths of fresh air when contrasted with such contortions as "highly integrated solution for cross-platform development."

The computer industry is still wet behind the EAROMs[3] relative to the legal, medical, political, and other professions that have had centuries of practice in crafting lingo that no one else can—or would particularly want to—understand. A big difference between computing and these other areas is that the public actually shows signs of being interested in the former's lexicon. How long that interest remains may relate to whether the computer industry can reverse its slide into the swamp of meaningless language. Given that it is less than a half century old, the industry has made depressingly rapid progress in developing some of the semantic habits of the military and other professional-group language offenders. The reason may well be that computer technology advances so quickly that it magnifies lexical trends—both good and bad—and that it has been heavily under the influence of the military.[4]

On the other hand, technobabble has truly enriched and enlivened the American language, which, as George Bernard Shaw and others have noted, is not the same as English, although the former is based on the latter.[5] English itself is a hybrid language, Germanic in structure but heavily indebted to Latin and the Romanic languages for its rich and diverse vocabulary. American English is even more of a melting pot than the British variety, reflecting the melting pot that is America. Analogies advanced about the openness of American democracy and the ease with which our language opens itself to accept disparate linguistic influences have validity. The American language has no institution like the French

Academy to "protect" it and maintain its purity. American English has always opened its arms to welcome vocabulary associated with new phenomena, and the computer revolution is just such a phenomenon.

America is the birthplace of the computer industry and the creation, for good or bad, of the language of high technology. For practical reasons, other countries have adopted this new and special language—to various degrees. The term *debugger*, for example, is demonstrably shorter than and, it could be argued, at least as descriptive as *aide à la mise au point*. *Bug* is more lively and crisp than the prosaic *erreur,* error. Conversely, *mémoire vivre* is literally more lively than *random-access memory*—but this fairly dull English phrase has already been shortened to form the explosive-sounding RAM.

The tendency is for the "worst" and the "best" of technobabble to slip into the mainstream. Obscure acronyms and technical terms, which lend themselves neither to extracomputer connotations nor to euphemistic obfuscation, are still almost solely the province of professionals: programmers, engineers, and the like. Terms such as *arithmetic unit, registers,* and *instruction set* cannot be readily coopted for other purposes and so remain restricted to professional industry use. The hundreds of acronyms beyond mainstream representatives such as ROM and RAM constitute a shorthand method of describing and communicating technical concepts that are increasingly complex. Besides, after acronyms are in use long enough, they become words unto themselves. People who know what RAM is and what it does may not even realize that it stands for *random-access memory.*

One could argue that some aspects of technobabble hold the potential to form a universal language of technology—a sort of "High-Tech Esperanto" that might actually succeed. One such effort is embodied in a consortium called Unicode, whose goal is to develop a universal digital code that computers could use to represent all the world's languages.[6] Collaborative notions are clearly sweeping through the industry. In the wake of German reunification and the emergence of fledgling democracies in Eastern Europe after decades of collectivist tyranny, the computer industry is beginning to sound downright socialistic, with terms such as "workgroup"[7] and "collaborative" computing. Along with notions such as rugged corporate individualism, "personal computing" seems to be becoming passé. Lots of people are still buying personal computers for their own use, but any contemporary discussion of PCs is likely to include the adjective *networked*. Workstation makers want to steal market share from PC manufacturers, but the former are not especially concerned about onesy-twosey machines; they want to muscle in on "environments" composed of "networked PCs."

Workgroup, interpersonal, network, distributed, enterprise computing—all the terms reflect the current and future focus in the industry on downplaying the individual. What this will do for the fabled strong-willed loners who buck the system and start up successful companies in Silicon Valley garages remains to be seen. *New York Times* technology writer John Markoff suggests that computing may be returning to centralism, although a version diametrically opposed to the earlier manifestation of "one computer, many users." Markoff says that the "shared interactive," or "distributed," computing model presented in chapter 2 will result in desktop computers that are "windows into a garden of computing delights: a variety of specialized systems, including parallel computers, database computers, graphics processors and supercomputers, all seamlessly drawn together by high-speed networks." One user, many computers.[8] As *Business Week* magazine put it in an article "Rethinking the Computer," "Connect [desktop computers] all together on a network and add specialized 'server' computers to do particular jobs. . . . Add the right software, and the network itself becomes 'the computer.' In computerese, it's known as the client-server model."[9]

The coming decade may put a collectivist spin on technobabble, but this lexicon is here to stay. The only development that may eventually stanch its spread is the disappearance of computers as we now know them: boxes connected to screens, keyboards, and peripherals. When and if that happens—when computers become nothing more than a component of the "integrated home entertainment center"—will much of the lingo now needed to talk about and explain them be necessary any longer? We do not hear people rhapsodize about interfacing their microwave-oven systems to recipe modules to implement culinary procedures; wags are fond of pointing out that we do not see dozens of home-appliance magazines with names such as *Toaster World* and *Optimized Washing Machine*.

Technobabble will increasingly become part of the general public's vocabulary as more and more people use computers at their jobs and buy them for their homes. With the depletion of the world's oil supply and the worsening nightmare of driving to work, more people will begin to engage in "telecommuting": working from home by way of a computer, a communication program, and a phone line. That inevitable cultural change will put even more people in close contact with computer technology. Even the "integrated home entertainment center" (which is presaged by Nintendo's "Famicom" machine) will have its ISDN and serial "ports" for connecting "peripherals."

Whither Technobabble?

Technobabble will continue to be a mirror of technology. If researchers at Xerox PARC are right, we will witness "information refineries," in which AI will extract relevant information from databases, or "information repositories." But the difficulty of artificial-intelligence "refineries," according to PARC, is that "they presume to 'understand' what users need to know." Users will need new tools, which will lead to "information theaters," which use "full-color graphics workstations to create three-dimensional, animated, intellect-augmentation tools." These tools, PARC notes, will act as "passageways to colorful universes of information— enabling users to 'fly' inside those worlds and give shape to thought."[10] A less hallucinatory, more amusing prediction comes from cartoonist Rich Tennant, who foresees "datamats." "Eventually all people will be required to do some personal computing on a regular basis. But not everyone will own a PC. As more homes and apartments come equipped with washers and dryers, we will see the inevitable conversion of laundromats into datamats," which will feature such devices as the "IBM front loader" with its "spin-cycle architecture."[11]

More seriously, four technological fields, two of which have been around for about thirty years and two of which are relatively recent, exemplify directions that the language of the computer industry is likely to take.

Artificial Intelligence

The term *artificial intelligence* (AI) was coined nearly thirty years ago, but it has yet to live up to some of its early, unrealistic promises. Even after the assassination of President Kennedy and the beginnings of the disillusionment that was to be the hallmark of the latter half of the decade, the mid-1960s was still a time of nearly boundless optimism in technical and scientific circles. We had put men into orbit and were striving to fulfill Kennedy's promise to put a man onto the moon before the decade ended. Against this backdrop, futuristic visions of cogitating computers ran through the brains of usually sober-minded scientists.

In 1963 AI pioneer Edward Feigenbaum edited a book called *Computers and Thought* that explored many of the precepts of AI and presaged much of the anthropomorphic technobabble that has become commonplace today. The first part of the three-part book, "Artificial Intelligence," posed questions such as "Can a Machine Think?" The answer was no—and yes, depending on the circumstances. The book also explained terms from the relatively new phenomenon of computing, placing such words and phrases as *memory*, *intelligent behavior*, and *arithmetic unit* within quotation marks. The essays in the book, written by such "heavyweights" as Alan Turing and Marvin Minsky, spanned a period from 1950 (Turing) to 1961; most were written between 1959 and 1961.[12]

Thirtysomething years later, robotic computers perform amazing feats (deploying satellites from the Space Shuttle) as well as more-mundane ones (welding cars together on assembly lines). Yet realization of what Yale's Roger Schank dubbed the "cognitive computer" remains elusive.[13] The term *artificial intelligence* has an uncomfortably foreboding ring to it and is semantically nebulous, so it most often goes by its abbreviation, AI. A more practically descriptive term that came along about a decade later is *expert system*.[14] Such a system embodies, through programming, the knowledge of experts in a given field and then performs related tasks.

Areas in the general realm of AI that will increase in sophistication and likely contribute to the lexicon are speech recognition and handwriting recognition. The latter has already given us *pen computer,* a device on which IBM, Grid, GO, Slate, and other companies are working and about which they may have made announcements by the time this book is published. Speech synthesis and recognition are likely to improve to a point where a machine can actually produce natural-sounding utterances and understand colloquial language. At least one Silicon Valley computer company is reported to be working on an operating system that can respond to spoken commands (will it be able to comprehend technobabble?). These fields are likely to expand the vocabulary of technobabble.

Virtual Reality

"Virtual Reality, Get Real" ran the headline over an article on the subject by Denise Caruso.[15] The term *virtual reality,* which according to Caruso was coined by Jaron Lanier of VPL Research in Redwood City, California, was preceded by the AI-inspired "artificial reality," coined by doctoral candidate Myron Krueger in his 1974 thesis on the subject. But he could not know, wrote Caruso, that "he was creating a media monster for the '90s. 'Virtual reality,' a buzzword of the highest water—delivered complete with its own buzzacronym, 'VR.'"[16]

Caruso did not supply a date for Lanier's purported coining of the term, but it already existed, if only in jest, in early 1983. A technobabble-laced parody of a user technical bulletin from the IBM Information Systems Group, dated February 4, 1983, read in part,

Because so many users have asked for an operating system of even greater capability than VM/370, IBM announces the Virtual Universe Operating System—OS/VU. Running under OS/VU, the individual user[17] appears to have not merely a machine of his own, but an entire universe of his own, in which he can set up or take down his own . . . planetary system. . . . Frequent calls to nonresident galaxies can lead to unexpected delays in the execution of a job. . . . Users should be aware that IBM plans to migrate all existing systems and hardware to OS/VU as soon as our engineers effect one output that is (conceptually and virtually) error-free. This will give us a base to develop an even more powerful operating system, target date 2001, designated "Virtual Reality." OS/VR is planned to enable the user to migrate to totally unreal universes. To aid the user in identifying the difference between "Virtual Reality" and "Real Reality," a file containing a linear arrangement of multisensory total records of successive moments of now will be established.

Sounds like a cosmological precursor to writer Markoff's model above: one user, many universes. It also sounds like some of the outlandish, but nonparodistic, descriptions of virtual reality being made today. Caruso believes that such claims have "sucked [virtual reality] almost dry of meaning since there is so little to substantiate" the claims. Caruso complains that "the viable concepts within VR, and there are many, are masked today by technology groupies who have become extraordinary media magnets by hyping VR as either 'electronic LSD' or the preferred mode of communication for the next century."[18]

Virtual reality is less complex than it appears, explained Caruso, and the phenomenon is developing along parallel paths, the most notable of which is "photorealistic, real-time 3D graphics animation. You can call

it cyberspace if you want, or virtual reality, or digitally mastered halluci-
nations if you must, but what we're really talking about here are simply
'simulations.' Not particularly romantic, but it certainly closes a few
'doors of perception' along the hallowed halls of hyperbole."[19]

"Groupies"? "Media magnets"? With people such as Timothy Leary
getting into the computing act, we should expect to see and hear a lot of
ludicrous lingo—as well as claims for new technologies' use and potential.
Even the serious work being done in virtual reality is cloaked in SF-
sounding technobabble: Witness the "Cyberspace Project" in Sausalito
(Marin County), California, and the "Virtual Environment Operating
System (VEOS)" project being developed at the "Human Interface Tech-
nology Laboratory (HITL)" at the University of Washington in Seattle.
Another virtual-reality–inspired acronym is VIEW (Virtual Interface
Environment Workstation), a "telepresence system."

The field of virtual reality has already started to spawn buzzphrases
such as "'virtual worlds technology'—the ability to create lifelike, computer-generated environments that can be 'inhabited' via eyepiece computer displays and manipulated by a new generation of input devices."
This description comes from Denise Caruso and is based on work being
done at the HITL, presided over by Tom Furness. He and his staff are
trying to develop a "virtual world knowledge base." To raise the estimated $5 million it needs, the lab has extended invitations to technology
companies, government agencies, and universities to join, at $50,000 a
head, the "Virtual Worlds Consortium."[20]

Fuzzy Logic

Fuzzy logic has existed since 1965, explains Paul Freiberger, a business
and technology writer for the *San Francisco Examiner*, but it has reached
public awareness only in the last few years. This technology was invented
at the University of California, Berkeley, by Lotfi Zadeh, a professor of
computer science. Zadeh discovered a way to convert concepts such as *tall*
and *hot* into mathematical formulae. He also devised the "fuzzy set,"
members of which can belong only in part. For example if a man is six feet
one inch tall, he might have a 0.8 membership in the set "tall men." Zadeh
characterized words as fuzzy sets and derived a logic, based on approxi-
mations, which he called "fuzzy logic." Fuzzy sets could be used to
summarize a given body of knowledge—controlling certain kinds of

machines, for example—in a way that defied the usual complex mathematical equations employed in expert systems.

In a now familiar pattern, American academics and scientists discounted the concept, but their Japanese counterparts did not. Today, Japan is the leader in research and development of "fuzzy" products and technologies, such as fuzzy washing machines, which automatically select the correct cycle and temperature; fuzzy camcorders, which eliminate jiggle; and fuzzy microwave ovens, which automatically cook food for the right length of time. Other products that are controlled by fuzzy logic include autofocus cameras, rice cookers, automatic transmissions, and braking systems. Sony has introduced a fuzzy palmtop computer, which reads handwriting.

The field has already spun off such disciplines as fuzzy arithmetic, fuzzy calculus, fuzzy statistics, and fuzzy control. Some people who are familiar with the overall phenomenon refer to it as "fuzziness." The word *fuzzy* has been incorporated into Japanese to mean "clever." As fuzzy logic proliferates, so, probably, will the fuzzy lexicon.[21]

Artificial Life

Virtual-reality critic Denise Caruso deals with technological developments and—either explicitly and implicitly—with technobabble in her *San Francisco Examiner* column and her newsletter about electronic media. In her February 11, 1990, column, she wrote about one of the farthest-out areas of computer technology: "artificial life." Right off the bat, Caruso contrasts artificial life, or "A-life," with AI, to which "A-lifers" refer "with a sneer as the 'top-down' approach . . . which tries to cram the human brain into a machine that can, for example, decide whether you're a good credit risk." According to Caruso, A-lifers believe that "AI blew its chance at understanding the big picture of life systems by focusing too much on detail." So A-lifers are taking a "bottom up" approach, starting with "the tiniest part of a living system (as tiny as a sliver of DNA), and use technology to figure out how it processes information, changes from one form to another, and learns from its surroundings; in other words, how it's born, grows, evolves, and dies."[22] Currently, however, "artificial life is much simpler than a fungus," according to Danny Hillis, an A-life researcher.[23]

So far, the most notable contribution of artificial life has been a destructive one. Computer "viruses" ("precursors to artificial life," according to some people[24]) are self-perpetuating pieces of software that wreak havoc on computer systems once they have "infected" them. The term *virus* first appeared in William Gibson's 1984 SF novel *Neuromancer*. By early 1988, the term had become more than a literary concoction. In that year, some commercial software became infected with harmless viruses planted as pranks.[25] According to the Associated Press, "virus was [Merriam-Webster Senior Editor James] Lowe's new word of the year."[26] By the end of the year, a Cornell graduate student named Robert Morris had dispatched a virus of a kind known as a "worm" through ARPAnet. It quickly spread and brought computers at several large companies, including DEC, and universities to their knees for hours. Morris was traced and arrested. At his trial, the defense attorney asked, "Once you released this worm, did you have the ability to control it?" "No," replied Morris. "Once I released it, I had essentially no contact with it. After it started, it was pretty much doing its own thing."[27]

Not to worry, though. In response to the virus problem, software companies are counteracting with products such as Disinfectant, Virucide, and Virex to combat viruses with names such as MDEF B (a.k.a. Top Hat), CDEF, Stoned, Devil's Dance, 1260, Jerusalem, Yankee Doodle, Pakistani Brain, Icelandic-2, Ping Pong, and December 24.[28] Several books deal with the problem, including one that applies one of technobabble's tried-and-trite techniques: reverse-engineering acronyms. Bantam released a book with the title *V.I.R.U.S. Protection: Vital Information Resources under Siege.*[29]

Millennial Technobabble

Strands of software that replicate themselves and spread—phenomena such as this increasingly fortify the notion that computers are alive. The terms *brain* and *virus* both personify computer technology, but they are nearly half a century apart in computing's lexicon. For the moment, A-lifers represent the ultimate in the computers-as-humans mentality. It is the A-life crowd, according to Denise Caruso, that coined the term *wetware* to refer to humans, "because of our high water content."[30]

If computer technology does take on the frightening proportions envisioned by Arthur Clarke, Aldous Huxley, George Orwell, Ray Bradbury, and other dystopian writers, we may see the opposite of what has been described as "computopia"[31] and "technoutopia."[32] At its worst, virtual reality, for example, can be thought of as the realization of Huxley's "feelies," a literary precursor to VR. As it is, many people are worried about the uncontrolled proliferation of information around them that is made readily available over networks and through such "demographic" software databases as Lotus Marketplace (a project that was eventually canceled after Lotus received demands from 30,000 people that it delete information about them from the database). People continue to be afraid of and seduced by computer technology. As we head into a new century and the second half-century of computing, certain areas are likely to be the most fertile grounds for new crops of technobabble.

"Nintendo War"

I mailed the manuscript for this book to The MIT Press on the same day that the United States and its allies attacked Iraq. During the second day of the war, two reporters on National Public Radio's "All Things Considered" interviewed an American pilot who had just returned from successfully shooting down an Iraqi plane. The elated flier talked about "locking on" to his target and "deltas." He also spewed acronyms like flak from antiaircraft artillery ("triple-A," as the military calls it). When the pilot had finished describing his "kill," one of the reporters said to the other, "Can you give us a translation?" The second reporter "translated" the military/technobabble into phraseology the audience could understand. On February 7, another NPR show, a call-in program about the war, received this comment from a listener: "This war seems to use the language of high tech." Two days earlier, at a Pentagon briefing, General Thomas Kelly had provided fodder for that assertion. "Intelligence is a mosaic," Kelly waxed poetic. "It's made up of thousands and thousands of bits of information."

The war with Iraq was quickly dubbed "the first television war," because of the immediacy of the satellite transmissions from the Middle East and because the Iraqis appeared to be timing Scud missile attacks to coincide with the evening news hour. Military-supplied video footage showing crosshairs on targets and bombs hitting those targets with pinpoint accuracy led to the nickname "The Nintendo War." Some media critics faulted TV news for presenting the war as "just another video game." One such critic was P.J. O'Rourke of *Rolling Stone* magazine, who wrote, "[This generation of soldiers] grew up in video arcades. This is the mother of all Mario Bros., the Gog and Magog of hacker networks, the devil's own personal core dump. And our soldiers have an absolutely intuitive, Donkey Kong–honed, gut-level understanding of the technology behind it." O'Rourke urged parents to help the war effort at home by getting their kids out of the Sunshine and into the house to play Nintendo. "The future of our nation may depend on it."[33]

From a technological point of view, the war was a testing ground for "smart weapons" such as the Patriot and Tomahawk missiles that had never been tested in battle and were in danger of losing funding from the Pentagon. Their apparent success under actual fighting conditions breathed new life into them and prompted commentators to note that this war was also the first "technology war." The war ended relatively quickly, but it gave people glued to their television sets the opportunity to listen to military spokespersons at briefings employ technobabble in their assessments of the fighting. The war has already propelled new terms into the mainstream lexicon. And wars of the future will be increasingly technological in nature.

SF

Science fiction is a genre regarded highly by many techies. Some terms in the hacker lexicon come directly from SF, most notably *grok*, "to understand," from *Stranger in a Strange Land* by Robert Heinlein. A more recent borrowing, and one that has strayed further into mainstream culture, is *cyberpunk*. For example, a *Time* magazine review of the Warren Zevon album "Transverse City" refers to three of the tracks as cyberpunk; *New York Times* writer John Markoff is working on a book about computer crackers entitled *Cyberpunk*. The term *cyberspace* comes from William Gibson's *Neuromancer*.[34]

The word cyberpunk has been around since the mid-1980s, when Rudy Rucker, William Gibson, Bruce Sterling, and John Shirley started writing science fiction that became known generically as cyberpunk. The genre is characterized by bleak technological landscapes, such as that portrayed in the film *Blade Runner*, in which robots have sex with people and people who use "decks" place their minds into a consensual hallucination. The latter practice is called "jacking in" by Gibson, the generally acknowledged founder of the Cyberpunk genre. Rucker noted in his novel *Software,* "A robot, or a person, has two parts: hardware and software. Your brain is hardware, but the *information* in your brain is software. A person is just hardware plus software plus existence. Me existing in flesh is the same as me existing in chips."[35]

Novels in the form of software have been around since the mid-1980s. Patterned after video games, these books on disks enable their readers to modify the plots each time they read one. This "interactive fiction" has contributed such terms as *electronic novel, computer fiction,* and *interactive text adventure* to our language.[36]

Throwaway Society

Consumer items are increasingly meant to be used and discarded. The Japanese are even more notorious than Americans for quickly disposing of products. Tales of nearly new television sets found in Japanese landfills are common. Reuters quotes Gordon Campbell, chairman of Chips and Technologies, as having said, "We can start to see, as we get to a single-chip product, a throwaway computer." Campbell refers to such devices as "disposable computers."[37] Disposable memory is already available in the form of "flash cards," battery-operated "nonvolatile" RAM that can hold as much as 60 megabytes of data. These cards slide into "pocket computers" (about 1 x 5 x 8 inches in size) and last for several years. When the batteries are about to give out, you back up the data, discard the card, and put in another one.

Japan's NEC has promised to soon sell a "diary-sized" computer system, and *PC Business World* reports that "the PC of the future will fit into the palm of your hand, have a flat LCD color display, respond to your every word and decipher your handwriting," according to a manager at Sharp.[38] The name for these devices? "Palmtops."

"Techno-Utopia"?

When Marshall McLuhan coined the term *global village* in the late 1960s, telecommunications technology was primitive by today's standards. Yet he likened the technology of the time to a central nervous system, presaging such notions as neural networks and Japan's "sixth generation" project, which is scheduled to start next year. The sixth generation follows the fifth, an unrealized attempt to "develop a computer that functions in ways similar to the human brain."[39] Japan's next-generation project involves "parallel computing," trillions of interconnected "neuronal" circuits, as well as further advances in fuzzy logic. Like fuzzy logic, neural networks imitate the brain by "learning through trial and error, instead of requiring a programmer to give detailed step-by-step instructions."[40]

Japanese writer Takemochi Ishi says that such technological developments will necessitate a new acronymic infrastructure: the CAPTAIN (Character and Pattern Telephone Access Information Network) system.[41] To take advantage of all this technology in the global village, Ishi notes, we will have to "reprogram our thinking."[42] (Pronouncements of this sort may heighten anxiety about technology's proliferation as much as computer invasion of privacy does.)

The term *global village* was a stroke of oxymoronic genius. In the 1990s, it shows signs of being supplanted by the prosaic *global network* ("the next big it," according to an article by Denise Caruso, who cites former Apple "visionary" Jean-Louis Gassée as predicting that global telecommunications and databases are the two big growth industries for the rest of this century).[43]

John Markoff has noted how e-mail and other network phenomena have had a profound influence on how we interact, form relationships, live, and die. In one of his articles, Markoff wrote about a California computer-network aficionado who committed "virtual suicide" before actually taking his life. Blair Newman used his technological expertise to seek out and destroy his contributions to the Well, a San Francisco-area computer bulletin board. Some Well subscribers were saddened by his death but also angered because they believed Newman's writing were no longer his to destroy. They were, rather, the property of the network community—a local network community in this case.[44]

Does this all sound like "techno-utopia" or "techo-dystopia"? In some ways, it smacks of cyberpunk. Whatever it turns out to be, it will continue to contribute to the lexicon of computing.

Technobabblers of the Future
Most children encounter computers in some form early in life—either in school as "interactive courseware," to use a term from a newspaper

article, or at home in the guise of video games or home computers. The first generation of kids who grew up with computers are adolescents today. "Children of the Computer Age See an Appliance, Not a Marvel," went a newspaper headline above an article in the *San Jose Mercury News* about how inured to computers kids may be becoming. It would seem natural, then, that this group would be among the primary users of technobabble. But according to writer Sue Chastain, that is not the case. The object of adolescent argot has always been to exclude adults. With the proliferation of computers and technobabble, too many parents may be on familiar terms with computer jargon. To incorporate it into "teenspeak," then, might not serve its purpose. Chastain does note occasional overlaps between adolescent and computer lexicons in such terms as *dweeb* and *nerd*.

In her article, Chastain quotes Paul Dickson, author of *Slang!: The Topic-by-Topic Dictionary of Contemporary Lingoes*. Dickson may be a slang expert, but he could not be further off the mark—except perhaps from the extremely limited perspective of adolescents—when he says that current teenspeak is "not like computer slang, which is moribund."[44] Quite the contrary, computer slang (a.k.a. technobabble) is alive and well—and spreading. Although teens may not use it overtly for fear of being understood, many are on familiar terms with it for reasons noted earlier. Like computer technology, adolescence moves fast, and after a few years, teenspeak will be sloughed off like an outdated computer. The adolescents and preadolescents of today will soon be the computer users of tomorrow, and technobabble will likely linger in their lexicons for a long time.

Appendix A
Internationalization: Technobabble in Other Languages

English is *the* language of high technology. Nearly everyone in the global computer industry is fluent in it; programming languages are based on it; and operating-system commands, often tied to English-language acronyms such as *PIP, DIR,* and *grep,* are also based on it. "Most computer-literate foreigners speak English as well as their own language," concluded a reporter on National Public Radio's December 20, 1990, "Morning Edition" program. "Some Soviet specialists speak DOS as well as *do svidaniya*" (good-bye; until I see you again).[1] The hegemony of English, however, has not restricted other countries to English only when it comes to technobabble. A brief look at French, German, and Italian computer jargon helps illustrate how three European countries have dealt with an inundation of English technobabble.

French

The French Academy and the French government are noted for their ongoing attempts to keep Americanisms out of the language, yet terms such as "le parking," "le drugstore," and "les jeans" have proliferated. In 1981, the French government banned "U.S.-derived" computer terms from official documents (see "Les Mots du Mal" box for a partial list of such terms, along with their sanctioned translations).[2] (According to National Public Radio, Iceland has tried a similar approach; instead of merely adding *computer,* for example, to the language, Icelanders have devised an Icelandic word for *computer.* Given that Icelandic is nearly identical to Old Norse, a medieval language, creating Icelandic technobabble must be quite a challenge.) In 1983 the French government went so far as attempting to fine violators for use of "Franglaisisms."[3]

Les Mots du Mal

Americanism	Sanctioned French Translation
backup	de secours
data	la donnée
database	la base de données
digital	numérique
display	la visu or le visuel
hard copy	le tirage or le fac-sim
hardware	la matériel
light pen	le photostyle
on line	en ligne
RAM	la mémoire vivre
ROM	la mémoire morte
software	le logiciel
word processing	le traitement de texte

Although not altogether successful, this campaign, a decade later, has borne fruit. The French computer industry has policed itself and managed to keep much American technobabble at bay—at least in formal correspondence and publications—but often at the expense of brevity; *workstation,* for example, becomes *station de travail.* Occasionally it is easier to graft the infinitive construction *er* onto an English verb. This technique produces *booter* for "to boot."

In some ways, the French have had an easier time of dealing with American technobabble than some other European countries. English belongs to the Germanic family of languages, but its vocabulary since the time of the Norman Conquest in 1066 has been greatly indebted to French. Words such as *interface, application, memory, architecture, environment,* and *support* were borrowed from French originals; thus the French can "borrow" them back and apply them to a computer context with relative ease.

Besides, an unyielding quest for bilingual purity could backfire, as almost happened to the *SunTech Journal* (of whose staff I was a member). We decided to produce annual French, German, and Japanese editions of the magazine. We contracted French and German translations out to a service bureau, whose orientation was more academic than technical. As long as the bureau stuck with commonly used terms such as *réseau* in place of *network* and *serveur* for *server,* everything was fine. A problem cropped up, however, in the case of *buffer,* for which the service bureau used *tampon,* a French word meaning, literally, *plug,* but also *menstrual tampon*—with an additional meaning of *buffer,* as in *servir de tampon entre deux personnes* (to act as a buffer between two people).[4] Manuscript reviewers at Sun's French office in Paris took one look at the offending word and changed it back to *buffer* in every instance. Cross-language usages, especially in the commercial arena, are always fraught with potential peril. A notorious example was Chevrolet's Nova, which did not sell well in Mexico because *no va* in Spanish means "does not go." In the computer industry, a telecommunications hardware product that in the United States was called the Chat Box became "the Cat Box" in France.[5]

German

The Germans have been less concerned than the French about restricting the use of American technobabble in formal documents. After all, German and English are members of the same language family. Given the German penchant for creating compound nouns, the German variety of technobabble has produced not only such pure compounds as *Benutzerschnittstelle* for "user interface" and *Speicherverwaltungssystem* for "memory-management system" but also such German-American hybrids as *Marketingstrategie* and *Syntax-Check mit Cursor.* For simplicity, apparently, the Germans adopted *cursor* in lieu of *Bildeschirmanzeiger* ("picture-screen indicator").[6] Some other German technobabble:

Hauptspeicher: "main memory"; literally, "main storage" (the primary meaning of *Speicher* is "granary," "loft," "silo")
Kupfersandwich: "copper sandwich"; used in reference to a Hewlett-Packard chip design
Resetknopf: "reset button"
Schreibprinter: "printer"; literally, "writing printer"

As in the United States, technobabble is increasingly visible in Germany. Enno von Lowenstern, deputy editor of the German newspaper *Die Welt,* wrote an article in late 1990 for the *New York Times,* a portion of which demonstrated the incursion of American technobabble into German (von Lowenstern "discovered to his horror that he can write an article in German [on numerous subjects including computers] using hardly any German words"): ". . . und sie müssen beim Handling ihrer Computer-Terminals fit sein, on-line und off-line, ihr Password nicht vergessen, mit dem Scanner umgehen können, das Register editieren, die Disks pflegen, sich mit Bits und Bytes auskennen, nicht Top News canceln."[7]

Italian

When it comes to freewheeling technobabble coinage, the Italians are in the forefront. Many of the words they have concocted appear to have come from a Chico Marx version of the Italian language. A predominant technique is to take American roots and cobble Italian suffixes onto them, resulting in such pseudo-Italian as

bootstrappare: to bootstrap
bufferizare: to buffer
computerizare: to computerize
debuggare: to debug
editare: to edit (the native word for edit is *corregere* or *rivedere*)
hardwarista: hardware designer
multiplexare: to multiplex
processare: to process
randomizzazione: random access
settato: a set
shiftare: to shift-key
softwarista: software designer
sortare: to sort

Other American-influenced Italian technobabble includes *un file:* file, pronounced as *file*, not "fee-lay"; *un flag:* flag, as in *settare un flag; set di istruzioni:* instruction set. Terms such as *personal computer, spreadsheet,* and *database* have been incorporated directly into the language.

Steve Fogel, an *InfoWorld* reader, contributed the following tidbits about Italian technobabble:

I was involved in a two-year project to design and implement a minicomputer operating system for Italy's second-largest computer manufacturer. All six of us on the team (I was the only American) took great pleasure in mutilating both English and Italian. The [term] that cracked us up the most was "IPLare" (pronounced "ee-pee-el-lar-ay"). This referred to bootstrapping our mini, since the term used by the mini supplier was to "IPL" ("initial-program-load"). My personal favorite was "backuppire"—to back up our large disks to tape. I decided that it was an *ire* verb, not an *are* verb. Why not? Also, what to do about gender? We always said "un bit" and "un byte," but "una word."

Fogel noted the confusion that could be caused by the Italian habit of appropriating American technobabble, even if the root of the borrowed word meant something entirely different in Italian. In Italian technobabble, *microprocessori* means "microprocessors." Yet *processo* in Italian does not mean a process, but rather a trial in court. He speculated that this discrepancy caused a writer for *La Republica* to mistakenly use the word *microcompressori* ("microcompressors") in an article about how the new microprocessors were going to change people's lives.

In spite of the best efforts to keep Americanisms out of French (or Icelandic, for that matter), the high-tech world increasingly conducts most of its affairs in English. America may be losing its preeminence in high technology, but it still effectively dictates the way the people of the world talk high tech.

Appendix B
Random Strings of TechnoLatin

Hodskins, Searls, and Simone is a Palo Alto, California, public-relations firm that serves high-technology companies. In that capacity, it has encountered a lot of technobabble. Alarmed by its proliferation and overuse, the people at Hodskins, Searls, and Simone have assembled what they call the Generic Description Table (nicknamed the Anesthesia-Induction Matrix). It is based on what they have dubbed TechnoLatin, a "language that makes things easy to describe but hard to understand." TechnoLatin is used "primarily to replace simple nouns with vague and nebulous substitutes."

The Generic Description Table employs the pick-one-from-each-column format familiar to patrons of Chinese restaurants. The firm's Doc Searls has written, "We give [it] to all our clients who are tempted to describe what they do using a generic language we call TechnoLatin. It's a table of words that are (or have been made by frequent use) so imprecise that they are . . . like the blank tiles in Scrabble. You can put them anywhere, but they have no value." The table contains adverbs, adjective "adnouns" ("nouns that serve as modifiers"), nouns, and "hyphixes" (hyphenated prefixes and suffixes). It works as an effective primer of technobabble descriptions. As Searls puts it, "See how many existing slogans you can find in the table."

Generic Description Table*
(TechnoLatin Noun Phrase Matrix)

Add none or one of these . . .	To any # of these . . .	To any # of these . . .	To any # of these	Put these anywhere
Adverbs	Adjectives	Adnouns	Nouns	Hyphixes
Alternatively	Advanced	Access	Alternative	-Access
Attractively	Alternative	Address	Analysis	-Active
Automatically	Architected	Analysis	Analyst	-Area
Backwardly	Attractive	Analyst	Application(s)	-Based
Centrally	Automated	Application(s)	Architecture	-Capable
Compatibly	Balanced	Architecture	Area	-Compatible
Competitively	Bridging	Area	Availability	-Connected
Completely	Central	Automation	Breakthrough	-Dependent
Comprehensively	Centralized	Availability	Business	-Determinable
Configurably	Committed	Breakthrough	Capability	-Driven
Considerably	Compatible	Bridging	Capacity	-Enabled
Consistently	Competitive	Business	Center	-Intensive
Continuously	Complementary	Capability	Chain	-Led
Cooperatively	Complete	Center	Channel	-Level
Corporately	Complex	Chain	Choice	-Optional
Credibly	Comprehensive	Channel	Client	-Oriented
Digitally	Conference	Choice	Clone	-Phase
Directly	Conferencing	Client	Commitment	-Ready
Efficiently	Configurable	Clone	Compatibility	-Referenced
Entirely	Configured	Commitment	Computing	-Structured
Especially	Consistent	Communications	Concept	-Time
Evidently	Contemporary	Compatibility	Conferencing	-Ware

Add none or one of these . . .	To any # of these . . .	To any # of these . . .	To any # of these . . .	Put these anywhere
Adverbs	*Adjectives*	*Adnouns*	*Nouns*	*Hyphixes*
Exceedingly	Continuous	Computing	Configuration	Backward(s)-
Exclusively	Convergent	Concept	Connection	Cross-
Externally	Cooperative	Conference	Connectivity	Data-
Extraordinarily	Credible	Conferencing	Context	Demand-
Extremely	Custom	Configuration	Contingency	Full-
Firstly	Customized	Connection	Control	Hyper-
Flexibly	Dedicated	Connectivity	Convergence	Inter-
Fully	Demand	Context	Design	Intra-
Functionally	Differentiated	Contingency	Developer	Multi-
Globally	Digital	Control	Device	Phase-
Graphically	Direct	Convergence	Differentiation	Power-
Highly	Directed	Core	Division	Super-
Incrementally	Distinguished	Credibility	Document	Tele-
Indicatively	Distinguishing	Custom	Empowerment	Time-
Inexpensively	Distributed	Data	Enhancement	Turbo-
Inherently	Efficient	Decision	Enterprise	Upward(s)-
Initially	Emerging	Demand	Environment	
Innovatively	Empowered	Design	Equipment	
Instrumental	Enabled	Developer	Evangelist	
Instrumentally	Enhanced	Device	Exchange	
Integrated	Environmental	Differentiation	Executive	
Integratedly	Excellent	Document	Facility	
Intelligently	Exclusive	Empowerment	Feature	

				Put these anywhere
Add none or one of these . . .	To any # of these . . .	To any # of these . . .	To any # of these . . .	Hyphixes
Adverbs	*Adjectives*	*Adnouns*	*Nouns*	
Intensive	Extended	Engine	Function	
Intensively	Extendible	Enhancement	Generation	
Interactively	Extensible	Enterprise	Groupware	
Interchangeable	External	Environment	Guideline	
Internally	Extraordinary	Equipment	Host	
Interoperably	Fast	Exchange	Impact	
Jointly	Fastest	Executive	Implementation	
Largely	Featured	Expert	Induction	
Logically	First	Feature	Industry	
Logistically	Flexible	Focus	Infrastructure	
Logistical	Framework	Framework	Initiative	
Majorly	Full	Function	Innovation	
Modularly	Functional	Generation	Integration	
Multiply	Global	Groupware	Intelligence	
Newly	Graphical	Growth	Inference	
Numerously	Horizontal	Guideline	Interface	
Objectively	Impactful	Host	Leader	
Openly	Incremental	Impact	Level	
Operationally	Independent	Implementation	Logic	
Optimally	Indicative	Induction	Machine	
Optionally	Inherent	Industry	Market	
Originally	Initial	Information	Matrix	
Particularly	Innovative	Infrastructure	Media	
Personally	Instrumental	Initiative	Medium	

Add none or one of these . . .	To any # of these . . .	To any # of these . . .	To any # of these	Put these anywhere
Adverbs	*Adjectives*	*Adnouns*	*Nouns*	*Hyphixes*
Positively	Integrated	Innovation	Method	
Primarily	Intelligent	Inference	Module	
Proactively	Intensive	Integration	Movement	
Procedurally	Interactive	Intelligence	Network	
Productively	Interchangeable	Interface	Objective	
Programmatically	Internal	Leadership	Objective	
Progressively	Interoperable	Level	Operation	
Reciprocally	Joint	Leverage	Option	
Responsively	Key	Logic	Paradigm	
Robustly	Large	Machine	Parameter	
Routinely	Leading	Management	Partner	
Seamlessly	Leveraged	Manipulation	Partnership	
Selectably	Logical	Market	Philosophy	
Significantly	Major	Marketing	Platform	
Specially	Modified	Matrix	Policy	
Strategically	Modular	Media	Position	
Structurally	Multiple	Messaging	Positioning	
Substantially	New	Method	Power	
Successfully	Numerous	Multimedia	Process	
Tactically	Objective	Network	Processor	
Technically	Open	Object	Product	
Totally	Operational	Objective	Production	
Transitionally	Optimal	Operation	Productivity	
Transparently	Optional	Option	Program	

Add none or one of these . . .	To any # of these . . .	To any # of these . . .	To any # of these . . .	Put these anywhere
Adverbs	*Adjectives*	*Adnouns*	*Nouns*	*Hyphixes*
Truly	Overall	Paradigm	Proposition	
Uncompromisingly	Parallel	Parameter	Protocol	
Uniquely	Particular	Partner	Provider	
Upwardly	Personal	Partnership	Quality	
Variously	Positive	Philosophy	Reference	
Virtually	Primary	Platform	Resource	
Visually	Proactive	Policy	Rule	
Wonderfully	Productive	Position	Sector	
	Programmatic	Positioning	Server	
	Progressive	Power	Service(s)	
	Reciprocal	Process	Shrinkage	
	Reinforced	Processing	Simulation	
	Responsive	Processor	Solution	
	Robust	Product	Standard(s)	
	Routine	Production	Strategy	
	Routing	Productivity	Structure	
	Seamless	Program	Supplier	
	Selectable	Proposition	System	
	Significant	Protocol	Technology	
	Sophisticated	Provider	Template	
	State-of-the-art	Quality	Tool(s)	
	Strategic	Reference	Topology	
	Streamlined	Resource	User	
	Structural	Routine	Vendor	

Add none or one of these....	To any # of these....	To any # of these....	To any # of these	Put these anywhere
Adverbs	*Adjectives*	*Adnouns*	*Nouns*	*Hyphixes*
	Successful	Rule	Wonder	
	Superior	Sector	Workgroup	
	Synchronized	Server		
	Tactical	Service(s)		
	Technical	Shrinkage		
	Total	Simulation		
	Transitional	Solution		
	Transparent	Standard(s)		
	Uncompromising	Strategy		
	Unique	Structure		
	Unparalleled	Supplier		
	Utilized	Support		
	Value-Added	System(s)		
	Various	Technology		
	Vertical	Tool(s)		
	Virtual	Topology		
	Visual	User		
	Wonderful	Vendor		
	Worldwide	Workgroup		

*Hodskins, Simone, and Searls, Inc. Used with permission.

Appendix C
Xerox and the Technobabble Quotient

On September 19, 1990, Xerox introduced several new products at its legendary Palo Alto Research Center (PARC). The event had a typically portentous title, "Opening the Future." Like many introductions of computer products, this one featured company bigwigs, videos with cliché computer graphics, refreshments, products demos, Q&A sessions, and a press kit—and what a press kit! Stuffed into it were twelve press releases, ranging in length from two to twelve pages; five bigwig biographies; seven 35mm color slides, and six black-and-white 8 x 10 glossies. The kit contained so much material that it needed a separate contents page. Best of all, much of the prose on the fifty-plus pages of materials extolled the virtues of electronic (i.e., nonpaper) documents.

What made all these pages stand out was their large technobabble quotient. It was as if someone had gone out of the way to include as much contemporary technomarketing parlance as possible, especially in the area of workgroup, interpersonal, networked, client/server—call it what you will—computing. After a while, it all began to read like a parody of that parlance. But why attempt to explain further? Let the materials speak for themselves.

A Very High TQ

Collaborative computing environment . . . integrated, multitasking document and information processing systems . . . Xerox-pioneered electronic desktop and graphical user interface (GUI) . . . client/server network architecture in which workstations, or "clients," are linked to shared networked servers . . . windows, icons, "What-You-See-Is-What-You-Get" (WYSIWYG) display, pull-down menus, and a mouse.

fully integrated set of applications . . . Users can perform multiple applications while automatically integrating information.

The initial 1981 product implementation . . . all standards of today's user-friendly interfaces.

richer array of network resources . . . a proprietary, multitasking, one-million-instructions-per-second (MIPS) computer.

The GlobalView environment represents one of the most highly integrated models of computing . . . intuitive user interface or "desktop" . . . users' personal desktops . . . are "portable."

GlobalView is really a multitasking network desktop environment.

"inter-personal" [sic] computing.

ease-of-use, transparent access to network resources, and transportability.

The hardware layer includes all the computing platforms that Xerox supports . . . It supports the management of windows.

The standard application user interface layer specifies how applications should behave . . . the application layer supports the use of "document agents" . . . all applications possess a high level of interoperability.

General purpose office productivity solutions; enhanced graphics and specialized applications; and advanced distributed processing teamwork solutions.

This capability was designed as an intrinsic part of the GlobalView architecture, making its implementation seamless across all applications . . . These applications use the GlobalView desktop as a front-end processor.

Each product supports a high degree of interoperability through interprocess communications, which allows a continuing dialogue between the user and the computer.

virtual keyboards.

extended language capability supporting Japanese, Chinese, Arabic, and Hebrew.

a suite of capabilities . . . across enterprise-wide networks.

integrated systems solution . . . user-friendly front-end processors.

moving from a paper-based documentation system to an electronic one.

it allows users to "hot-key" between . . . environments.

the dawn of "interpersonal [sic] computing" . . . designed to support teamwork.

with peer-to-peer, client/server distributed computing environments rapidly replacing yesterday's hierarchical MIS-dominated mainframe/dumb terminal/isolated PC configurations.

delivering complete "TeamWare" solutions today.

its capacity to create a "virtual workspace" . . . The GlobalView environment is so highly integrated and network-centric.

DocuTeam is not a single application; rather it is a set of capabilities that enables many applications.

The next generation of computer products, the so-called "Third Generation," will provide some level of teamware functionality.

Intelligent Information Access Solutions

user-friendly, object-oriented, mouse-enabled environment.

The . . . desktop environment is very "friendly" and intuitive.

industry-standard open architecture product configuration.

a very robust typographic capability.

DEC Virtual Machine Systems (VMS)[1]

personal augmentation.[2]

An advanced computing solution for the Xerox user-friendly, icon-based GlobalView software environment.

So here is Xerox, pushing electronic documents in a forest-decimating, technobabble-laced, redundant press kit that could easily have contained less than half the material it did, eliminated the gratuitous jargon, and conveyed the story much more clearly and simply in the process. Did the Xerox PR and marketing people seriously expect that anyone would read all this nonsense?

When it comes to introducing new products, some companies still adhere to the concept of the "technobabble quotient"—the higher the better. The fact is that very few people outside those in the company who produced it have any desire to plough through all this stuff; several people from the press who attended the Xerox event complained about and ridiculed the bloated press kit. The marketing types have to appear to be doing their jobs; their salaries, in cases such as this, seem to be proportional to tonnage produced.

As any company does when it introduces new products, Xerox wanted to make a big splash with its announcement. Instead, it made a large thud when the bulging press kit was dropped onto a desktop.

Appendix D
Psycho/Technobabble

When you sit down and interact on a network, you experience it as a whole. It's real fuzzy. You can't really say at what point a collection of neurons becomes a mind in our heads. And likewise, if you conceive of the world brain as a collection of individuals, you can't say really say at what point the network becomes volatile and takes on a life of its own. It is mystical, I guess—in the sense that information itself is mystical.

—Sandy Stone, CommuniTree sysop[1]

As noted in chapter 1, technobabble bears some similarities to psychobabble. Psychobabble was a product of the 1960s and 1970s, a reaction against, among other things, the perceived depersonalization wrought by computer technology.[2] Although computerese has been around for several decades, technobabble can be viewed as having come into full flower in the 1980s. Much as the 1960s and 1970s fostered a widespread awareness of self-awareness, with the attendant profusion of psychobabble, the 1980s, coming on the heels of the personal computer, produced a widespread awareness of computers, with the attendant profusion of technobabble.

One reason for the similarity is that many promulgators of psychobabble became active in the computer community, or sometimes in its fringe areas. Furthermore, "self-actualization" often went hand in hand with the campus radicalism of the 1960s. Computer hacking was born on college campuses—at the time, practically the only place anyone could get access to computers—and the attitudes it represented tended to parallel many of those that were being increasingly and stridently expressed elsewhere on campuses. Ironically, while many students were overtly protesting the Vietnam war and, by implication, the march of computer technology—in the form of "smart" weapons and computerized grading—hackers were seeking more computing freedom.

In spite of their idealism and naïveté, many radicals of the 1960s went on to embrace computer culture, including its lexicon (see "Counterculture Computerphiles" box). The most notable representative of sixties radical turned computerphile is Timothy Leary, the one-time Harvard professor who "tuned in, turned on, and dropped out" in the early 1960s to become LSD's major apostle. In the 1990s, Leary has become one of the advocates of "virtual reality," a fringe area of computing that has been equated with LSD experiences.

Counterculture Computerphiles

Steward Brand. Brand, an associate of 1960s icons Ken Kesey and Paul Krassner, started the *Whole Earth Catalog*, an assortment of items for people of alternative outlooks. In the late 1970s, personal computers began to show up in the *Catalog*'s pages. Brand is credited by the Merriam-Webster publishing company with the first recorded use of the word *hacker*—in *Rolling Stone,* the quintessential journal of the 1960s–70s counterculture.[3]

Ray Mungo. As editor of the *Boston University News* in the mid-1960s, Mungo was probably the most radical man on a relatively staid campus. By the 1980s, Mungo was living in Pacific Grove, California, after having tried and failed at communal farming in Vermont. He coauthored a computer baseball program. Mungo and Brand both shared the same literary agent—John Brockman, a man who had staged "happenings" in the 1960s.

Ted Nelson. Probably the most influential of those in the counterculture who have embraced computers. In his legendary book of the same title, Nelson gave the computer lexicon the term "computer lib." Nelson and other aficionados organized groups with such names as the Homebrew Computer Club,[4] Community Memory, People's Computer Company (PCC), Community Computer Center, and the Whole Earth Truck Store.

Jerry Rubin. In 1968, the scruffy Rubin was one of the "Chicago 7." By the late 1970s, however, he was sporting a three-piece suit, was impeccably coiffed, and was conducting "networking" parties at hip discos in New York for Wall Street types. Rubin was largely responsible for promoting networking in its personnel context.

Steve Jobs. Although Jobs was too young to have been a product of the 1950s or 1960s, he was a carryover from the latter decade. In the mid-1970s, he was a fructarian who went off to India "in search of himself." He was the subject of a book with a mock-spiritual title[5] and reportedly gave the computer industry the psychobabblish term "interpersonal computer."

About the same time that Leary was getting booted out of Harvard because of his experiments with LSD, Joseph Weizenbaum, an MIT computer-science professor with a skeptical attitude concerning technophilia, wrote the famous Eliza computer program. Weizenbaum is one of the seminal forces in modern computing. Author of *Computer Power and Human Reason*, he created "a program with which one could 'converse' in English." Weizenbaum connected a typewriter to a computer. Questioners could "ask" the computer questions by typing them, and the computer would type "answers" in response. He named the program Eliza, after the heroine of *Pygmalion*, because "it could be taught to 'speak' increasingly well" about a variety of subjects, information about which was provided by "script" programs. A "language analyzer" related to the lexicon of the script enabled the computer to make seemingly relevant responses.

"For my first experiment, I gave Eliza a script designed to permit it to play (I should really say parody)," Weizenbaum noted, "the role of a Rogerian psychotherapist engaged in an initial interview with a patient." Weizenbaum explained that such therapists were easy to imitate because their techniques consist largely of drawing their patients out by reflecting their statements back to them. For example,

Woman playing patient: My boyfriend made me come here.
Eliza: Your boyfriend made you come here?
Patient: He says I'm depressed much of the time.
Eliza: I'm sorry to hear you are depressed.
Patient: It's true. I am unhappy.
Eliza: Do you think coming here will help you not to become unhappy?
Patient: Perhaps I could learn to get along with my mother.
Eliza: Tell me more about your family.

On the MIT campus, the program acquired the moniker Doctor and became famous, mainly because it easily and effectively demonstrated information processing and was interactive. Soon, Doctor gained national prominence, and people began to play it. But three subsequent events "shocked" Weizenbaum.

1. He discovered that some practicing psychiatrists seriously believed that the program could grow into a nearly completely automatic form of psychotherapy.

2. He was startled to see that some people who conversed with Doctor became emotionally involved with the computer and quickly anthropomorphized it.

3. He worried about a growing belief that his program demonstrated a general solution to the problem of computer understanding of natural language.

He was all the more disappointed by these occurrences because he had discounted their likelihood of happening in a paper in which he had introduced the program.[6]

By the early 1980s, it seemed that psychobabble and technobabble might merge into a psychotechnical lingua franca (see "Psychotechnobabble" box).[7]

Psychotechnobabble

Person A: I have a really meaningful interface with my computer.

Person B: I can really get behind your output on that. My system is very friendly, and I can relate to it almost any time I boot it up. Once in a while it gets negative and generates glitches, but usually it's just going through some heavy changes and has to get its CPU together. Basically it's responsible for its I/O.

A: Do you ever feel any glitch anxiety when that happens, or can you deal with it OK?

B: Most of the time, I'm OK and my system's OK.

A: Generally, I access the same feelings. But I noticed that you referred to your computer as a "system." Do you have any problem verbalizing that kind of output? *System* seems to have negative parameters.

B: Do you really conceptualize my output that way? I think that *system* feels good. A system to me covers the whole gestalt of number crunching. You should think of the universe as one big micro chip. Computing is more than just numbers, it's being.

A: I'm starting to relate to what you're saying. At first I was as down as my computer is when power spikes and bad vibes don't go with the data flow, but now I think I'm beginning to feel a sense of wellness.

B: Yeah, and if you think of bad vibes on a power line as an analogue to bad vibes in the central nervous system, you've really accessed something important. People are really computers. They relate to each other and interface with each other; people interface with each other; people interface with computers. Really cosmic parameters!

Richard Seltzer captured the spirit of the merger of psycho- and technobabble, as well as the introverted nature of many technophiles, in defining his neologism *interfacelift:* "n. (*interface* + *facelift*): Attendance at a seminar on interpersonal communication and human interaction. 'Jack, you have gotten so involved in this software project that I don't think you have said hello to anyone in months. I would say it's time you had an *interfacelift.*'"[8]

Many practitioners of psycho/technobabble are seekers of planes beyond those at the back of a computer,[9] and many of them are situated in California. If, as these people believe, "information is the key to a whole new world, a mystical universe where magic comes alive"—wrote Frank Rose in a *Vanity Fair* article entitled "Wired to God"—"the computer might be some sort of philosopher's stone, an alchemical tool that will transmute baser consciousness into gold." Rose profiled some of the denizens of what the marketing manager of a Santa Cruz software company called "Oz." He accumulated some New Age technobabble in the process.

The Pit: disparaging term for Silicon Valley

evolutionary technology: catchphrase from Allan Lundell and Geneen Haugen. Proclaimed Lundell, "We're just taking the tools to their next level of sophistication, and as they evolve so do we."

"With a personal computer, you can reprogram your own brain and you can be in control":   wisdom from Robert Dilts, software engineer and head of an outfit called Behavioral Engineering. Dilts was working with Timothy Leary on a series of seminars and programs.

SMI²LE: acronym standing for "space migration, intelligence increase, and life extension"

information artisan: programmer, probably working on nonmainstream software

information ecology: "The flow of data, knowledge, and ideas through the culture"

biofeedback-controlled, interactive holograms: precursor to what is now known as virtual reality

technological alchemy: another Lundell/Haugen catchphrase

post-industrial/cybernetic/computopia: description from the user manual of CommuniTree, a computer network of information artisans, technological alchemists, and the like. According to Rose, "computopia" was coined in Japan and picked up by artisan and CommuniTree-manual author Dean Gengle as "an alternative to '1984.'"

self-transmuting information sculpture: another description of CommuniTree *cosmic switchboard:*   what "contemporary paganism" is trying to plug into.[10] CommuniTree's sysop (quoted at the beginning of chapter 9) noticed that the ideas generated by a network conference called Start-a-Religion resembled the "precepts of contemporary paganism."[11]

With This Token Ring, I Thee Interface[12]

In 1980, Ron Jaenisch was a "minister" in the Modesto, California–based, 13,000,000-minister mail-order Universal Life Church. When he called the offices of *InfoWorld* magazine in November of that year, he announced that he was going to perform the world's first "computer wedding," with the assistance of "Reverend Apple," in Sunnyvale, California. Jaenisch had programmed a standard wedding ceremony, complete with vows, into his apostolic Apple II. The scripture popped up onto the screen, giving the bride and groom the choice of answering Y for *yes* and N for *no* when the computer asked them if they took each other for husband and wife. It was a strictly binary ceremony, although Jaenisch later added flourishes such as sound and synthesized speech. The irreverent Reverend Jaenisch had his tongue firmly in cheek, but in the process he got a lot of press, which redounded to the success of his real business: recruiting (a.k.a. "headhunting") for computer companies in Silicon Valley. At about the same time, serious psycho/technobabble was going on to the north, in Marin County, the psychobabble capital of the known universe.

The party at the Marin house had all the requisite trappings: large windows, redwood deck, hot tub. One of the party-goers looked like Marin, but she talked like Atlanta. The contrast was startling. More startling was her revelation that among her pastimes was "channeling" with her personal computer. So earnest did she seem to be in this endeavor that no one even asked her to contact Elvis. She never explained exactly how she accomplished her activities, but one could only assume that she had a powerful modem and telecommunications program.

The party's host was one of Silicon Valley's noteworthy psycho-technobabblers, a man for whom the term *space cadet* was surely invented. After writing about "meditation and prayer" software in a computer journal, he received a letter from a Southern California minister affiliated with a group called Teaching of the Inner Christ. "I would very much like to obtain your meditation and prayer computer programs.

What a wonderful way to bring forth Truth into the world! You are truly spreading your light and love upon the world in this beautiful new age." The letter's salutation read, "In Peace and Light."

Götterramerung

California holds no monopoly on computer cosmology. In 1982 a man named Alan Rogers claimed to be able to contact God through his TRS-80 computer. Originally from Nova Scotia, Rogers made his way to New York, although not before taking a correspondence course from the San Jose, California-based Rosicrucian Society. In New York, Rogers conceived the Infinity Project about the same time the star-directed Nancy Reagan was moving from California to Washington. The basis for Rogers's endeavor was an attempt to understand the workings of prayer, which friends of his who prayed could not explain. "I was struck by the fact that if you succeeded, you succeeded by accident," Rogers concluded. He then decided that the problem lay in "transmission." People's memories are so short and their minds so confused that they cannot clearly define a prayer.

At the time, Rogers had no direct computer experience, but he "surmised that their circuitry might prove a good conduit for transmission." After buying the computer, Rogers set out to write a program to help people pray more efficiently. But he discovered that "there were some people who were into meditation who could not accept a program that was full of religious connotations. So I rewrote it for people who were into meditation." The result was the Infinity Program.

How did it work? In part, Rogers postulated, because "the crystals within the computer, vibrating at the rate of one hundred million times a second, set up an electromagnetic field that interacts with one's own aura, drawing one into the 'infinity circuit.'" Upon starting, Rogers's program displayed this message on the screen: "I am the electronic unit for using the soul circuit."[13]

In the computer cosmos, most aficionados are content to "evangelize" and seek the guidance of "gurus." Some, however, view the computer as a direct link to a higher state of consciousness and meld psychobabble and technobabble in the process.

Notes

Chapter 1

1. David Roth, "William Safire, Eat Your Dictionary: Here Comes TechnoBabble," *Franson's Business Report on Technology*, 2, no. 4 (1984), 1.

2. Language-watcher Richard Lederer wrote about a female baby boomer who waded through some of the jargon of the 1980s. "CDs were no longer just certificates, and the computer had thoroughly befuddled her sense of crash, hacker, menu, mouse, virus, and window." (From an e-mail posting; no publication information provided.) But not all these terms are 1980s concoctions; *hacker*, for example, dates from the 1950s.

3. Joseph Weizenbaum, *Computer Power and Human Reason* (San Francisco: W.H. Freeman and Co., 1976), 41.

4. According to the *Random House Unabridged Dictionary of the English Language*, 2d ed., unabridged (New York: Random House, 1987), "[The suffix] -ese occurs in coinages denoting in a disparaging, often facetious way a characteristic jargon, style, or accent: Brooklynese, bureaucratese, journalese, computerese." The *Oxford English Dictionary* states that "a modern application of the suffix is to form words designating the diction of certain authors who are accused of writing in a dialect of their own invention."

5. As of January 1990, Computer Literacy Bookshops, arguably the most comprehensive source of computer books in the U.S., had seventeen different computer dictionaries in stock. A Bookshops spokesperson said, "It's safe to say there are twenty to twenty-five." These are only the commercially available titles; numerous computer companies publish dictionaries for in-house and contractor use.

6. In *Computer Power and Human Reason*, Weizenbaum writes of this obsession: "Bright young men of disheveled appearance, often with sunken glowing eyes, can be seen sitting at computer consoles, their arms tensed and waiting to fire their fingers, already poised to strike, at the buttons and keys on which their attention seems to be as riveted as a gambler's on the rolling dice." For a comprehensive examination of computer obsession, see the work of another MIT professor, Sherry Turkle, *The Second Self* (New York: Simon and Schuster, 1984).

Chapter 2

1. Robert McCrum, William Cran, and Robert MacNeil, *The Story of English* (New York: Viking, 1986), 37.

2. The hopelessly archaic, from a technological viewpoint, 1971 edition of the *Oxford English Dictionary* gives *computor* as a secondary spelling but defines the word in terms of people who perform computations; it makes no mention of devices.

3. Jack Rochester and John Gance, *The Naked Computer: A Layperson's Almanac of Computer Lore, Wizardry, Personalities, Memorabilia, World Records, Mindblowers, and Tomfoolery* (New York: William Morrow and Company, 1983), 182, 183.

4. According to Rochester and Gance, the "first known computer" was Martin Zacharias Dase (1824–61). Dase could correctly multiply two 100-digit numbers in his head. The first reference to a computer of the human variety, *computist*, was made in 1398, according to the *Oxford English Dictionary*.

5. Bernard Lacroute, "Computing: The Fourth Generation," *SunTechnology*, Spring 1988, p. 9.

6. Ibid.

7. Ibid.

8. For years, Ted Hoff of the Intel corporation was credited with having invented the microprocessor in the period 1969–71. But in 1990 the U.S. Patent Office credited an obscure engineer, Gilbert Hyatt, with its creation in 1968. (Richard Behar and Patrick E. Cole, "Who Invented Microprocessors?" *Time*, September 10, 1990, p. 62).

9. An operating system created at AT&T's Bell Laboratories.

10. Lacroute, "Computing," 10.

11. Probably a wise idea, since *Modern Data* sounds like some sort of consumer magazine along the lines of *Modern Bride*.

12. S. Henry Sacks, "So What Am I Doing Here?" *SunExpert*, March 1990, p. 10.

13. None of these dates are fixed, and overlap occurred between generations.

14. According to the Random House unabridged dictionary, the term *e-mail* was coined between 1975 and 1980.

Chapter 3

1. Charles C. Smith, "Spreading the Words," *TWA Ambassador*, November 1983, p. 110. Smith's article examined technobabble's journey from the industry to mainstream dictionaries. The article focused on two Webster's dictionaries, the *Third New International* and the *Ninth New Collegiate*, and their criteria for admitting technobabble to their pages.

2. A joke floating around the computer industry: What's the difference between a computer salesman and a car salesman? The car salesman knows when he's lying.

3. John Bear, *Computer Wimp* (Berkeley, California: Ten Speed Press, 1983), 48. This book contains one of the earliest recorded uses of the word *technobabble*.

4. For example, the November 1990 issue of *USAir Magazine*, in a section called "Execatech," ran an article entitled "Programs That Work." The author, Robert Bixby, an associate editor at *Compute* magazine, even included a glossary of terms such as *80386, autotrace, digitizing, megabytes,* and *PIM* (personal information management [software]). The definitions themselves included such well-worn terms as *slots, ASCII, bit map,* and *operating system* (p. 38).

5. Everett Rogers and Judith Larsen, *Silicon Valley Fever* (New York: Basic Books, 1984), 107.

6. The heading above Zilber's commentary was "Say the Secret Word," *MacUser,* November 1990, p. 28.

7. John Flinn, "Does User-Friendly State of English Need Debugging?" *San Francisco Examiner,* November 25, 1984, p. A-1. This article included a tongue-in-cheek glossary called "The Best of Technobabble," which demonstrated how technobabble was infiltrating mainstream conversation and being used to sound important. It featured definitions such as these: **"debug:** To work problems out, as in 'Leonard, it's time we debugged our relationship.' **downtime:** People used to have coffee breaks. Now they 'have downtime.' It originally meant the period when a computer wasn't working. **input:** People used to throw in their 2 cents' worth. Now they 'give input.' **queue:** A list. Sounds computerish."

8. Dick Pothier, "In Pursuit of Clear Communication," *Philadelphia Inquirer,* December 4, 1983, p. B-13.

9. For example, the long-winded set of manuals (affectionately known as the "docubox" or "docucrate") that accompanies Sun Microsystems' workstations totals more than 2,000 pages of wildly diverse prose. No one attempts to—because no one has time to—standardize the style of the multifarious books in the set. Writers are left on their own, with the result that one manual may have a florid, metaphorical tone, whereas another may read like a scientific paper. Not infrequently, the information presented is misleading and/or inaccurate. Technophiles can take all this in stride, but clerks, marketers, assembly-line workers, and others may be lost when they encounter it.

10. Bob Davis, "Hundreds of Coleco's Adams Are Returned as Defective; Firm Blames User Manuals," *Wall Street Journal,* November 30, 1983, p. 4.

11. Copyright 1981 by William Horton.

12. Heavenly bodies have provided many product names in the computer industry. North Star, a now-defunct company, was initially called Kentucky Fried Computers, however.

13. Paul Freiberger and Michael Swaine, *Fire in the Valley* (Berkeley, California: Osborne/McGraw-Hill, 1984), passim.

14. Ibid.

15. Rory O'Connor, "Fitting Yourself to a Computer," *San Jose Mercury News,* August 5, 1990, p. F-1.

16. Smith, "Spreading the Words," 11.

17. Ibid.

18. Ibid.

19. Ad copy provided by Hill, Holiday, Connors, Cosmopulos Advertising. Used with permission.

20. Jeffrey S. Young, *Steve Jobs: The Journey Is the Reward* (Glenview, Illinois: Scott Foresman and Company, 1988), 235. The self-aggrandizing, grandstanding

ad not only implied that IBM had just entered the computer business, but it also accorded Apple credit for inventing the personal computer. Xerox has a more valid claim to the honor, as noted by Xerox vice president William Lowe, who once called Xerox PARC "the home of the personal computer." The ad also implies that Apple invented the term personal computer, which may be valid in a generic sense. The Random House unabridged dictionary places the term's origin in the 1975–80 time frame. By 1978, for example, the "hobbyist" magazine *Kilobaud* was replacing the term *microcomputer* with *personal computer*. Whether Jobs can claim credit for coining the term *personal computer* is open to dispute, but he is generally credited with coming up with *interpersonal computer*. Further, the ad manifests the early 1980s vogue term *computer literacy* and the industry's preoccupation with third-person-singular constructions—in this case, "the individual."

21. The term first cropped up in the early 1980s. An October 27, 1983, press release from the Computer and Business Equipment Manufacturers Association cautioned, "A new communications network that will integrate voice, text, pictures, and video poses significant challenges for the Federal Communications Commission. . . . The proposed offering, the Integrated Services Digital Network (ISDN), currently under development, is a breakthrough technique to integrate many forms of digital communication."

22. One company reportedly ran a TV ad that was laced with technobabble and printed "translations" on the bottom of the screen.

23. Phillip Godwin, "Modulators and Multiplexers, Take Note," reprinted from the *Washington Post* in the *San Francisco Chronicle*, March 27, 1983, p. 2 of "Punch" section.

24. Michael Miller, "High-Tech Hype Reaches New Heights," *Wall Street Journal*, January 12, 1989, p. B-1.

25. Ibid.

26. Ibid.

27. Ibid.

28. Ibid. Note the uppercase CASE. For more on this typographic technique, see chapter 6.

29. Steve Lopez, "Trying to Access the Local Dialect," *San Jose Mercury News*, April 1983 (exact date and page number unknown).

30. "'Windows' Software," *Peninsula Times Tribune*, May 29, 1990, p. C-5.

31. According to Jobs, in 1984 America had 25,000,000 "knowledge workers."

32. Copyright 1990, Jonathan E. Sisk, John Treankler, Dick Pick, and Zion, Pick Systems.

33. Mark Hall, "The Oral Tradition," *Datamation*, August 1, 1985, p. 127. In this essay, Hall explains how the oral tradition works in the computer industry. Although it operates outside official company channels, it has its own hierarchy and is similar to oral traditions that have preceded it—Renaissance artisans learning by word of mouth from masters, for example.

34. A 1983 book was aimed at just such people. *Computer Bluff* (Sunbury, Middlesex, England: Quartermaine House) by Stephen Castell explained that "to hold your own—in conversation or at work—from now on you are just going to have to know how to call the bluff of all those computocrats. This book helps you fight back."

35. William Briggs, "High-Tech Firms Need More Than Engineers," *San Jose Mercury News*, October 21, 1984, p. PC-1.

36. The definition of regular expression, according to Don Libes and Sandy Ressler, in *Life with UNIX* (Englewood Cliffs, New Jersey: Prentice Hall, 1989) is "a theoretical classification of certain patterns—it is not necessary to know the theory, but the end result is extremely powerful" (p. 194). And that's a powerfully vague statement, replete with the tautological "end result."

37. Bill Tuthill, "UNIX System Jargon," *UNIX World*, December 1985, p. 86.

38. Peter Birns, Patrick Brown, and John C.C. Muster, *UNIX for People* (Englewood Cliffs, New Jersey: Prentice Hall, 1985), 491.

39. Libes and Ressler, *Life with UNIX*, 149.

40. Paul S. Want, *An Introduction to Berkeley UNIX* (Belmont, California: Wadsworth Publishing, 1989), 114.

Chapter 4

1. Timothy Taylor, *San Jose Mercury News*, August 13, 1984, p. B-7. Taylor began by noting that the acronym OSIM could stand for Overseas Station for Industrial Mechanization, or Ocean Surveys for Intercontinental Mapping, or Oil Shipping Import Management. But in the computer industry, it meant Open Systems Interconnect Model (a set of seven protocols that measure the abilities of computer systems to intercommunicate). "OSIM is more than just another acronym," wrote Taylor. "It is a sort of grammar book for computers." Only six years old as of the writing of this book, Taylor's article is dated, outlining as it does the profound difficulties involved with getting disparate computer systems to communicate. Today, accomplishing this task is not simple, but it is considerably easier than it was in 1984, when proprietary-product thinking still ruled the industry. In a single sentence, "It's difficult to define standards for any industry that is changing and moving as quickly as the computer industry," Taylor provides a synopsis of this chapter.

2. IBM's open approach was inadvertent; the giant company eventually regretted its open approach to the PC and made its subsequent line of personal computers more difficult to clone.

3. And it followed the evolutionary pattern of technobabble delineated in the previous chapter.

4. Or GOD (from Jeffrey Armstrong's computer-humor book, *The Binary Bible of Saint $ilicon* [Santa Cruz, California: Any Key Press, 1987]).

5. A term coined in the mid-to-late 1950s, according to the Random House unabridged dictionary, s.v. "language."

6. For now, nearly all programming languages are based on English, but efforts such as the JLE (Japanese Language Environment) have translated interaction with UNIX into Japanese.

7. A California company called Natural Language, Inc., makes a product by the same name that is "a database tool that enables end-users to access and analyze relational database management systems in English."

8. Letter to *InfoWorld*, December 8, 1983. Another *InfoWorld* reader, who signed the letter "Confused," wrote, "How about a computer lingo dictionary— and if the definitions are different for different companies, please include the

differences for the major companies in each definition. Eventually they may settle for one!"

9. Jeremy Campbell, *Grammatical Man: Information, Entropy, Language, and Life* (New York: Simon and Schuster, 1982), passim.

10. In this case, FIFO is an adjectival acronymic abbreviation for "FIFO (first in, first out) memory." A buffer is a holding place for bits—a file to be printed, for example, while another printing job is in progress.

11. "LSI Logic Markets MIPS-Based MPU," *Electronic News*, October 22, 1990.

12. Writing to subscribers of the *Whole Earth Software Review* in August 1984, editor Art Kleiner indicated support's overuse by putting the word within quotation marks.

13. *Oxford English Dictionary*, 1971 compact edition, s.v. "interface."

14. Now out of vogue, apparently because of the gender-specific connotation, is the term *man-machine interface*.

15. Audrey Billet, "Measuring Graphics Performance," *SunTech Journal*, July/August 1990, pp. 36–49.

16. Freiberger and Swaine, *Fire in the Valley*, 276. Even this designation wasn't quite fixed. The operating system became known both as PC-DOS and MS [for Microsoft]-DOS.

17. This is the denotation favored by the Random House unabridged dictionary. CPM, minus the slash, also stands for "critical-path method" (for project scheduling) and "cost per thousand" (in the publishing business). In a letter to *InfoWorld*, Bruce Foster wrote, "CPM does not equal CP/M. CPM may not be older than CP/M—I don't know—but I heard of it before I heard of CP/M."

18. This sentence is also interesting because it shows the use of desktop as a noun meaning *desktop system*. In this instance, the "disk-crepancy" was at least departmental. In the case of a company called Optical Software Solutions, an optical-disc maker, two different press releases, released on the same day and emanating from the same person, both employed the acronym WORM in the first sentence. In the first release, WORM was identified as standing for "write once read mostly," with no punctuation. The second release indicated that WORM stood for "write-once, read many."

19. *Oxford English Dictionary*, 1971 compact edition, s.v. "disk."

Chapter 5

1. Howard Baldwin, "It's All in the Game," *UNIX World*, July 1990, p. 43. To prove her point, Goldberg concocted a "meaning" for the Place in the name of her company, ParcPlace, spun off from Xerox PARC (Palo Alto Research Center). When someone asked what Place stood for, she replied, without blinking an eyelash, "Programming Languages and Communication Environment."

2. Not strictly neologisms, such coinages could be called "neosemanticisms."

3. Guy Steele, et al., *The Hacker's Dictionary* (New York: Harper & Row, 1983), 33.

4. The *Oxford English Dictionary* cites *The Little Red Book Bristol*, 1408, as having the first use of this term, in the Middle French phrase "*la dusseyne de*

souliers applez Courseware" (a dozen shoes called Courseware). This phrase appears to have something to do with the meaning of *course* in the sense of *run*.

5. Published in the heart of Silicon Valley, in Sunnyvale. The May–June 1990 issue is listed as vol. 5, no. 3, indicating that the term *shareware* has been around for at least six years.

6. As of late 1990, the problem had become so pressing that some software companies formed the Software Business Practices Council to combat vaporware and other dubious practices.

7. Denise Caruso, "Coming Soon: Meaning of (Artificial) Life," *San Francisco Examiner*, February 11, 1990, p. D-18.

8. Press release dated May 15, 1990.

9. Caruso's weekly column once dealt exclusively with Silicon Valley happenings, but it has lately ranged wider to include general technological subjects. By its nature, the column often touches on technoargot.

10. In spite of their verb-to-noun predilections, computer people sometimes unwittingly have etymological precedent on their side, as in the terms *compute-intensive* and *compute engine*. Even though it is employed as a verb outside the computer industry, the word compute first entered the language in 1588 as a noun—a synonym for *computation*—half a century before it became a verb in 1638. It was not until 1646 that the noun *computer* came into use; it took on its current meaning in the twentieth century.

11. Anecdote recounted by former Harper & Row editor Michael Bessie at the 1984 Stanford Publishing Course.

12. David Roth, "William Safire, Eat Your Dictionary: Here Comes TechnoBabble," *Franson's Business Report on Technology*, 2, no. 4 (1984), 1.

13. April 4, 1986, installment of "Frank and Ernest" by cartoonist Bob Thaves.

14. Doug Clapp, "Clapp-Trapp," *InfoWorld*, October 31, 1983, p. 20. After the column appeared, an "anonymouse" reader from Milwaukee responded, "'Mouse' is becoming a verb! Ugh!"

15. "Keeping Your Versions Intact," *MacUser*, March 1991, p. 2.

16. *Architecture* is a favorite word among computer people. Brochures, press releases, and other pieces of collateral are replete with references to hardware, software, networking, processor, and other "architectures." *Webster's Ninth New Collegiate Dictionary* defines the noun *architecture* as "the art or science of building" and "a unifying or coherent form or structure."

17. He could not have been more wrong. The Lisa vanished after a short, unsuccessful life.

18. David Sheff, "New Ballgame for Sun's Scott McNealy," *Upside*, November–December 1989, p. 49

19. Particularly in a labyrinthine, process-laden operating system such as UNIX, which was developed by hard-core computer hackers. Many of its "verbs" look and sound like monosyllabic proto-Indo-European grunts: *sed, diff, grep*. Much hacker terminology consists largely of nonsense words that could well have come from the works of Lewis Carroll and J.R. Tolkien: *foo, frobnitz, gritch, gronk*. A couple of more processes as verbs: The *vi* (for visual, pronounced "vee-eye") editor in UNIX is "*troff* without the formatting commands." "We say 'vi it' to compose or edit a document," notes Ron Richardson, a UNIX maven. "Years ago I used to 'tar it' on DEC LSIaa/23 systems. *Tar* is a character editor not unlike

using vi in open mode (I think that's the terminology)." (*tar* is also an acronym standing for *tape archive*.) A stripped-down version of vi, developed by Nick Vituli and David Wise at Indiana University, was called VW because it was considered an "editor for everybody."

20. Eclipsed by other, more powerful and flexible operating systems, CP/M is for all practical purposes dead. Some diehard aficionados of the system live on, however, as does "CP/M-ese"—barely. By the turn of the century—if not sooner— CP/M-ese will be a dead language. Sic transit gloria—CP/M illustrates the volatile and often short-lived nature of computerese.

21. Three-letter acronyms and abbreviations are common in the industry—so common that an apt abbreviation, TLA (three-letter abbreviation), has been coined to describe them.

22. John Ciardi, *Good Words to You* (New York: Harper & Row, 1987), 2.

23. William and Mary Morris, *Dictionary of Word and Phrase Origins*, 2d ed. (New York: Harper & Row, 1988), 4.

24. Ibid. Also, according to *Tech Speak* by Edward Tenner (New York: Crown Publishing, 1986), the *Acronyms, Initialisms, and Abbreviations Dictionary* was first issued in 1960 (p. 3). More than thirty years ago—before acronyms really began to spread—this reference book had more than 12,000 entries.

25. Ibid. Probably people similar to the ones in the marketing department of a computer company who came up with SCAM for their Sales Customer Administration Module. Or the company that named itself Modular Advanced Design (or MAD for short) Intelligent Systems; "Craig Sweat joins MAD" read a May 4, 1990, press release from the company.

26. Ciardi, *Good Words*, 2.

27. It's almost a sure bet that an *I* in an acronym that is going to be reverse-engineered will come out either as integrated, interface, or interchange—as in the reverse-engineered Locally Integrated Software Architecture for Lisa.

28. This typographical twist may have been designed to avoid legal hassles with Sony, which makes a line of workstations called NEWS. Press material sometimes refers to Sony's "NEWS workstation," a redundancy, since the WS in the acronym stands for workstation. With this name, Sony may be proclaiming that its NEWS workstation is new, not JAWS (just another workstation, a disparaging term applied by vendors to their competitors' latest product announcements).

29. A RIP is a component of a laser printer, imagesetter, or typesetter that produces raster images.

30. OAR is also an IBM acronym meaning *operator authorization record*.

31. As with XDR—and others, such as NFS, NCR , NSE—is an acronym an acronym if you cannot reasonably pronounce it, or is it merely an abbreviation? Sometimes approximation is the *onym* of the pronunciation game, as in "scuzzy" for SCSI.

32. Wade D. Petersen, The *VMEbus Handbook* (Scottsdale, Arizona: VITA, 1989), passim.

33. A couple of companies that apparently want to differentiate their products from UNIX have employed nested acronyms and recursion to make their point. GNU is not only a homonym of *new*, but it also supposedly stands for "GNU's Not UNIX." In a similar vein, Mt. XINU is UNIXTM backward—a jab at AT&T, which is renowned for its fanatical insistence on designating UNIX's trademark status. XINU reportedly stands for "XINU Is Not UNIX."

34. William Bulkeley, "Technology" column, *Wall Street Journal*, date and page number unknown.

35. Jack Rosenthal, "Yo! Word Up!," reprinted from the *New York Times* in the *San Francisco Chronicle*, August 12, 1990.

36. James Gaskin, "A Classic Case of Acronymaphobia, Clearly Caused By the Complications Of Computer Burnout," *UNIX Today*, August 20, 1990, page number unknown. The camouflaged acronyms in Gaskin's anecdote include NCR (National Cash Register), AT&T (American Telephone and Telegraph), SNA (System Network Architecture), MAP (Manufacturing Automation Protocol), CAD (Computer-Aided [or Assisted] Design), CAM (Computer-Aided [or Assisted] Manufacturing), IBM (International Business Machines), TCP/IP (Transfer Control Protocol/Internet Protocol), ISDN (Integrated Services Digital Network), and ITT (International Telephone and Telegraph).

37. All Xerox had to do to come up with its name was capitalize the *x* in *xero*, a Greek root meaning "dry," and append an *x*.

38. Paul Somerson, "Box Scores," *MacUser*, October 1990, p. 26. The article concerned Apple's stormy relationship with its pseudoindependent software-development arm, Claris.

39. When I worked at Sun Microsystems as manager of the Editorial Services department, Sun lawyers routinely routed to me AT&T's threatening letters concerning the inviolability of UNIX.

40. Two chip companies overdid their efforts, though. Zilog and Intel tried unsuccessfully to trademark, respectively, the letters *Z* and *I*.

41. A marketing manager from a large computer company once caught herself in midsentence after uttering the word *productize*: "Did I just use that horrible computer word? Is that even a word?" In one of the daily Pentagon briefings during the U.S.-Iraq war, General Thomas Kelly talked about "optimizing" targets. A reporter said, "I have to ask you about some of your jargon. What do you mean by optimizing targets?" The general was clearly taken aback by the questioning of military/technical gobbledygook.

42. William Bulkeley, "An Electronic Critic Tells Today's Typist How to Write Better," *Wall Street Journal*, September 29, 1983, p. 23.

43. "How to Find a Name for Your Cadicon, Nulavak, or Quisicac," reprinted from the *Washington Post* in the December 21, 1986, *San Francisco Chronicle*; no byline, page number unknown.

44. Other examples of real, nondescript company names are Associative Design Technology, Digital Consulting Group, Government Technology Group, Mass. High Tech., and International Technology Group.

45. Robert Mamis, "Name-Calling," *Inc.*, July 1984, pp. 67–74.

46. "High-Tech Company Names May Have Been Selected by Whimsy or over Six-pack," reprinted from the *Orlando Sentinel* in the *Peninsula Times Tribune*, February 25, 1984, p. B-3; no byline.

47. Everett Rogers and Judith Larsen, *Silicon Valley Fever* (New York: Basic Books, 1984), 14.

48. The name of a Silicon Valley database company may derive from a French neoclassical painter, although the company's title is pronounced ING-res. If the company is named for Jean Auguste Dominique Ingres (pronounced AN-gre), its software is surely written in "La Source" code.

49. Not eponyms per se are such street names as Disk Drive and Semiconductor Drive, located in in Silicon Valley and other high-tech venues.

50. *Iconify* is a coinage of the late 1980s, coming several years on the heels of the first commercially available iconified computer, the Apple Macintosh.

Chapter 6

1. Entry for March 16 on a 1980 novelty calendar.

2. Roth, "William Safire, Eat Your Dictionary," 5.

3. Alan Rogers (see appendix D) called his TRS-80 computer "she."

4. *Life* magazine listed Von Neumann as one of "the 100 most important Americans of the 20th century." "His major breakthrough," *Life* noted, "was inventing internal programs—now called software" (Fall 1990 special issue, p. 24.)

5. Random House unabridged dictionary, s.v. "engineer."

6. *Oxford English Dictionary*, 1971 compact edition, s.v. "engineer."

7. According to the Random House unabridged dictionary (1987 edition), a supercomputer is "a very fast, powerful mainframe computer, used in advanced military and scientific applications." As integration advances, however, and computers get smaller and more powerful, this definition has already become inadequate.

8. Theodore Roszak, *The Cult of Information* (New York: Pantheon Books, 1986), 45.

9. Miniaturize is a common *-ize* word in the industry.

10. By personifying hardware and software entities, computerphiles have minimized use of the pronoun *it* in their vocabularies.

11. Richard Bolles, *What Color Is Your Parachute?* (Berkeley, California: Ten Speed Press, 1984), ix.

12. Ada, who studied math all her life, is noted for her work with Charles Babbage, inventor of the Difference and Analytical engines, nineteenth-century precursors to computers. According to the *Sun Observer*, Babbage asked her to translate a paper on the Analytical Engine written by an Italian engineer. In the process of translation, she took a few notes. "Ada, of course did not use our contemporary computer argot, but the notes read almost like one of the popular books of our day that describe the possibilities of electronic computers" ("Who Is Ada?" sidebar in September 1990 issue, p. 22). Did technobabble begin with a poet's daughter?

13. Then again, *Time* drops essential commas from restrictive appositives, as in "His wife Joan is an editor." Perhaps the Time Warner [Time-Warner?] combine is infested with polygamists.

14. This distressing example of ignorance was delivered in the form of an e-mail message from a computer-company training-course manager to a marketing writer: "In the hardware and course descriptions, I've found a couple of instances of 'it is' abbreviated it's instead of 'its.' Something to watch for!"

15. So it must have been a little embarrassing when MicroPro Corporation, maker of the popular WordStar (with the SpellStar checking program) sent a letter to an *InfoWorld* reader, in which the letter's writer wished the reader "continueed success." *InfoWorld* carried an ad from a company that produced

a word-processing program. The ad ran twice with the words "compramise" and "secratary" before someone at the agency spotted the gaffes and corrected them. Word-watcher Richard Lederer tells of a spelling checker that, of course, did not flag *graphite*, even though the writer meant *graffiti*.

16. Anonymous, "On the Uselessness of an Editor in the Presents of a Spell Checker," "borrowed" by Dana Curtis for "Silicon Valley Connection," December 1989, p. 7.

17. Bill King and Don Steiny, "Writer's Workbench: Automated Grammar?" *Unix World*, p. 58; issue unknown. Apparently King and Steiny, or their editors, did not use the product about which they raved, for one sentence reads, "Typical word processing systems are designed to be typing stations for the typist but rarely serve writer's or editor's needs."

18. William Bulkeley, "An Electronic Typist Tells Today's Typists How to Write Better," *Wall Street Journal,* September 29, 1983, p. 1.

19. Appeared in 1982; date and page number unknown.

20. Michael Shrage, "Are Computers Message Maimers?" *San Jose Mercury News*, August 13, 1990, p. D-4.

21. This example was provided by an *InfoWorld* reader who called the use of the future for no reason "beloved of engineers."

22. No, this is not another example of anthropomorphism, even though *lazar* means "a person afflicted with a repulsive disease; specifically, leper," according to *Webster's Ninth New Collegiate Dictionary.*

23. Thomas Moroney, a columnist for the *Middlesex* [Massachusetts] *News* put it more strongly: "There is a sad shortage of computer jokes. And the ones out there are just awful." ("In the High Tech World, Humor Does Not Compute," August 25, 1983.)

24. Karla Jennings, *The Devouring Fungus* (New York: W.W. Norton & Company, 1990), 99, 100.

25. Well into the 1990s, many humorists with no apparent understanding of the current state of computing still portray the machines as paper-devouring behemoths—an increasingly anachronistic choice as more and more of the general populace becomes "computer literate."

26. During an HBO comedy show, Carlin took a poke at technobabble. "No, we will not interface tonight . . . we will not network."

27. Name of a presentation at the 37th annual International Technical Communication Conference held in May 1990, sponsored by the Society of Technical Communicators, a group dedicated to fostering effective communication in high tech. "For the purposes of our audience," wrote one of the authors (three tech writers at IBM) of "Demythifying Technobabble: A Play in Three Acts," "we identified 'technobabble' as jargon or gobbledygook we often encounter in technical jobs. Technobabble basically hides what a product or person really does; it inhibits communication."

Chapter 7

1. Here, Ray, a person, is trying to make (a computer command, by the way) a program named Julie. In the film *Demon Seed,* on the other hand, a computer is trying to make a woman named Julie.

2. Patty Bell and Doug Myrland, *Silicon Valley Guy Handbook* (New York: Avon Books, 1983), passim.

3. Sherry Turkle, *The Second Self* (New York: Simon and Schuster, 1984), 202.

4. Steven Levy, *Hackers: Heroes of the Computer Revolution* (Garden City, New York: Anchor Press, 1984).

5. Based on my presentation, "Sex, Drugs, and Computers," at the West Coast Computer Faire, San Francisco, 1985.

6. Frank Hayes, "Virtual Reality," *UNIX World*, August 1990, p. 58.

7. Rory O'Connor, "Tripping into 'Virtual Reality,'" *San Jose Mercury News*, October 8, 1990, p. A-7.

8. With words such as *dildonics* in its vocabulary, virtual reality might also be termed "venereal reality."

9. Paul Panish and Anna Belle Panish, *Mother Goose Your Computer: A Grownup's Garden of Silicon Satire* (Berkeley, California: Sybex, 1984).

10. Guy Kawasaki, *The Macintosh Way* (Glenview, Illinois: Scott, Foresman and Company, 1990), passim. SUM stands for Symantec Utilities for Macintosh.

11. Once the graphics improved, commercial sex games, such as MacPlaymate, began to appear. Some of the games were clandestine programming efforts, circulated among friends.

12. Not surprising—readers of computer publications are overwhelmingly male.

13. Wellington Long, "Commodore Turns to Nudes," *Advertising Age*, September 24, 1984, p. 66.

14. Charlene Canape, "Computer Books Grow, Bit by Bit," *Magazine*, issue unknown, p. M-11.

15. Gerald Youngblood, "Give Me That Old Time Religion," *Workstation News*, December 1990, p. 38.

16. In 1982, Harry Henderson of the Graduate Theological Union Library in Berkeley, California, ran across a print of Christ overseeing His flocks (children and animals) from Victoria-era religious art inscribed "Behold, I Send You Forth." He was kind enough to let me borrow the print, and in a note he included with it, Henderson wrote: "[The print] suggests that my favorite computer language may have a sanction even higher than that awarded to Ada by the DoD."

17. It might be said that some people get joy from their religion; UNIX devotees get their religion from Joy.

18. Sun Microsystems junkmail.

19. Saint $ilicon is not the only one preaching the computer gospel. Arthur Naiman, author of a "Goy's Guide to Yiddish," is the editor of the self-published, nearly 800-page *Macintosh Bible*. Doug Clapp is the author of *The NeXT Bible*, a reference book for users of computers from Apple cofounder Steve Jobs's current company. The "Reading List" in the computer section of the June 3, 1990, *San Jose Mercury News* led off with a capsule review of *The Printer Bible* by Scott Foerster (Que Books). "'Printer Bible' can be a savior," read the headline.

20. Jeffrey Armstrong, *The Binary Bible of Saint $ilicon* (Santa Cruz, California: Any Key Press, 1987).

21. Kawasaki, *The Macintosh Way*, passim. Kawasaki reveals that the term *software evangelism* was coined by Mike Murray of Apple's Macintosh division. "It meant using fervor and zeal (but never money) to convince software developers to create products for a computer with no installed base."

22. A play on DMA (direct memory access).

23. Steve Ditlea, ed., *Digital Deli* (New York: Workman Publishing, 1984), 92, 93.

24. Stefan Arngrim and Warren Zevon, 1989, Dark Victory Twins (BMI)/Zevon Music, Inc. (BMI).

25. The Random House unabridged dictionary, in definition number 4, defines *icon* as "a picture or symbol that appears on a monitor and is used to represent a command, as a file drawer to represent filing." A UNIX programmer prone to visual puns added to the operating system an icon called "eyecon." It consists of a pair of eyes that follow the mouse-manipulated cursor around the screen.

26. The Random House unabridged dictionary, s.v. "icon."

27. William Safire, "I Like Icon," reprinted from the *New York Times* in the February 11, 1990, *San Francisco Chronicle*, page number unknown.

28. The most popular semioticist of our time, Umberto Eco, employed a computer as a mystery-solving device in his novel *Foucault's Pendulum*. Ironically, Eco's computer displayed only alphanumeric commands—no icons.

29. Safire, "I Like Icons."

30. *Visix* stands for Visible, or Visualized, UNIX.

31. Steve Hamm, et al., "Walking on Water," *San Jose Mercury News*, September 19, 1990, p. D-1.

32. NB: *who*, not *which*.

33. Dennis Hayes, *Behind the Silicon Curtain* (Boston: South End Press, 1989), 12.

34. Sharon Begley, Karen Springen, Susan Katz, May Hager, and Elizabeth Jones, "Memory," *Newsweek*, September 29, 1986, p. 48.

35. According to *Digital Deli*, p. 25, when Dijkstra married in Amsterdam in 1957, he noted his profession on the marriage license as "programmer." City authorities claimed no such job existed and changed the entry to "theoretical physicist." This was probably the first use of the term *programmer* in a computer context.

36. Edsger Dijkstra, "On the Cruelty of Really Teaching Computing Science," *Communications of the ACM*, December 1989, pp. 1402, 1403.

37. Turkle, *The Second Self*, 17.

38. Denise Caruso, "The Brain Is Called 'The Competition,'" *San Francisco Examiner*, February 18, 1990, p. D-14.

39. The Random House unabridged dictionary, s.v. "cycle."

40. Gassée made this statement at a 1987 launch party for his book *The Third Apple* (New York: Harcourt Brace Jovanovich).

41. This example comes from computer salesman Dave Buchanan, who says, "The real interesting examples [of mechanistic] thinking come from operating-system types, who regard their thought processes as being similar to a multitasking operating system."

42. Weizenbaum, *Computer Power and Human Reason*, passim.

43. According to *The Handbook of Computers and Computing* (New York: Van Nostrand Reinhold, 1984), edited by Arthur Seidman and Ivan Flores, "Not only are the traditional computer-based systems being reduced in price and therefore invading new markets, but also new systems which include the computer as a component are becoming feasible. These latter systems, termed *embedded*

computer systems, include functions which previously existed only as hardware now provided as software."

44. According to *The Hacker's Dictionary*, "to mung" means to destroy. Also, "This word is said to be a recursive acronym: Mung Until No Good."

Chapter 8

1. Adding to the folkloric gestalt of this film, the *Realist* magazine once claimed that its director, Stanley Kubrick, was so enamored of *Citizen Kane* that he had the word *Rosebud* inscribed on the monolith that appears in *2001*.

2. Rochester and Gantz, *The Naked Computer: A Layperson's Almanac of Computer Lore, Wizardry, Personalities, Memorabilia, World Records, Mindblowers, and Tomfoolery*; Steve Ditlea, ed., *Digital Deli: The Comprehensive, User-Lovable Menu of Computer Lore, Culture, Lifestyles and Fancy* (New York: Workman Publishing, 1984); Karla Jennings, *The Devouring Fungus: Tales of the Computer Age* (New York: W.W. Norton & Company, 1990).

3. Then again, perhaps e. robert wallach was also a UNIX aficionado. Remember him? He was the crony of Edwin Meese who was indicted in the Wedtech scandal. Maybe he was trying to get Wedtech to adopt UNIX so the Air Force would be more inclined to accept the company's bids.

4. Libes and Ressler, *Life with UNIX*, 150.

5. Bill Tuthill, "UNIX System Jargon," *UNIX World*, December 1985, p. 86.

6. Ibid.

7. According to Jennings in *The Devouring Fungus*, Multics stands for Multiplexed Information and Computing Service; she also indicates that someone at Bell Labs suggested calling UNIX Eunix—to no avail.

8. Tuthill, "UNIX System Jargon," 86.

9. John Barry, "What's in a Code Name," *A+*, January 1987, p. 45.

10. Letter to the author, May 19, 1983.

11. Wozniak was working for the giant computer and instrumentation company Hewlett-Packard at the time. His superiors viewed his design for a single-board small computer as worthless and gave him the rights to it. That "worthless" design became the basis for the Apple I computer, which launched a multibillion-dollar business.

12. Several years later, Sun Microsystems was using Phoenix as a code name for one of its products.

13. Barry, "What's in a Code Name," 45.

14. Raskin, letter to author.

15. The Random House unabridged dictionary, *Webster's Ninth New Collegiate Dictionary*, *The Hacker's Dictionary*, *Good Words to You*, and *Dictionary of Word and Phrase Origins*.

16. Webster's *Ninth New Collegiate Dictionary* and the Random House unabridged dictionary at least give credence to these suggested dates, with the former dictionary putting the first use in 1962 and the latter putting it more broadly in the period 1960–65.

17. NB: "was noticed" and "was seen" instead of "I noticed" and "I saw." Engineers love that passive voice.

18. This story seems to be as tall as Kravitz's unit.

19. Author Jeffrey Young confirms this assertion in *Steve Jobs: The Journey Is the Reward* (p. 155). So, obliquely, does Jef Raskin, a one-time Apple engineering manager, who wrote in a letter, "As you suggest, Apple Computer's Lisa was named by Jobs for someone he knew."

20. Dr. Seuss, *If I Ran the Zoo* (New York: Random House, 1950), no page numbers.

21. Perhaps in this stance the nerd is uttering the word *nerts* (1930–35), a variation on *nuts* and an expression of defiance, according to the Random House unabridged dictionary.

22. The article's title, "Revenge of the Nerds," later became the basis for a series of low-budget films.

23. The original meaning of *geek*, dating from the early twentieth century, according to the Random House unabridged dictionary, is a carnival performer who entertains by biting the heads off live chickens or other animals. (The Random House unabridged dictionary suggests that the term is a variant of the Scottish *geck*, fool.) By the latter part of the century, the word had all but become synonymous with *nerd*. A couple of other monosyllabic synonyms for *nerd* are *dweeb* and *wonk*. The origin of the former term is in doubt; the latter possibly derives from British slang *wonky*, meaning unreliable, stupid, boring, unattractive. The Random House unabridged dictionary, from which the foregoing definitions come, places the origin of *wonk* in—no real surprise—the period 1960–65. In American slang, a wonk is a "midshipman," whereas in Australian slang, it is a "white person" or a "homosexual."

24. Mary Corey, "Rise of the Neonerd," reprinted from the *Baltimore Sun* in the June 25, 1989, *San Francisco Chronicle*, "Punch" section, p. 3.

25. Ibid.

26. Sun Microsystems' RISC effort was called SPARC, and the company named a large cafeteria in one of its buildings Sparcy's. When the company acquired a large building and remodeled it, the new floor plans called for a cafeteria. Inspired, apparently, by Sparcy's, the cafeteria-naming committee decided to call the new eatery Riscy's, a dubious moniker because of the word's double-entendre. The sign painters took a look at their assignment and decided they had caught a typo. Without bothering to query Sun, they took it upon themselves to correct the error. The freshly painted signs went up over the entrances to the cafeteria: Risky's. And there they stayed for about a month, until Sun had the painters fix them, prompting endless jokes in the interim about ptomaine and salmonella.

27. From an interview with Patterson by the author. In an extracomputer sense, CISC stands for a New York organization called the Communications Industry Skills Center (Steve Radlauer, "Mau-Mauing the Moviemakers," *Spy*, October 1990, p. 61).

28. This is the computer industry, after all, home of acronymophilia, and it turns out that SPIM is an industry acronym of ParcPlace, itself an acronym-inspired name. SPIM stands for Small Portable Imaging Model, and the Parc in ParcPlace derives from Xerox PARC (Palo Alto Research Center), where the founder of ParcPlace once worked.

29. Andrew Ould, ed., "Overheard," *UNIX World*, July 1990, p. 18.

Chapter 9

1. Another computer magazine, *MacUser*, prepared a Q&A column, in which the author wrote, "A phone line is a phone line, and the hardware you mention is perfectly happy wherever it can find a dial tone."

2. Lewis Beale, "Technological Advances Bring a Brave, Rude World," *San Jose Mercury News*, October 2, 1990, p. C-1.

3. Michael Shrage, "It's Them—Those People with Voice Mail," reprinted from the *Los Angeles Times* in the October 22, 1990, *San Jose Mercury News*, p. C-4.

4. L.M. Boyd, "Grab Bag," *San Francisco Chronicle*, September 30, 1990, "Punch" section, p. 5.

5. Songwriter Warren Zevon noted the anthropomorphic implications of the term in his composition "Networking," a parody, among other things, of technobabble: "Networking, I'm user friendly; networking, I install with ease."

6. This statement is based on the optimistic assumption that the documentation is comprehensible to the user.

7. Steele et al., *The Hacker's Dictionary*, 128, 129.

8. This complaint could be directed at a great deal of technobabble. What, for example, is a "cross-development solution," or a "support package for next-generation industry standards"?

9. Paul Heckel, *The Elements of Friendly Software Design* (New York: Warner Books, 1984), xi.

10. "Bundled" software is application or utility software that is included in the price of a computer. The nominal use of *bundle* here is uncommon.

11. Barbara Bailey, "Home Design Gets User-Friendly," *San Francisco Examiner*, August 26, 1990, p. E-14. According to the article, a "user-friendly home" is one that is "designed not according to tradition, but for the way the people in it really live."

12. Kevin Cowherd, "In His Own Way, a Most Computer-Friendly User," reprinted from the *Baltimore Evening Sun* in the *San Jose Mercury News*, August 15, 1990, p. C-8. Incidentally, *get* and *go* are programming-language commands.

13. Denise Caruso, "Turning Point: Productivity and Computers," *San Francisco Examiner*, May 13, 1990, p. D-14.

14. In the spring of 1990, Sun apparently was serious about using this phrase as the company's tag line. By the summer of that year, the company had changed its corporate mind and instead opted for the anthropomechanistic line "Computers that network people."

15. Lee Gomes, "A New Project for Mac Team," *San Jose Mercury News*, July 12, 1990, p. F-1.

16. John Hillkirk, "New Poor: Computer Illiterates," *USA Today*, date unknown.

17. Ernest Baxter, "Computer Literacy: Is It Worth the Effort?" *Personal Software*, February 1984, pp. 37, 39.

18. Kenneth Sherman, "'Computer Literacy' and Test Patterns," *Wall Street Journal*, date and page number unknown.

19. Fall 1984.

20. Published by Dell.

21. Arthur Luehrmann and Herbert Peckham, *Computer Literacy Survival Kit* (New York: McGraw-Hill, 1984).

22. "Eradicating the Scourge of Computer Illiteracy," *World Press Review*, October 1983, p. 34.

23. Donald Lichty, "Computer Literacy: Where to Begin," *Perspectives*, September 1983, p. 10.

24. Barbara Wallraff, "The Literate Computer," *Atlantic Monthly*, January 1988, pp. 64–71.

25. Denise Caruso, "Empowerment's Mixed Blessing," *Media Letter*, July 1990, p. 1.

26. Leonard Soltzberg, *Sing a Song of Software* (Los Altos: California: William Kaufmann, Inc., 1984), passim.

27. According to the Random House unabridged dictionary, this term was coined in the early 1970s.

28. In Aldous Huxley's *Brave New World*, pharmacologically and psychologically sedated and technologically tyrannized residents of a future London attend movies called "the feelies." Not only can they see what goes on on the screen, but they can also feel and sense the action.

Chapter 10

1. Takemochi Ishi, "Building Techno-Utopia," *San Francisco Examiner*, May 15, 1990.

2. Steve Lopez, "Brave New Words," *PC*, August 1983, p. 419.

3. Electrically alterable ROMs.

4. A couple of examples are the terms *launch* and *deploy*, employed in discussions of starting up systems or putting applications onto a screen.

5. Shaw observed that England and America are two countries separated by a common language.

6. "Consortium Plans Code to Cover All Languages," reprinted from the *New York Times* in the *San Jose Mercury News*, February 20, 1991, p. E-1.

7. At least one company has worked this buzzword into its name. In 1986 a company called CAD/CAM Technologies formed in Waltham, Massachusetts. Later in the decade, the name had changed to Workgroup Technologies. Expect to see more organizations with this word in their names. Amazingly, the entire industry seems to have settled on the closed-up spelling of the word. Although you will encounter *workstation*, *work station*, and *work-station*, you will probably find only *workgroup*.

8. John Markoff, "Research Aims for One User, Many Computers," reprinted from the *New York Times* in the *San Jose Mercury News*, November 18, 1990, p. F-6.

9. John Verity, "Rethinking the Computer," *BusinessWeek*, November 26, 1990, pp. 116, 117.

10. From a PARC press release.

11. From a cartoon in the January 7, 1991, *San Jose Mercury News*.

12. Edward Feigenbaum and Julian Feldman, eds., *Computers and Thought* (New York: McGraw-Hill, 1963).

13. Schank wrote a book with this title (Reading, Massachusetts: Addison-Wesley, 1984).

14. Even *expert system* is a misnomer, according to *InfoWorld*—at least in the business world. "Although artificial intelligence projects are often generically referred to as 'expert systems,'" begins a "Perspectives" piece in the October 1, 1990, issue, "that is a misnomer. In actuality, they are more often *knowledge-based* systems. . . . Both systems are based on 'rules'—pieces of information containing knowledge about how to address a particular business problem. . . . But whereas expert systems are based on knowledge acquired from one human or expert [the implication being that there are experts of a nonhuman kind], a knowledge-based system offers a much broader spectrum of rules." The perspective concludes with what may be the forever insurmountable obstacle to realization of computer "intelligence": "AI technology will not be magic, just good solid programming and design work."

15. Denise Caruso, "Virtual Reality, Get Real," *Media Letter*, August 1990, pp. 1, 2.

16. Denise Caruso, "A New Art Form Comes of Age," *San Francisco Examiner*, April 8, 1990, page D-14.

17. Note the misplaced modifier. Technobabble is replete with this kind of construction, in which humans are seemingly interchangeable with hardware and software. This particular phrase evokes the image in a *Realist* magazine poster of the 1960s: a portly Jehovah sitting atop a prostrate Uncle Sam and bearing the legend "One Nation Under God."

18. For example, regarding the former assertion, UNIX guru Bill Joy has referred to virtual reality as "the drugs of the 90s," and the media have picked up on the theme, as in this headline from the *San Jose Mercury News*: "Tripping into 'Virtual Reality.'"

19. Caruso, *Media Letter*, 1.

20. Denise Caruso, "News from the Virtual World," *San Francisco Examiner*, mid-1990, exact date unknown.

21. Based on material provided by Freiberger. For more on the history and implications of fuzzy logic, see the upcoming book on the subject by Freiberger and Dan McNeil, due from Summit Books in 1992.

22. Denise Caruso, "Coming Soon: Meaning of (Artificial) Life," *San Francisco Examiner*, February 11, 1990, p. D-18.

23. Nancy Shulins, "Is It Alive? Not Yet, But . . . ," *San Francisco Examiner*, December 23, 1990, p. D-13.

24. Ibid.

25. Jim Bartimo, "Virus Found in Commercial Software," *San Jose Mercury News*, March 15, 1988, p. 1.

26. Associated Press, *Peninsula Times Tribune*, December 19, 1989, p. F-4.

27. Jonathan Littman, "The Shockwave Rider," *San Francisco Chronicle*, "This World," July 8, 1990, p. 7.

28. Associated Press report in *Peninsula Times Tribune*, mid-1990, exact date unknown.

29. Pamela Kane, *V.I.R.U.S. Protection: Vital Information Resources under Siege* (New York: Bantam, 1989).

30. Caruso, "Coming Soon," D-18.

31. As noted in Frank Rose, "Wired to God," *Vanity Fair*, August 1984, p. 104. Also, see appendix D.

32. Term used in a headline for a newspaper article.

33. P.J. O'Rourke, "Another Round at Club Scud," reprinted from *Rolling Stone* in the *San Francisco Chronicle*, "Punch" section, February 24, 1991, p. 3.

34. In what is considered to be the first "cyberpunk" SF novel, *Neuromancer*, author William Gibson defines cyberspace as "A consensual hallucination experienced daily by billions of legitimate operators, in every nation, by children being taught mathematical concepts. A graphic representation of data abstracted from the banks of every computer in the human system. Unthinkable complexity. Lines of light ranged in the nonspace of the mind, clusters and constellations of data. Like city lights, receding."

35. Richard Sheinen, "Crossover Dreams," *San Jose Mercury News*, August 24, 1990, pp. C-1, C-2.

36. David Lehman, "You Are What You Read," *Newsweek*, January 12, 1987, p. 67.

37. Gordon Campbell, quoted in "Official Says 'Disposable' Computers on Horizon," *IDG/P Daily News*, December 6, 1990, p. 5.

38. "Sharp Exec Foresees 1-Pound, Color LCD Palmtop Computer," *IDG/P Daily News*, October 24, 1990, p. 3.

39. Don Johnson, "Much Learned from Japan's Fifth-Generation Project," *Sun Observer*, September 1990, p. 48.

40. Robert Boyd, "Machines Starting to See, Hear, Understand," *San Jose Mercury News*, September 30, 1990, p. E-8.

41. Note the use of an English acronym to describe a Japanese phenomenon. In spite of Japanese ascendance over the last chronological generation or so in computer technology, the language of the latter-day global village will continue to be American, on which any possible universal techno–lingua franca of the future will be based.

42. Ishi, "Building Techno-Utopia," A-21.

43. Denise Caruso, "Global Networks the Next Big 'It,'" *San Francisco Examiner*, May 16, 1990, p. E-18.

44. John Markoff, "Virtual Death, Death, and Virtual Funeral," reprinted in the *San Francisco Chronicle*, "Punch" section, September 9, 1990, p. 2. If "virtual death" is possible, so is "virtual life." With the proliferation of the word *virtual* in technobabble, the French are someday likely to shrug their shoulders at certain technical glitches and say, "C'est la vie virtuelle."

45. Sue Chastain, "So You Can't Understand Your Teen? That's the Idea," *San Jose Mercury News*, August 26, 1990, p. L-8.

Appendix A

1. Those are the IBM PC specialists; Soviet UNIX mavens speak SVID (System V Interface Definition) as well as *do svidaniya*. The reporter also noted that "as more people master the use of user-friendly computers, fewer people are interested in studying computer science."

2. Fabrizio Franzi, "Micro English: A New Language," in *Digital Deli*, Steve Ditlea, ed. (New York: Workman Publishing, 1984), 262.

3. David Gelman, "Le Counterattack," *Newsweek*, March 7, 1983, p. 47.

4. *Collins Robert French-English, English-French Dictionary* (London: Collins Publishers, 1984). *The International Microcomputer Dictionary* (Berkeley, California: Sybex Books, 1981) gives *mémoire-tampon* for *buffer*.

5. Robert Mamis, "Name Calling," *Inc.*, July 1984, p. 69.

6. Franzi, "Micro English," 262.

7. Enno von Lowenstern, "English Über Alles," *New York Times*, November 9, 1990, page number unknown.

Appendix C

1. DEC's minicomputer operating system.

2. Appearances to the contrary, not self-actualization, but rather "the period in which personal computers and workstations empowered individuals to work electronically on their personal applications." Xerox called this period (the 1970s and 1980s) the "second generation" of computing, the first being the 1960s and 1970s, which was data processing. The third, of course, will be "interpersonal." This pattern of generations reflects those outlined in chapter 2.

Appendix D

1. Quoted in Frank Rose, "Wired to God," *Vanity Fair*, August 1984, p. 104. A "sysop" is a system operator, someone who monitors and maintains a BBS (bulletin-board system).

2. A popular anticomputer slogan of the 1960s was "I am a human being. Do not bend, fold, spindle, or mutilate," a reference to the warnings found on computer cards. In 1967 the folk-rock group Jefferson Airplane sang sardonically, "Data control to IBM, science is mankind's brother." A year later, the alienated narrator of the Rolling Stones' "2000 Man" lamented, "Though my wife still respects me, I really misuse her, 'cause I'm having an affair with a random computer."

3. Charles Smith, "Spreading the Words," *TWA Ambassador*, November 1983, p. 111.

4. *Homebrew* means either a computer built from scratch (noun) or to build such a computer (verb); although popular from the mid-1970s to the mid-1980s, the term is now out of vogue.

5. Young, *The Journey Is the Reward*.

6. Weizenbaum, *Computer Power and Human Reason*, 2–7.

7. Psychobabble and technobabble share some of the same terms, although the implications may be different. Both stress the need for "connections," for example, as in "Millions of us do have an awareness that all life is interconnected . . . that starts to shift the whole collective mind-set." The quote comes from Carolyn Anderson, director of the Marin County–based Global Family and one of the moving forces behind the so-called Harmonic Convergence of 1987. This event was the topic of much electronic discussion among the "alternative lifestyles" e-mail group at Sun Microsystems.

8. Richard Seltzer, "What's the Word for . . . ? *Harper's*, February 1990, p. 48.

9. The panel on the back of a computer that reveals ports and connections is called the backplane.

10. When the technobabble-titled *Intelligence Machines Journal* metamorphosed into generic-sounding *InfoWorld* in late 1979, the editorial staff consisted of three self-styled "neopagans."

11. Rose, "Wired to God," passim.

12. Token ring is a type of network "topology."

13. Teresa Carpenter, "How I Found God through My TRS-80 Computer," *Village Voice*, October 19, 1982, pp. 21, 22.

Glossary

This glossary lists, defines, and comments on some of the terms in the lexicon of technobabble that have not been covered elsewhere in this book and expands on a few that have. My list is not intended to be comprehensive. For much more on hacker terminology, consult The Hacker's Dictionary. *Scores of computer-industry dictionaries are also available. Words set in* SMALL CAPS *are defined elsewhere in the Glossary.*

access (n., v.) Like numerous computer terms, this one started lexical life as a noun but is now more frequently seen as a verb, as in "Can you access that code?" Also employed anthropomorphically—for example, "He tried to access her, but she turned him down."

algorithm (n.) A set of rules for solving a problem in a finite number of steps. Coined in the late nineteenth century as a variant of *algorism,* the art of computation using Arabic numerals. The early computer language ALGOL is putatively an acronym for Algorithmic Language, but given the difficulty of some algorithms, it may derive from the Greek *algos,* pain.

architecture (n.) A fundamental design. Spectrum, for example, is a hardware architecture on which to build RISC microprocessors; the operating system that runs on the system has a software architecture. Sometimes used as a highfalutin substitute for *design* or *product.* Overused in the computer industry.

baud (n.) A measure of data communication that has come to be synonymous with the number of BITS per second (bps) that can be transmitted; for example, 1,200 baud is equivalent to 1,200 bps. The term, which entered the language in the early 1920s, was named after

French inventor J.E. Baudot and originally referred to the communication of telegraphic pulses. Dictionaries give *baud* as a synonym for BIT, but the latter word was not coined until twenty years after the former. A person with a low "baud rate" is laid back or lethargic.

benchmark (n.) A measurement, usually of the speed at which a computer completes a particular operation, to evaluate performance. One of the first such measurements was the "whetstone"; in strange examples of wordplay, later benchmarks were called "dhrystone" and "khornerstone."

binary (adj., n.) Having two components. Computers are binary devices whose circuits are either off (0) or on (1). Binary arithmetic uses 1s and 0s to count—0101, for example, is a 4-BIT binary representation of 5. Binary code is the lowest level of computer programming, consisting of binary numbers (cf. SOURCE). The binary code for a program is called its "binaries."

bit (n.) A portmanteau word standing for *bi*nary digi*t*. As noted above, 0101 is a 4-bit number, 1010 1010 is an 8-bit number, etc. Eight bits equals a BYTE, whereas 4 bits constitutes a nybble, or nibble. A 32-bit processor can deal with 32 bits at a time. Bit is a combining word that spawned some not-so-clever puns, but it may derive from monetary slang. Etymologist John Ciardi noted that Colonial America lacked an official mint and was always short of small coins, so coins of many nations were accepted in the making of change. The most common of these coins was the Spanish piece of eight, which was similar to the later dollar and named as it was because a large Arabic 8 was stamped on it. The 8 meant the coin was worth eight Spanish *reals*, with a *real* being valued at about 12 1/2 cents. Because an entire piece of eight was quite valuable, it was often chopped into halves and quarters called "bits." In about 1798, the Philadelphia mint started to issue silver quarters and half dollars, which were called by their already established monikers: two bits and four bits. By extension, a bit was 12 1/2 cents and 6 bits was 75 cents.

boot (v., adj.) To start a computer running by activating operating-system or other software. Derived from *bootstrap*, to help oneself without the aid of others.

bootleg (v., adj.) To copy software illegally; illegally copied software. Those who engage in the illegal reproduction of software are called bootleggers or software pirates.

box (n.) The hardware component of a WORKSTATION, including the boards, DISK, and enclosure. One company's box is essentially indistinguishable from another's; what differentiates computers is the software they can run. As a result, the word has taken on a slightly disparaging tone, unless the product in question is a "hot box." Some shallow, square computer enclosures are called "pizza boxes." Auxiliary disk and tape drives are sometimes called "lunchboxes," or "shoeboxes," perhaps because of their small FOOTPRINTS.

bulletin board (n. phrase) An information service on which subscribers can electronically post notices and other information to each other. Similar to E-MAIL.

bus (n.) A circuit that connects the computer with other devices, or PERIPHERALS, such as printers and disk drives. Some examples of buses are VMEbus, NuBus, and SBus. Various bus specifications are in use, including Microchannel, TurboChannel, EISA, SBus, ATbus, NuBus, and VMEbus. They come in various sizes, or "form factors," with arcane designations such as 6U and 9U. One type, which fits into a slot and hovers above a larger bus, is called a "mezzanine bus." Although the plural of *bus* shows up as both *buses* and *busses,* the former is preferable, because the latter also means *kisses,* which may be appropriate, given that a bus is one of numerous types of interface.

button (n.) A stylized representation of a button on a computer screen that you can "push" by *clicking* on it with the MOUSE *pointer.*

byte (n.) Eight BITS. By combination with Greek roots, a kilobyte is a thousand bytes, a megabyte is a million, a gigabyte is a billion, and a terabyte is a trillion. And, according to *UNIX World* magazine, a petabyte is 1-to-the-power-of-52 bytes.

cache (n., adj.) A type of memory that is "stashed away from" main memory and used as needed. From the French verb *cacher,* to hide. A company called Dilog (short for Distributed Logic) makes a disk drive that serves as a front end to larger disks; this product is called the CACHEbox.

card (n.) A circuit board that plugs into a slot of a computer. The board may accomplish graphics, audio, or other functions. In earlier days, a card was a form of input, a piece of stiff paper punched with patterns of holes.

chip (n.) An integrated circuit; so called because it is composed mainly of a small fragment of SILICON. The source of many bad puns, such as "fission chips," components for nuclear reactors, and "chocolate chips," candies shaped like ICs.

click (v.) See POINT AND CLICK.

client/server (n., adj. phrase) Physical entities as well as a metaphor. A client computer is in network thrall to a *server* computer, although the relationship is viewed as being *peer-to-peer*. The server doles out various kinds of resources, depending on whether it is a FILE, DATABASE, or other kind of server, and all work together as if they were one machine. In more disciplinary days, the relationship was known as master/slave. In a metaphorical sense, a client/server relationship is one in which one entity serves the needs of another. The entities can range from software to CHIPS or portions of memory inside the BOX. A client can also be a server. The terminology depends on the technical milieu.

clone (n., v.) A computer that mimics the functions of another, or SOFTWARE that is similar to another program. Computer clones are cheaper to manufacture than the name-brand products they replicate, because the clone-maker can bypass the R&D costs and go straight into production. In order for a company to produce clones, the replicated product must be OPEN and the OPERATING SYSTEM readily and cheaply licensable. The first computer to spawn large numbers of clone makers was the IBM PC. As a verb, to produce clones. *Clone* is not restricted to the hardware realm.

code (n., v.) The lines of alphanumeric or BINARY characters that make up a program. As a verb, to write code.

compatible (n.) Derived from the adjective in the phrases *compatible computer, system,* and the like. Serves as a noun for the entire phrase. A nominal or adjectival variant is *plug-compatible*. See CLONE.

computer science (n. phrase) The study of computers and programming. Formed from the models "political science" and "social science," but probably has a more truly scientific identity.

cracker (n.) A HACKER with destructive tendencies. Derives from the verb *crack,* in the sense of "cracking a safe" or "cracking code."

curse (v.) Pseudoverb meaning "to use a cursor," the placekeeper on the screen that shows where you are typing or performing some action with a mouse.

data (n.) Pronounced "day-tuh" rather than "dat-uh," this omnipresent word is actually the plural of the Latin *datum,* meaning "something given." In the computer industry—as just about everywhere else—*data* is used as both plural and singular, more often the latter.

database (n., adj.) A large amount of computer DATA stored in memory and accessible by *records* and *fields.* If the database is relational, users can cross-reference by posing questions in an SQL (*standard* [or *system*] *query language*). A database program. The term is noteworthy for being one of the scores of compound constructions upon whose spelling the industry cannot agree: *database* versus *data base.* Also, a metaphor for a person's knowledge of a subject, as in "That's not in my database."

dedicated (adj.) Set aside for a specific use, as in "That's a dedicated printer for reports."

desktop (n., adj.) As a noun, this word has several meanings. Occasionally it actually refers to the top of a desk. With the creation of the Apple Macintosh *object-oriented user interface* in 1984, it came to mean the appearance of the computer's screen when no *applications* are running on it, because the screen was supposed to resemble a desktop. Currently, the term is most frequently seen as shorthand for *desktop computer,* a computer small enough to fit on top of a desk.

desktop publishing (n. phrase) Use of relatively inexpensive DESKTOP computers, page-composition software, laser printers, and imagesetters (what used to be called typesetting machines) to produce materials ready for printing. Reportedly coined in the mid-1980s by Paul Brainerd, founder of Aldus Corp., producer of the seminal desktop-publishing software package, PageMaker. Not quite a synonym for computer-aided publishing (CAP) or electronic publishing (Epub), as these two often involve expensive, dedicated systems.

digital (adj.) Relating to BINARY digits. Derives from digits (fingers or toes) as counting mechanisms. Also, a shorthand method of referring to Digital Equipment Corporation (DEC).

dialog[ue] (n., adj., v.) Spelled either way, a method of interaction with a computer. Interacting with the computer is dialoging. A dialog box is an object on a computer's screen that enables users to choose some course of action in a seemingly interactive fashion. For example, a box may give you the choice of saving or not saving changes to a file by using the buttons "yes" or "no."

disconnect (n.) A gap in communication, a lack of understanding. A similar construction is the noun-once-verb *interconnect,* meaning interconnection.

disk, disc (n.) A flexible mylar or rigid metal platter coated with magnetic material and used for storage of computer DATA. Flexible disks are called floppy; rigid ones are called hard. Diminutive: *diskette.* Another type of disc is the CD-ROM (compact disc-read-only memory); these look like the discs for audio CD players, except they store vast amounts of digital data. As of early January 1990, San Jose disk-maker Insite Peripheral had developed a prototype disk drive that could write data to and read it from conventional disks as well as to and from "super floppies," disks that can store more data than the conventional variety. Insite calls these disks "flopticals."

display (n., v.) As a noun, synonymous with the screen of a computer; as a verb, to show something on said screen. Also called *CRT,* for cathode-ray tube ("tube" for short), and *VDT,* for video display terminal.

distributed computing (n. phrase) The "fourth generation of computing," in which files and other computer resources are distributed across networks.

dot (n.) Period, point. (An exclamation point is a "bang," and an asterisk is a "splat.") The 4.2 version of Berkeley UNIX, for example, is called "four dot two." A dot command is one preceded by a period—the DOS command .dir, for example. Also refers to the resolution of a laser printer or typesetting machine or display screen, based on the number and fineness of tiny dots that the digital output device can cram into an inch. The more dots, the better: A resolution of 1,200 dpi (dots per inch) is much crisper than one of 300 dpi.

download (v.) To move a computer FILE, for example, from E-MAIL to a directory, or from a communication program to a directory. Used anthropomorphically in SF (William Gibson's *Neuromancer*) and pop music (Warren Zevon's "Networking").

drive (n., v.) A transport mechanism for a computer DISK or tape. The infinitive of *driven,* a component of such favorite industry terms as "customer driven," "technology driven," and "marketing driven."

e-mail (n., v.) Short for "electronic mail," messages sent among people on a computer network. Recipients of these electronic missives can call them up and read them on a computer screen. To send such a message is "to e-mail." See FLAME, JUNKMAIL, and SNAILMAIL.

enabling technology (n. phrase) A technology that assists in the implementation of some other technology.

end-user (n. phrase) The final user of a computer in a trail that stretches from manufacturer through VARs (value-added resellers) and OEMs (original-equipment manufacturers). Essentially synonymous with *user*.

environment (n.) One of the great catchall terms of technobabble. Derived from the Old French *environ*, around; dates from the sixteenth century. The Random House unabridged dictionary offers five definitions for the word, one of which is specific to computers: "The hardware or software configuration, or the mode of operation, of a computer system."

ergonomic (adj.) A buzzword involving computers and furniture that have supposedly been designed for optimum comfort and efficiency. "With a Greek etymology, *ergonomic* means the study of work; with a Latin etymology, it means the study of *therefore*," noted an industry observer.

execute (v., n.) Cause to happen; specifically in computing, "to run a program or routine, or to carry out an instruction in a program"—as in "he executed the program" or "the program executed an instruction." Part of the thanatotic undercurrent of technobabble—e.g., *terminal, terminate, abort, die, [brain] dead, hit.*

fiber (n., adj.) Optical fibers are replacing metal wires as a means for moving data, as in fiber-optic networks and FDDIs (fiber-distributed data interfaces).

file (n.) A carryover term from the days when offices stored information on paper in file folders in file cabinets. Files are now digital entities— "streams of bytes," as an Apple manual once put it.

filter (n.) Software that removes formatting commands from one program's FILE so that it be imported into the format of another.

flame (n., v.) A (usually electronic) diatribe about some subject. To dispatch such a diatribe.

footprint (n.) The amount of space a computer occupies. A small DESKTOP machine such as a Macintosh SE has a small footprint; a mainframe that fills a room has a large footprint.

gating (adj.) Crucial, important, as in a "gating item." In electronics, a gate (or logical gate) is a signal that makes a circuit operative or inoperative for a short period of time.

generate (v.) Often a hifalutin substitute for *produce, make,* or *build.*

generation (n.) Advances in computer technology—from prosaic to significant—are called generations. Sometimes the term serves merely as a marketing buzzword, as in the popular phrase "next-generation product." Other times, it refers to an accepted, quantifiable phase of evolution, as in "fifth-generation computer" or "fourth-generation language."

graphics (n.) In the most general sense, visual representations on a computer screen. Computer graphics, however, can run the visual gamut from simple, static DIALOG *boxes* in user interfaces; to complex scientific VISUALIZATION of geologic and atmospheric data; to the moving, swirling, exploding images that are all too familiar to television viewers. The adjective *graphic* is rarely seen in the computer industry, having been supplanted by the bastard variant *graphical.*

hacker (n.) According to Steven Levy, author of *Hackers: Heroes of the Computer Revolution, hacker* means software virtuoso and aficionado. The term originated in the late 1950s within the Tech Model Railroad Club at MIT. "The most productive people working on Signals and Power called themselves 'hackers' with great pride." At MIT elaborate pranks were called hacks. The word *hacker* is constantly misused by the media to signify someone who illegally breaks into computer systems; CRACKER is the correct term for such a person.

hard (adj.) A word with many uses (e.g., *hard disk, hardwired, hardened*). Means durable or fixed in place, unalterable. For example, a hard key is one whose purpose is fixed. The purpose of a soft key (or softkey), on the other hand, can be altered by programming. *Soft* is often synonymous with "programmable."

help (n., adj.) Usually, electronic assistance that users can invoke as they NAVIGATE through the workings of a computer and its software. Obtaining such aid generally involves pushing a help button to get a help screen full of online help. Although this approach is faster and easier than trying to find assistance by slogging through a manual, the prose called up is often as deadly and convoluted as that found in printed documentation.

high-resolution (adj. phrase) "If you stand more than four meters away, you can see the DOTS" is one acerbic definition of the term. In addition *high* is used, frequently, in conjunction with *end, performance, speed,* and *technology.*

high tech (n.), **high-tech** (adj. phrase) Abbreviation for *high technology.* Also denotes a style of minimalist industrial design.

hyper- Popular suffix. Hypertext, for example, is a Byzantine, though rapidly traversed, labyrinth of software cross-referencing. *Hyper* meant "over" in Classical Greek and usually implied excess or exaggeration. The prefix has become so hyperused in the computer industry that a software company called Owl International headlined the full-page ad for its Guide hypertext product "Hyperbabble."

implement (v.) Rarely in the computer industry will you hear the more prosaic *do, accomplish, build,* or *perform* in reference to something re-alized. Cf. GENERATE.

import (v.) Bring FILES from one program into another. Antonym: *export.*

incompatible (adj., n.) Nonfunctional with a similar entity. The Macin-tosh operating system and DOS (two popular operating systems) are inherently compatible. Thus, each is an incompatible.

integrated (adj.) Blended. An integrated program may include a spread-sheet, a word processor, and a database. An integrated person is someone who "has his act together."

interactive (adj.) Responding to input and producing output to which a user can respond. There's nearly a 50 percent chance that the I in any computer acronym will stand for interactive—another likely possibility being *integrated.*

interoperability (n.) The ability of disparate systems to work recipro-cally—an extremely important capability for heterogeneous networked environments. The term is beloved of data-communication aficionados. A trade show for them is called Interop.

interrupt (n., adj.) Often used with *mode,* as in "He's in interrupt mode." When not used anthropomorphically, a break in the flow of a computer program.

junkmail (n.) A component of E-MAIL devoted to personal tirades, jeremiads, pontifications, solicitations, sales pitches, and the like.

knowledge engineer[ing] (n. phrase) Grandiose term for someone who works in field of artificial intelligence.

knowledge worker (n. phrase) Another ego-inflating term. Basically means "white-collar worker in the computer industry." Derives from KNOWLEDGE ENGINEERING and *knowledge base.*

laptop (n.) Another adjective substituting for a noun phrase—the phrase in this case being *laptop computer,* one that is small and light enough to sit on someone's lap. Cf. DESKTOP. Synonym: *notebook,* owing to surface dimensions approximating the size of a notebook.

look and feel (n. phrase) The appearance and operation of a computer program.

Luddite (eponym) After Ned Ludd, nineteenth-century British antitechnology crusader whose followers smashed machines of the industrial revolution because they feared that the machines would put them out of work. Today the term refers to people who fear HIGH TECH.

macro (n.) A piece of code that can be "invoked" as a shorthand method for accomplishing a task. For example, typing the relatively short *pdq-abc* might cause a program to produce a "template" (a canned layout) for a page.

menu (n.) A list of actions, as presented by a graphical user interface, from which to choose by the POINT-AND-CLICK method.

metaphor (n.) A liberally employed term meaning anything from "representation" to "method of operation." The phrase "drag and drop metaphor," for example, refers to the way you "drag" a representation of, say, a file across a screen and "drop" it into a representation of, say, a folder.

micro- (prefix) Small, minute. Specifically one-millionth part of a unit (for example, *micro*gram). Frequently combined with various words, most notably *computer* and *processor*. A microcomputer is smaller than a minicomputer, although the prefix *mini-* also means small. A minicomputer is smaller than a mainframe. *Mini* and *micro* are abbreviations, respectively, for *minicomputer* and *microcomputer*.

mode (n.) State or condition; for example, "telecommunications mode." Often used anthropomorphically, as in "She's in work mode," an example of an overly complex way of saying something simpler, namely, "she's working." In 1981, William Safire discussed the word's use in fashion, food, and physics, among other areas. "*Mode* could now use a rest. Whenever a scientific term is embraced by jargonauts, the parameters are stretched beyond recognition. Let us return *mode* to fashion, and to the large dollop of ice cream that lands squarely on top of the pie."

module (n.) A component of hardware or (more often) software. Also used generally to refer to a portion of something. For example, a chapter can be a "module" of a book.

mouse (n., v.) A one-, two-, or three-button device—used in conjunction with or as an alternative to a keyboard—for entering data. With its cable "tail," a mouse vaguely resembles a rodent. Possible inspired by the "turtle" in the Logo programming language. No relation to *cat*, the concatenate command in UNIX. The mouse and the keyboard have been blended into the "keymouse," a "mouselike pointing device," according to *InfoWorld*. A keymouse is a pressure-sensitive key on a LAPTOP computer that enables people to move a cursor around on the LCD (liquid-crystal display) screen. Another variant is the "trackball," a device holding a golfball-sized orb, over which you roll your hand to move the cursor on the screen.

multi- (prefix) A big favorite in the computer industry. Among the constructions wrought with this prefix: *multitasking, multithreaded, multivendor, multinode, multinetwork,* and *multimedia.* The last term meant slide shows, movies, and sound when it was coined in the mid-1960s but today is a much-hyped buzzword involving video, audio, animation, files, and other computer attributes. *Multiple* is another favorite industry buzzword, often substituting for the more mundane *many.*

nanosecond (n.) Used technically, one-billionth of a second. Used loosely, in relation to human activity, very fast, as in "I'll interface with you in a nanosecond." Derives from the Greek *nânos*, dwarf.

navigate (v.) To move around within a (usually) conceptual environment, such as software. Dictionary definitions stress the physical, nautical aspects of *navigate*, which derives from the Latin *navis*, ship. For several years, Apple has been touting the possibility of a notebook-sized, hypermedia computer reference tool called the Knowledge Navigator— similar to a concept that has been around the industry for years, that of the "Dynabook."

neural network (n. phrase) A method of computing for artificial-intelligence applications in which the computer circuits are said to resemble neurons in the brain. Also called artificial neural networks (ANN). One company that works in this area is called Neuron Data.

node (n.) A usually diskless computer on a network but can refer to any device or entity that is in a subservient position to another (cf. CLIENT/ SERVER). Disparaging term for a person: "He's a diskless node."

nonlinear (adj.) Derived from mathematics, this term is applied to people who lose their cool or to situations that get out of control, as in "This situation can go nonlinear in an instant!"

nontrivial (adj.) Difficult. Antonym: *trivial,* meaning "easy."

object (n.) A class of data or a visual representation of something on a computer screen. Object-oriented programming (OOP) employs canned "modules" that programmers can incorporate into their code by moving them around on the screen, rather than by keying in lines of code.

off line (adv. phrase) One of many terms originally descriptive of computer phenomena but since transported to the realm of human interaction. Imagine that you are in a meeting and someone raises an issue that is not on the agenda; you respond by saying, "I'll talk to you about that off line." Antonym: *on line.*

open (adj., component of product nomenclature) This word started to receive significant use in the industry in the early 1980s, most notably in the phrase *open systems,* a term that originated in the late 1930s in the field of thermodynamics. A de rigueur buzzphrase meaning, loosely, nonproprietary (cf. PROPRIETARY). The word *open* has been incorporated into numerous products, philosophies, and company names.

Open for Buzziness

Use of the word *open* and the term *open systems* is out of control in the computer industry. In an article entitled "Open Systems Defined" in her newsletter with the tag line "Guide to Open Systems," industry analyst Patricia Seybold wrote: "*Open systems* is becoming the protective mantle for vendors and users alike." *Open systems* is so nebulous that the monthly magazine *UNIX World* devoted a cover story to the meaning of the term, in which industry chiefs defined what it meant to them. As Patricia Seybold suggested, the word *open* has been incorporated into numerous products, philosophies, and company names, among them: "Open Systems Advisor" (newsletter); Open Network Computing, Open Systems Computing, Open Windows, Open Fonts (Sun Microsystems); Open Look (AT&T); Open Software Foundation, X Open, 88 Open, User Alliance for Open Systems; Open Systems Interconnection [or Interconnect, depending on your verbs-into nouns predisposition], Government Open Systems Interconnect Profile [GOSIP] (organizations); Open View (Hewlett-Packard); Open Networking Environment (NCR); OPEN/server Technology (Wang); Open Desktop (Santa Cruz Operation); Open Prepress Interface (prepress specification); Open Systems, Inc.; Open Connect Systems (and its newsletter, "Open Connections"). In an attempt to get in on the frenzy, several companies changed their names or their products' names—even if the changes were spurious or ridiculous—just to get the word *open* into them. One example was Rabbit Software, which changed the name of its Rabbit PLUS product to Open Advantage.

---

operating system (n. phrase) Also known as system software, an OS, as it is abbreviated, controls the operations of a computer system. The overworked metaphor for an OS in the industry is "traffic cop."

parameter (n.) This word, whose original meaning concerned mathematics, now denotes anything from "boundary" to "factor." Root of verb *parameterize*.

pen-based computer (n. phrase) A small computer that employs an electronic "stylus" and "notepad" in lieu of a keyboard. The devices are called, more simply, "pen computers," although the November 5, 1990, issue of *InfoWorld* used the grandiose term "pen-input platform" to refer to these little machines. Computer technology moves fast, but as of July

22 of that year, *San Francisco Examiner* columnist Denise Caruso wrote of "the newest buzzword in the business . . . pen-based hardware and software system."

peripheral (n.) An adjunct device such as a disk drive or a printer for a computer.

plug and play (v. phrase) A sometimes optimistic phrase suggesting that a computer user can take a new machine out of a box, plug it in, and begin to use it immediately.

point and click (v. phrase) To use a MOUSE to move an arrow on the screen to a desired FILE, operation, or other entity and then click a button on the mouse to effect an action on the entity.

port (v., n.) Move. If, for example, your product runs on DEC minicomputers, and you port it to the Data General "platform," you move it over from a DEC machine to one from Data General—although it still runs on the DEC machine. The code is said to be *portable*. Upon success, you have completed the port. Also, a connector on the back of a computer into which you can plug PERIPHERALS. Depending on how they handle DATA, these ports are serial or parallel.

portable (n., adj.) Cf. DESKTOP, LAPTOP. A lightweight computer. Occasionally employed adjectivally, as in "portable code." Portables that weigh more than about ten pounds are sometimes called "luggables" or "transportables."

proprietary (adj.) "Closed" or "nonportable." The Macintosh operating system is proprietary, meaning that it works only on Macs. MS-DOS, on the other hand, works, more or less, on IBM personal computers and on "PC clones." Proprietary technology is rapidly becoming passé.

raster (n., adj.) The pattern of closely spaced dots on a computer screen. Also the pattern formed on a CRT by the back-and-forth and up-and-down pattern of a scanning electron beam. The latter definition is the original, dating from 1934. The word derives from the Latin *radere,* "to scrape." *Raster* graphics are based on patterns of dots, whereas *vector* graphics are based on lines.

real time (n. phrase), **realtime** (adj.) Dealing with real-world events. In *The Macintosh Way,* Guy Kawasaki writes that "real time means people responding to events as they happen without having to wait for something or someone to give them control. It shouldn't be confused with 'surreal time,' which is the time between when a software company announces a product and ships it."

real estate (n. phrase) The available space in or on a given entity. Circuit-board real estate is at a premium, thus the importance of miniaturization—integrating circuits and other components to make them as small and tightly packed as possible.

seamless (adj.) Sans seams. A figurative term related to INTEGRATED. Seamless integration of one module of code with another, for example, means that both pieces blend perfectly, with no indication of where one was "stitched" to the other. As with other computer terms, seamlessness is relative. What is seamless to a veteran hacker may look like the work of Dr. Frankenstein to someone with less experience.

signage (n.) Signs, posters, and the like—generally for trade shows.

silicon (n.) The basic material from which most computer chips are made. New, more efficient materials, such as ceramics and gallium arsenide (GaAs, pronounced "gas"), are under development. "To have silicon" or "to be in silicon" means to have a chip design actually imprinted onto a chip.

Silicon Valley (geog. phrase) The Santa Clara Valley of Central California, bounded roughly by San Jose to the south, the East Bay foothills to the east, the Santa Cruz mountains to the west, and San Francisco Bay to the north. Also known more colloquially as "Silicon Gulch"—as in *Silicon Gulch Gazette,* the name of a defunct rag published by personal-computing pioneer Jim Warren. The term *Silicon Valley* was coined by Don Hoefler, editor of *Microelectronic News,* but Hoefler credited Ralph Vaerst, president of a company called Ion Equipment, for suggesting the name. Although Silicon Valley remains the predominant high-technology area in the United States, other locations that are attempting to court computer companies have altered the moniker accordingly. The New Orleans area, for example, has its "Silicon Bayou"; the Dallas area has its "Silicon Prairie"; and Scotland has a "Silicon Glen."

smart (adj.) Intelligent. A computer-controlled home is a "smart home"; a computer-guided missile is a "smart bomb."

snailmail (n.) The United States Postal Service.

software (n.) Computer programs and documentation. Generally speaking, "media" such as audio and videotape that are not hardware. Also, the movie-industry term for entertainment and the title of an SF novel by Rudy Rucker.

solution (n.) Generally synonymous with *product*. Most often seen in marketing materials, although engineers are also prone to using this euphemism.

source (n., adj.) As a noun, short for *source code*. Source code is a level above BINARY code in its direct relationship to the workings of a computer.

standalone (adj., n.) A standalone computer is one that runs on its own and does not have to be plugged into a server (cf. CLIENT/SERVER) or network to operate. Someone who is laboring without assistance is said to be "working standalone."

state of the art (n. phrase) The Random House unabridged dictionary defines this industry buzzphrase as "the latest and most sophisticated or advanced stage of a technology, art, or science" and puts its date of coinage in the middle 1960s. But columnist William Safire provides a citation from 1956, from the *U.S. Air Force Dictionary:* "The level to which technology and science have at any designated cutoff time been developed in an industry." Whenever it was coined, it has devolved into a meaningless buzzphrase in the computer industry. As Safire put it, "[This term] has seized technocrats by the throat." Industry wag Bill Tuthill defines the term thus: "When referring to hardware: about five years behind the best research labs. When referring to software, about ten years behind the best research labs."

strategic (adj.) Based on a strategy. Nearly all decisions in the computer industry, especially those made in marketing, are "strategic."

super- (prefix) This Latin prefix means "above," "beyond," "in addition," "to an especially high degree." The latter sense predominates in the computer industry, when it is appended to *computer, conductor, microcomputer, minicomputer, scalar, workstation,* and a seemingly endless list of other entities.

systems integrator (n. phrase) A company that buys various components from different suppliers and assembles them into a computer system, which it then sells under its own name. More or less synonymous with OEM (original-equipment manufacturer) and VAR (value-added reseller), both of which do pretty much the same thing.

talk to (v. phrase) Communicate, as in "I'll have my computer talk to your computer." In addition to being one of many anthropomorphic technobabble terms, it also exemplifies a shorthand method of describing an action that would otherwise require a lengthy explanation. Synonym: *interface with.*

technobabble (n.) Popular and/or professional overuse of computer jargon. Synonyms include

compuspeak: computer slang; also, chapter title in *The Devouring Fungus* by Karla Jennings

computalk: n. [computer + talk + double-talk + doublethink]: jargon, consisting of computer terms applied to business and human relations, especially in the use of nouns as verbs

tech speak: "Postcolloquial discourse modulation protocol for user status enhancement"; also, the title of a book of the same name by Edward Tenner, subtitled "How to Talk High Tech"

techno-talk: the metalanguage of machines, according to an article in *Harper's* magazine

technojive (techno + jive): Glib, fast, deceptive, and abbreviated use of technobabble. Computer salespeople tend to speak technojive.

technoweeny [or **weenie**] (n.) One of several synonyms for *nerd,* others being *digit head, wirehead, geek, wonk, dweeb, dork, Twinkie-eater, beanie head,* and *propeller head,* the latter two referring to the perceived penchant of hackers for wearing propeller beanies.

terminal (n.) A keyboard and display connected directly to a computer or a network. Called terminal because it is at the end of the line. Before terminals had monitors, they were keyboards with paper-tape punches. An early moniker for the monitor was "glass Teletype." Anthropomorphically, most terminals are considered "dumb," because they merely alphanumerically manipulate information served to them.

tower (n.) A tall, vertical STANDALONE computer that sits on the floor, often under a desk. Trademark for a machine of this type made by NCR. Towers have given way to "minitowers," which sit on desktops.

transparent (adj.) Malapropism meaning *invisible.* People in the computer industry use the word transparent when they mean invisible (e.g.,

"The operations of the system are transparent to the user."). In a computer context, transparent is applied to software and systems that hide from their users the complexities that make them run. For example, someone who is employing a word-processing program wants to write and edit easily and effectively. Such users have little or no interest in how the program works to enable them to perform this task. In fact, a manifestation of the program's inner workings would get in the way of its intended purpose. For the program's user to concentrate on the word-processing characteristics of the program, the intricate and detailed processes by which it works must remain *invisible,* not transparent. If the processes were transparent, the user could see right through them, to their baroque—and for the purpose of word processing—annoying, irrelevant, and counterproductive complexities.

transverse (v.) Frequent misspelling of *traverse.*

tweak (v., n.) To adjust or finesse something. Such an adjustment is a *tweak.*

under (adv.) Application software "runs under" an operating system, which controls it. Obversely, graphical user interfaces, which control user interaction with the operating system, run on top of it. Would you rather be on top or underneath?

upload (v.) The opposite of DOWNLOAD.

value-added (adj. phrase employed as n. phrase) Added value, as in "I think that a winning publishing strategy should emphasize five key factors. The first is value-added."

vector (n., adj., v.) See RASTER. As a verb, generally means to move toward some sort of convergence. Also the root of *vectorize.*

virtual (n., adj.) A word much beloved in the computer industry. It is used to form technical terms such as *virtual memory* and *virtual cache,* and trendy terms such as *virtual reality,* but it also shows up frequently in the writing and speech of industry people.

visualization (n., adj.) Glorified substitute for GRAPHIC(S).

widget (n.) Canned code component used for building user interfaces. Overheard at the keynote address for Xhibition 1990: Audience member

1: "They're like widgets that run other widgets." Audience member 2: "Sort of like widget macros?" Audience member 1: "Yeah."

window[ing] (n., v.) You could call it a "virtual workspace" or a "virtual vitrine," but a window is a (usually) square or rectangular area on a computer screen in which you write, draw, program, and the like. A window system enables you to work on several files simultaneously in different windows. The word *window* dates from the eighteenth century and comes from an Old Norse word meaning "wind eye." Its use in the computer industry dates from the 1960s, when "windowing" technology was developed at Xerox PARC. The term has prompted numerous jokes about computer systems that do and do not "do windows."

workgroup (n., adj.) A buzzword for the 1990s, meaning a group of people that work together in collaborative, enterprisewide environments using "teamware" and "groupware."

workstation (n.) Although the distinctions between "workstation" and "networked high-end PCs" is blurring, a workstation is generally considered among those who are familiar with computers to be a high-performance, 32-BIT, networked, multitasking computer system running UNIX and having a WINDOW system. *San Francisco Examiner* technology writer Paul Freiberger equates the public's knowledge of the term to its familiarity with *personal computer* in 1981. "In 1990, the average person thinks a 'workstation' is perhaps a cubicle or a position on an assembly line." In a sense, the average person would be right, as that is the original meaning of the term, which dates from the early 1930s. The confusion is understandable, since many items, including office typing tables, are called workstations. The word has also given rise to variants such as the Datastation, from Structural Concepts Corp., "computer support systems furniture" that complements the company's Personalized Air System (which "delivers fresh air to 2–12 workstations"), and Multistation 550, an IBM microcomputer of the early 1980s. In a 1984 press release, Vivid Software Corp. used the terms *work station* and *workstation* in the same paragraph to refer to the Facility Manager, a workstation in the original sense of the term.

Bibliography

One my reasons for writing *Technobabble* was the paucity of comprehensive treatments of the subject. Several books deal in passing with computer argot, and some of the numerous general-interest and trade magazines for industry professionals and users touch on it occasionally.

Books

Armstrong, Jeffrey. *The Binary Bible of Saint $ilicon.* Santa Cruz, California: Any Key Press, 1987. This self-published effort is chock-full of religious-imagery wordplay—for example, "Boota, the on-line one who taught us how to achieve nerdvana."

Ditlea, Steve, ed. *Digital Deli.* New York: Workman Publishing, 1984. This "comprehensive, user-lovable menu of computer lore, culture, lifestyles, and fancy" features several "appetizers" about technobabble.

Freiberger, Paul, and Swaine, Michael. *Fire in the Valley.* Berkeley, California: Osborne/McGraw-Hill, 1984. Now out of print, this book chronicles the "making of the personal computer." A useful history of the development of PCs and, analogously, technobabble.

Howard, Philip. *The State of the Language.* New York: Oxford University Press, 1985. As literary editor of *The Times of London,* Howard had enough of an interest in technobabble to devote a couple of pages to it.

Howe, Irving, ed. *Orwell's Nineteen Eighty-Four: Text, Sources, Criticism.* New York: Harcourt, Brace & World: 1963. A notable essay in this collection is Orwell's classic "Politics and the English Language." Although Orwell writes primarily about the ruinous effect of politics on language, some of his comments could apply to technobabble, or any professional argot. For example: "Never use a foreign phrase, a scientific word, or a jargon word if you can think of an everyday English equivalent."

Jennings, Karla. *The Devouring Fungus: Tales of the Computer Age*. New York: W.W. Norton & Company, 1990. This follow-on to *Naked Computer* and *Digital Deli* has a chapter entitled "Compuspeak" that deals with problems in human-computer communication, wordplay, computer "grammars," and technobabble style.

Kelly-Bootle, Stan. *The Devil's DP Dictionary*. New York: McGraw-Hill, 1981. Now out of print, this take-off on Ambrose Bierce's *The Devil's Dictionary* must be special-ordered.

Levy, Steven. *Hackers: Heroes of the Computer Revolution*. Garden City, New York: Anchor Press/Doubleday, 1984. Levy traces the history of hacking over nearly three decades—from the mid-1950s at MIT up to the mid-1980s.

McCrum, Robert; Cran, William; MacNeil, Robert. *The Story of English*. New York: Viking, 1986. Published as a companion piece to the Public Broadcasting System series of the same name, this book devotes a page or so to technobabble.

Rochester, Jack, and Gantz, John. *The Naked Computer*. New York: William Morrow and Company, 1983. Now out of print, this "almanac of computer lore, wizardry, personalities, memorabilia, world records, mindblowers, and tomfoolery" touches occasionally on technobabble as it comprehensively explores technotrivia up to the early 1980s.

Guy Steele, et al. *The Hacker's Dictionary*. New York: Harper & Row, 1983; revised edition, The MIT Press, 1991. The definitive work on the hacker lexicon has been revised after its first appearance in 1983. It also continues to exist and proliferate on computer networks.

Tenner, Edward. *Tech Speak, or How to Talk High Tech*. New York: Crown Publishers, 1986. A primer on how to turn simple designations into impressive-sounding Latinate jargon. For example, Tenner would have you call a spade not a spade but a "geomorphological modification instrument" (GMI).

Weizenbaum, Joseph. *Computer Power and Human Reason*. San Francisco: W.H. Freeman and Company, 1976. Classic study of computers and humans' reactions to and interactions with them.

Magazines

Byte, [published by] McGraw-Hill (general technical articles)

Computerworld, IDG Communications (articles for DP [data-processing] professionals)

Dr. Dobb's Journal, M&T Publishing (articles for accomplished programmers; originally called *Dr. Dobb's Journal of Computer Calisthenics and Orthodontia,* with the tag line "Running Light without Overbyte")

IEEE Spectrum, Institute of Electrical and Electronics Engineers (notable for its "Technically Speaking" column, an examination of the computer-industry's lexicon)

InfoWorld, IDG Communications (articles for business users of PCs; has many technojive headlines)

MacUser, Ziff-Davis (technical articles for users of Macintosh computers)

MacWeek, Ziff-Davis (weekly news about "Macs")

MacWorld, IDG Communications (general articles about Macs)

PC, Ziff-Davis (mammoth mag about IBM and IBM-compatible desktop computers)

PC Computing, Ziff-Davis (computer magazine for the "literati," complete with articles by computer-using celebrities)

PC Week, Ziff-Davis (weekly news about IBM and IBM-compatible desktop computers)

PC World, IDG Communications (mammoth mag about IBM and IBM-compatible desktop computers)

Publish, IDG Communications (magazine about desktop publishing)

SunWorld, IDG Communications (magazine about Sun and Sun-compatible workstations; "/lex" column examines technobabble use and etymology)

UNIX Review, Miller-Freeman (monthly for UNIX users; more technical than **UNIX World**; features language column by Stan Kelly-Bootle, author of *The Devil's DP Dictionary*)

UNIX Today, CMP Publishing (newsmagazine for UNIX users)

UNIX World, McGraw-Hill (yet another monthly for UNIX users)